Counseling Single Adults

Other books by Douglas L. Fagerstrom

Single to God
The Lonely Pew
Single Adult Ministry

Counseling Single Adults

A Handbook of Principles and Advice

Douglas L. Fagerstrom, ed.

Foreword by Jim Smoke

Baker Books
A Division of Baker Book House Co
Grand Rapids, Michigan 49516

©1996 by Douglas L. Fagerstrom

Published by Baker Books
a division of Baker Book House Company
P.O. Box 6287, Grand Rapids, MI 49516-6287

Printed in the United States of America

Library of Congress Cataloging-in-Publication Data

Counseling single adults : a handbook of principles and advice /
   Douglas L. Fagerstrom, ed.
    p. cm.
   Includes bibliographical references.
   ISBN 0-8010-9008-3
   1. Church work with single people. 2. Single people—Pastoral counseling of. I. Fagerstrom, Douglas L.
   BV639.S5C68 1995
   253.5—dc20
                                     95-21480

Contents

Contents

Foreword

Jim Smoke

Listening to the struggles of others is exhausting work. Most of us listen with our heads when we need to listen with our hearts.

Hurting people make heart sounds. Our task as counselors is to listen for those sounds, pray about them, and offer wisdom that comes from the heart of God through us.

Counselors today need a great reservoir of compassion. Our example is Christ Himself who was moved by people's needs because He "felt compassion" toward them. Out of His feeling for the hurts and pain of others He was able to bring healing and wholeness.

Today's men and women who offer lay and professional counsel can do no less. Many who share their knowledge and expertise in this book I have known personally. They have a calling and desire to strengthen the wings of weary single adult hearts. Their passion for those who hurt has turned around many lives as they have shared what God has taught them.

You will be enriched as you read this book and use its sound principles in your ministry to single adults.

Solomon, wise writer of proverbs, sums up good counsel with these words:

"Listen to advice and accept instruction, and in the end you will be wise" (Prov. 19:20).

This is my prayer for all those who struggle to find answers in their lives and for the gifted men and women who share answers in this book.

Preface

A Single Adult

How long must I wrestle with my thoughts and every day have sorrow in my heart?

—Psalm 13:2

Two years ago I entered therapy to overcome the effects of an abusive childhood. I am excited to share my reflections on the counseling process, yet these words are written with great emotion and tears. To share what counseling has meant to me is to share my brokenness, loss, and continual healing. Some days I experience great joy because of the inner growth I've experienced; other days are filled with pain and grief of deep losses. I believe God is using counseling to help me see the truth about who He really is and who I really am.

Why Did I Need Counseling?

In college, due to the transformation I saw in my friends who became Christians, I committed my life to Jesus Christ. That decision radically changed my life. As a young, eager new adherent to the Christian faith I believed the past was behind me. After all, God wanted me to experience the abundant life. I thought spiritual growth was what I needed to overcome my emotional difficulties. Over the following decade I studied the Scriptures diligently, enrolled in discipleship groups, and even did some teaching myself, but my emotional life always seemed to be in turmoil. Mostly, I just sucked down the pain and the intensity of feelings I didn't understand. No amount of spiritual growth made the pain go away. I experienced "shame attacks" when I would recount every mistake I'd ever made. And I'd fall into long periods of depression.

Finally, my emotional life reached a crisis point and crumbled. God did not satisfy; friendships felt hollow; success didn't fulfill me. The world appeared black. I experienced difficulties in my most significant relationships. No amount of love and support could take away the pain. I had to do something, but what?

For several months I lay awake at night sobbing as I relived old memories. The deep-seated issues of the past could not be resolved by my good intentions. I needed intervention; I needed the intervention of an objective, third-party professional trained in helping abused people. I placed a call to my pastor who put me in touch with a Christian counselor. The long painful journey began; I had broken out of denial.

"The purposes of a man's heart are deep waters, but a man [woman] of understanding draws them out" (Prov. 20:5).

Why Is Counseling Important?

The defenses I had used to protect myself failed, and reality hit home. During my first year of therapy I experienced an overwhelming sense of devastation in trying to own the truth: I had survived an abusive home but the poison I experienced still affected my life deeply. The crushing load of pain had never been lifted from my soul.

Children from abusive homes rarely get to talk about their feelings, so I learned to minimize them and deny my pain to survive those childhood years. Never learning how to experience or express emotions crippled my emotional (and spiritual) life.

To grow up in an abusive home is to learn many false notions about yourself, God, and others. My parents typically reacted to any request in a punitive, angry manner. I learned early to take care of myself and to not trust others. I survived by becoming super-involved in school and staying late at friends' homes. Whenever I had to go home I grew tense. I was physically threatened at times but most of the damage came from angry verbal assaults and heartless controlling behaviors. I learned to withdraw from people to survive. The very adults who were supposed to teach me how to function in the world as a healthy adult turned on me. They considered their lives normal, yet they were terribly messed up. If I dared to make a request or ask to talk, they denied there was any problem with them; I was the problem.

My father died when I was sixteen years old—to my relief. Thousands of people in therapy admit feeling a sense of release when the abusive parent dies. Pia Mellody, in her classic workbook *Breaking Free*, points out a curious aspect of growing up in an abusive home: "Our minds are so powerful that although we can bury memories in our unconscious mind and 'know but not know,' our bodies never forget and will keep trying to get us to see the truth about ourselves."[1]

God used counseling in my life to reveal truth. Facing the truth about my brokenness could not have been accomplished by any other means. To explore the full impact of emotional difficulties requires an extended period of counseling and support. It is not uncommon for people to be in therapy two or more years, depending on the level of trauma caused by the abuse. Sexual abuse victims may require several more years of therapy.

The church is not equipped to handle all the emotional difficulties people face. In his book *A Place for You,* the late Christian therapist Paul Tournier says that the role of the psychologist is to help wounded people become whole; the role of the church is to call whole people to serve others in the name of Jesus Christ.

When my shroud of denial fell off, I felt helpless to find support systems in the church that would accept without judgment my anger, pain, and losses. The most progressive churches have support groups for drug and alcohol abuse, but it is secular agencies that provide the bulk of support groups available for adult children of abuse.

Sharing my struggles with Christian friends brought about painful changes in my relationships. Some condemned the counseling process and urged me to find healing in Jesus. Others were skeptical about the long process. I have lost significant friendships and gained others. One dear friend struggles with allowing me to feel my pain fully. Overall, I have found that most people want to be supportive but are afraid of the process.

Denying pain in favor of religious activity is dangerous to the person in recovery. To deny pain is to not be real. At times I feel social pressure to be "religiously correct" rather than real in a church setting. God is interested in the deepest parts of our being. I guess that prompts many to wear masks in God's house because to face the truth is to face the pain.

"Praise the LORD, O my soul, and forget not all [H]is benefits— who forgives all your sins and heals all your [emotional] diseases, who redeems your life from the pit and crowns you with love and compassion, who satisfies your desires with good things so that your youth is renewed like the eagle's" (Ps. 103:2–5).

What Counseling Does for Me

Healing through emotional pain has affected every area of my life. Perhaps the greatest benefit is clearing up the distortions of myself and others. I have burned up a great deal of energy trying to cope with life with limited skills. The process of identifying the pain and of feeling and grieving the losses has allowed me to become much freer in my emotions. I am free to build intimacy with safe people and to protect myself against further abuse.

Purging those old childhood feelings has given me the opportunity to experience God in a new, positive way. My mother would invoke Scripture when she wanted absolute control, so I grew up with the idea that God is wrathful, punitive, and selfish. My concept of God is changing, and I am beginning to shed some unhealthy theological beliefs.

One of the big issues I've had to resolve as a Christian is why God allowed me to grow up in an abusive home. The responsibility for the abuse rests on my parents' shoulders, not God's. My parents made poor, sinful choices with painful consequences. Although they are responsible for the abuse, I am responsible for my recovery. Some people in Christian circles are skeptical of counseling because of those in therapy who blame their own poor choices on their parents. Working in a recovery program has increased my sense of being able to influence others. God holds the universe under His divine control but allows us freedom to make choices. We each have a circle of influence whether we do or do not accept our personal responsibilities as adults.

Recovery is a lifelong process of emotional maturing. The lies I believed about myself are slowly being replaced with truth. I am becoming more real and more able to express the full range of emotions. The shame attacks have stopped altogether. Recovery requires me to be honest about myself and accountable to others.

Recommended Resources

Collins, Gary. *Christian Counseling.* Dallas: Word, 1980.

Fagerstrom, Douglas L. *Single Adult Ministry: The Next Step.* Wheaton: Victor, 1993.

Hiltner, Seward. *Preface to Pastoral Theology.* Nashville: Abingdon, 1963.

Holifield, E. Brooks. *A History of Pastoral Care in America.* Nashville: Abingdon, 1983.

Hunter, Rodney J., ed. *Dictionary of Pastoral Care and Counseling.* Nashville: Abingdon, 1990.

Jaeckle, Charles, and William Clebsch. *Pastoral Care in Historical Perspective.* New York: Prentice-Hall, 1964.

Kemp, Charles. *The Caring Pastor.* Nashville: Abingdon, 1985.

Oates, Wayne. *When Religion Gets Sick.* Louisville: Westminster, 1970.

Oden, Thomas C. *Pastoral Theology.* New York: Harper and Row, 1983.

Introduction

Doug Fagerstrom

There is a knock at my office door. With hesitation, a single adult pushes it open a crack. A downcast profile appears and a small voice whispers, "Can I talk with you?"

"Sure," I respond, "come on in."

Two hours later the phone rings. A frustrated and frantic single adult at the other end of the phone connection stammers, "I have to talk to you. Can you see me sometime today?"

"Sure," I respond, "come on over."

The knocks at the door continue and the phone calls fill my voice mail with the countless needs and hurts of single adults in our church and community.

Overwhelming? Without question!

Every day single adult leaders spend hours trying to help people. When they finally retire late in the evening, they are exhausted, and they wonder if what they said or did was any help at all.

This book offers encouragement and help for the single adult ministry leader whose phone continues ringing and whose doorway is crossed every day by people with an array of stories, needs, cries for help, and desperate circumstances. Each chapter guides leaders through a counseling issue common to single adults. The chapters are not the final word on therapeutic or clinical counseling. Nor are they a shortcut or a substitute for professional counseling or long-term spiritual guidance. They are brief, easy-to-use summaries to begin the process of helping another.

This book is for the pastor, associate pastor, lay leader, and others who come alongside single adults to encourage them through life's struggles and hurts. The format makes it simple to use. Several resources are suggested in each chapter, along with portions of God's Word for additional support and encouragement.

This book is unique to most counseling tools in that it was written by those who practice every week what they have written about. In offices, homes, restaurants, or wherever it is convenient for single adults to meet, these people are doing their best to help. Their theological training, educational background, and personal experience have given them insights and skills that enable them to help those who hurt.

Jesus said, "Come unto me, all you who are weary and burdened, and I will give you rest." Many will come to you for that kind of help. When you point them to Jesus, they can find rest.

Blessings as you share your life. Blessings as you minister to single adults. Blessings as you use this book.

Part 1

Overview of Counseling in the Church

1

The Need for Counseling in the Church

Robert Duffett

The question in need of an answer today is not *"Is* there a need for counseling in the church?" The question is *"How* should the church do pastoral counseling?"

People today are familiar with the term *counseling*. Most students have had guidance counselors or camp counselors. Television commercials have introduced us to diet counselors. Lawyers are called counselors-at-law. And many others—psychiatrists, psychologists, marriage and family therapists, and social workers—make their living as professional counselors.

Church is another term that is familiar to most people. Almost 40 percent of the American population went to church last Sunday and will be there again this Sunday.

Until recent decades the practice of counseling and the work of the church were closely related. In his book *The Caring Pastor*, Charles Kemp points out that for generations personal counseling in America was done by the family doctor, church pastor, or trusted friend. In fact, counseling was done almost exclusively in the church.

That is not true today, however. Most people no longer associate counseling with church. Although ministers are often the first to be called when tragedy strikes, most Americans think that serious counseling is done in a clinic, outside the church, by a professional.

The professions of psychology and psychiatry began rather recently. According to E. Brooks Holifield in *A History of Pastoral Care in America*, the first laboratory for the scientific study of psychology was established in Europe by Wilhelm Wundt in 1879. William James and G. Stanley Hall followed Wundt's lead by starting America's first psychological lab at Johns Hopkins University in 1883. The American Psychological Association, the society that oversees the profession of psychology, was founded in 1892 and incorporated in 1925. In 1934 psychiatry established its own specialty board and became a distinct branch of medicine.

Surely it would be a mistake to say there was no psychiatry before 1934 and no psychology before James and Hall at the turn of the century. However, these dates underscore Kemp's point. From the time of Jesus until the beginning of this century, ministers and priests shouldered virtually all personal counseling.

Perhaps, therefore, the subject of this chapter should be "*Reclaiming* the Church's 2000-year Counseling Heritage."

Pastoral Care and Pastoral Counseling

The terms *pastoral care* and *pastoral counseling* are often used synonymously. In recent years, however, the words have taken on separate meanings. In the *Dictionary of Pastoral Care and Counseling* Rodney Hunter argues that pastoral care is the totality of pastoral work that supports and nurtures people within the broad range of pastoral activities. Pastoral counseling, on the other hand, refers to more structured, intense conversations on specific issues, concerns, or needs. Such conversations usually require more than one session.

The distinction between pastoral care and pastoral counseling reflects the emergence of complex problems in our society that need prolonged attention and the rise of a profession of ministers specially trained to deal with them.

Pastoral care is a natural and important function of church ministry that most churches provide in a variety of ways. Sermons address people's needs and provide help, care, and encouragement. Christian education frequently focuses on personal needs. Worship, while emphasizing adoration, praise, and celebration of God's goodness, is linked to people's needs and concerns. One of the goals of pastoral prayer is to bring the needs of the congregation to God. As the congregation worships God, people feel hope and encouragement, and when people have hope they experience pastoral care. Even serving on church boards and committees is an opportunity to give and receive pastoral care! People linked in a common task often develop supportive and trusting relationships.

The chief value of regular church attendance may well be the opportunity to know and be known by others. This interpersonal connection allows the giving and receiving of pastoral care. Perhaps the reason the writer of Hebrews advised regular church attendance was his recognition of the need for pastoral care. "Don't neglect meeting together . . . but encourage each other" (see Heb. 10:25).

This ancient biblical text partially explains the popularity of singles bars as well as singles ministries. Humans are incurably relational. We seek close encounters with others. To feel loved, encouraged, helped, and cared for we must be with other people. We long for places where, to borrow a phrase from the situation comedy *Cheers*, "everybody knows your name."

There simply is no substitute for human presence. Watching religious television programs or listening to taped Christian music or sermons will not provide relational connection or pastoral care. Why? Surprisingly, the writers of *Cheers* and the writer of Hebrews agree: Encouragement comes through contact with others!

Although distinct, the goals of pastoral care and counseling are similar. Both seek to heal, sustain, and guide. Charles Jaeckle and William Clebsch, in *Pastoral Care in Historical Perspective*, define healing as the pastoral function that aims to overcome some impairment and to restore a person not to mere functioning but to wholeness that moves the person beyond the mere removal of the impairment. In other words, biblical healing does not seek to "fix or repair," but to restore and to move a person to wholeness.

Seward Hiltner, in the preface to *Pastoral Theology*, defines sustaining as standing by people. The difference between healing and sustaining is that healing holds open the possibility of change and the hope of wholeness; sustaining relates to situations that cannot be changed (e.g., divorce, death, terminal illness, job loss, physical disability). Sustaining is the ministry of support and encouragement.

Guiding is the ethical dimension of ministry. It helps individuals make decisions about life. Guiding should not be confused with what Ann Landers does (as good as her advice may be). Guiding brings the teaching, wisdom, and resources of the Christian faith to contemporary problems, options, and questions. The ministry of guiding assumes a sophisticated understanding of Scripture, the ability to distinguish biblical teaching from cultural and religious tradition, and the knowledge of whatever concern is presented.

A Biblical Rationale for Counseling in the Church

There are two primary reasons counseling belongs in the church. First, life as we know it is not as God intended it to be. Genesis 1 and 2 affirm the goodness, beauty, and harmonious balance of the created world. The human male and female, the apex of creation, were at the same time complete in themselves yet incomplete without the other; they found relational completeness only in union with one another (Gen. 2:23–24). Equality of the sexes is affirmed from the very beginning. Eve was taken from Adam and the children of their union were taken from Eve and given back to Adam. The couple was naked yet not ashamed, which means their relationship was based on trust and openness.

Adam and Eve lived in harmony with the environment as well as with one another. The phrase "till and keep the garden . . . and freely eat of every tree of the garden" (see Gen. 2:15–16) suggests a relationship between human beings and the natural world that was healthy in that it worked two ways: Humans cared for the garden and the garden sustained the humans.

The first humans also lived in harmony with God. Direct communication existed between God and God's beloved human creations until something went dreadfully wrong. Genesis 3 tells the story of how sin fragmented their lives and ours.

It is the reality of this fragmentation that necessitates both spiritual leadership and pastoral counseling. This old story, rightly understood, explains why life as we know it is not as God intended. By choosing to disobey God's directive, human beings fragmented the harmony of God's created order in three ways.

1. *Interpersonal fragmentation.* Adam and Eve, once "naked and not ashamed" (see Gen. 2:25), became aware of their nakedness after they disobeyed God. Awareness of their nakedness is the Bible's poetic way of describing shame and the dissolution of open and trusting relationships. By disobeying God, humans brought to themselves interpersonal fragmentation. The first consequence of disobedience is the fragmentation of human relationships.

Adam and Eve blamed others for their own decisions (Gen. 3:12–13). Adam implicated Eve, "the woman you gave me, *she* gave me the fruit" (see 3:12), while Eve accused the serpent, "the *serpent* tricked me" (see 3:13). Interpersonal fragmentation led to the practice of blaming others for personal disobedience.

2. *Environmental fragmentation.* Adam and Eve's disobedience led to environmental fragmentation. Not only were they removed from their beautiful physical environment, but basic life functions (e.g., work and childbearing) became burdensome and painful.

3. *Spiritual fragmentation.* Humanity's unique relationship with God was fragmented. Adam and Eve's open and trusting relationship with their loving Creator became one of fear and distrust. Afraid of what God would do to them, they attempted to hide (Gen. 3:8). And that is what people have been trying to do ever since.

The fragmentation spoken of in Genesis 3 is repeated daily in contemporary America when people reject God. And the refusal to accept God's sovereignty and to live within the limitations established by God is the reason for all pain and suffering, then and now. It is not simplistic or naive to suggest a correlation between the drama of Genesis 3 and many of the chapters of this book (e.g., low self-esteem, bitterness and pain, guilt and rejection, death, divorce, alcoholism).

The reality of Adam and Eve is our reality. We live in a world fragmented by our own choices as well as those of others. Scripture teaches and history testifies to the chaos and suffering that result when humanity refuses to acknowledge God's sovereignty and live ethically.

The second reason counseling belongs in the church is that God took the initiative in Jesus to restore and heal our fragmented world and life. Romans 5 is the apostle Paul's answer to the question "Who can undo the fragmentation of Adam and Eve that continues to plague humanity?" The apostle shows how Jesus' life, death, and resurrection undid the results of Adam's disobedience. Note the summary of contrasts in Romans 5:12–21.

	Adam	**Christ**
Act	Disobedience, v. 19	Obedience, v. 19
Result	Many made sinners, v. 19	Many made righteous, v. 19
	Many died, v. 15	Many benefitted, v. 15
	Death reigned, v. 17	Righteousness will reign, v. 17
Future	Condemnation for all, v. 18	Justification and life for all, v. 18

Through Adam and Eve, humanity experiences fragmentation, sin, and death. Through faith in Jesus, humanity experiences wholeness, restoration, and life. Paul stresses that Jesus' accomplishment is far more powerful than the fragmentation of Adam. Three times Paul adds the words "much more" (vv. 9, 15, 17) to emphasize the power of Jesus' actions to overcome Adam's chaos.

The reason, then, for having pastoral counseling in the church may be stated simply: The world is filled with broken and hurting people who, through faith in Jesus, can be healed, sustained, and guided to wholeness.

The basis of pastoral care and counseling is the life, death, and resurrection of Jesus. Through faith in Jesus humanity is healed, sustained, and guided. Christians affirm Immanuel—God with us! In Jesus, believers are justified, forgiven, liberated, and reconciled.

The thesis of this book and the theological and psychological foundation of pastoral counseling are the same: People whose lives are fragmented—by divorce, depression, high levels of stress, unabated bitterness, unintended pregnancy, sexual struggles, or some other debilitating force—need specialized and often prolonged help.

It is irresponsible for church leaders to suggest that prayer, sermons, attendance at church functions, or positive thinking will solve these problems. Single adult leaders face an important decision at precisely this point. When an individual has not been healed, sustained, or guided by the pastoral care ministries of the church, the role of the single adult leader must shift. While continuing to provide pastoral care, the leader should encourage the person to seek pastoral counseling. It is not that pastoral care has failed this person. Rather, the needs of the person demand something more—specialized pastoral counseling.

Most single adult leaders have neither the time nor the training to move from pastoral care to pastoral counseling. Some ministries have staff counselors. Referral in such cases is easy. In other cases leaders need a well-developed network of pastoral counselors, Christian psychologists, and marriage and family therapists to whom they can refer those in need of specialized help. (See chapter 4.)

Counseling Suggestions

Perhaps the most important question for single adult leaders to ask themselves is whether or not the "climate" of their ministry is conducive to pastoral care and counseling.

Often the climate of a church or singles ministry is one that emphasizes appearances. Although hurting people are all around, the ministry and the church are focused on performance. Single adults in that environment feel pressure not only to conform to the prevailing attitudes and economic status of the group but also to hide their pain to keep from marring the image of success.

This type of climate discourages people from discussing their needs and hinders the meaningful ministries of pastoral care and counseling. If the subtle but prevailing message is "look good to impress others" why would anyone share his or her pain?

The climate of a ministry is not set by members but by leaders. If leaders are image-conscious, performance-oriented, and success-driven, members will take the cue and share only that part of their lives that conforms to image, success, and performance. This climate of ministry leaves out the person whose life is being torn apart. It's hard to feel successful, vital, and alive when your spouse has walked out. It's hard to find a reason to "dress for success" when you have gained weight, lost your job, or found out you have a serious health problem.

Few single adult leaders want to create a climate that is hostile to pastoral care and counseling. How then can we keep it from happening? How can we create instead a climate that is friendly to pastoral care and counseling?

Reaffirm the Healing Nature of the Gospel

Through teaching and preaching emphasize the power of the gospel to heal. A careful study of the New Testament reveals that the gospel of Jesus Christ is *less* information and *more* inspiration; less concerned with data to believe than power to receive! The result of Jesus' teaching and preaching was healing for those who believed. His message still heals. Regardless of how successful and secure a person appears to be, he or she still needs healing. Everyone experiences the ravages of sin, sickness, death, temptation, and evil. Whether as a result of our own choices or those of others, we all experience broken dreams, relationships, promises, and goals.

Make Healing a Priority

If the gospel does indeed heal, then logic causes us to conclude that the church is to be a healing community. One way to evaluate the effectiveness of any church, therefore, is by the degree to which it helps its members heal. Pastoral care and counseling should be major priorities of ministry, and any ministry that is serious about pastoral care and counseling must be open to the full range of emotions and problems people face.

Create a Climate of Openness

The success of pastoral care and counseling depends on the degree of openness people sense. It is not an overstatement to say that Jesus was the world's best example of someone being open to people's needs. He left us an example to follow and a goal for ministry. Jesus demonstrated His openness in four ways:

1. *Jesus was open to people others despised.* He associated with tax gatherers, lepers, prostitutes, and those who were ceremonially unclean. His non-separated life incurred the wrath of the religious leaders of His day. However, His ministry to those whose lifestyle was "suspect" enabled them to experience God's presence and love.

2. *Jesus was open to questions.* He was not angered or ashamed when people asked questions. Nor did He ever shame a person for asking them. The following is a sample of questions Jesus was asked:

- "Why do you eat with sinners?" (Mark 2:16).
- "Why do you speak this way?" (Mark 2:7).
- "What is most important?" (Mark 12:28).
- "Is it lawful for a man to divorce his wife?" (Mark 10:2).
- "Is it lawful to pay taxes to Caesar?" (Mark 12:14).
- "What must I do to inherit eternal life?" (Mark 10:17).
- "Is there a resurrection?" (Mark 12:18–27).

Perhaps the best example of Christ's openness to questions, however, is found in the question He Himself asked His Father: "My God, my God, why have You forsaken Me?" (Mark 15:34 NKJV).

3. *Jesus was open to people's doubt.* Matthew 11 records a fascinating story of doubt from an unlikely source. John the Baptist,

while in prison, sent emissaries to Jesus. The purpose was to express his doubt about Jesus and openly question whether Jesus was the Jewish Messiah. The question reflects the serious doubt John had regarding Jesus' being and ministry. Jesus replied to John with kindness and affirmation. He pointed to the results of His ministry (Matt. 11:4–6).

4. *Jesus was open to His own emotions.* Jesus cried at His friend's grave (John 11:30–38). He asked to be relieved of the suffering He was about to endure (Luke 22:42). And, in the end, He questioned whether God was even with Him (Mark 15:34).

If single adult leaders follow Jesus' example of openness in these four areas, the climate of their ministry will be conducive to pastoral care and counseling.

And when spiritual leaders see that biblical counseling can indeed bring healing to people wounded by the effects of sin, they will be convinced of the need for counseling in the church.

Counseling Single Adults: An Overview

Kay Collier-Slone

The number one rule for counseling singles is a major rule for all counseling but one that is particularly important in working with the single adult: *The counselor must take responsibility for the dynamics, ethics, and boundaries of the counseling relationship.*

In any counseling situation, the professional (i.e., counselor, therapist, or minister) is the person in power, regardless of whether or not the professional perceives it that way. The client legitimately expects to deal in a safe place with whatever issues he or she has to bring. The counseling relationship is established the moment an individual says, "I'd like to talk to you about a problem."

All those who counsel single individuals must understand that it is their responsibility to keep the therapeutic environment a safe place by maintaining their own professional boundaries and by knowing and not exceeding their own limits of expertise.

Know Your Limits

Most clergy are not trained for psychological counseling just as most psychological counselors are not trained for spiritual counseling. Each needs to know when it is appropriate to refer a client to someone else. Many ministers set a limit of three sessions with an individual. If in-depth work is needed, they refer the person to a mental health professional with expertise in the needed area. Mental health professionals need to have the same referral system in place and know when to send those with spiritual problems to someone trained in giving spiritual direction.

Know the Dangers

People who offer counseling need to understand the issues of transference, countertransference, and shadow-self.

Transference. This occurs when counselees transfer feelings toward a person in their life onto the counselor. For example, clients grieving the loss of a relationship begin to believe they are in love with the counselor. Single individuals who are without a significant other in their lives can easily transfer emotions onto the counselor. (This is also true for people with mates, but a special warning is necessary when working with singles who may be looking for a relationship.)

Countertransference. This occurs when counselors experience emotional attachment to the client. For example, a counselor experiencing criticism in the workplace or stress at home may come to rely on the admiration and dependence of a counselee and begin to believe the person's feelings extend beyond the professional relationship.

Shadow-self. This occurs when counselors exhibit personality characteristics that are opposite of the ones they believe about themselves. Everyone has these but they remain in the subconscious until times of stress, anger, need, or fatigue. Counselors who believe themselves to have high and impeccable morals and who assume they can operate with integrity in any situation, even while carrying a heavy stress load, may agree to see a distressed client after office hours. In the more intimate setting, surprising, lustful feelings surface that the counselor is not prepared to deal with. Later, the counselor will protest, "I have no idea what got into me. It wasn't like me at all!"

Counselors who do not understand transference or counter-transference, or who are carrying around unresolved issues of their own, may cross the boundary of professional counselor to inappropriate intimacy before they even realize what is happening.

Know Yourself

Those who have not experienced the need for affirmation and affection that follows rejection or broken relationships must be aware of the extreme vulnerability of individuals who are dealing with such issues.

Counselors experiencing these issues in their own lives should place themselves under supervision and be actively working on their own problems, or they should withdraw from all counseling responsibilities.

While these guidelines may seem stringent, it is critical to realize the extreme vulnerability of the counselor as well as the client. There are hundreds of cases of known sexual and emotional abuse, and the responsibility for maintaining the ethical boundaries of the situation belongs with the counselor.

Entering the Counseling Relationship

When a person arrives for counseling and begins to tell his or her story, what the counselor hears is the presenting issue—the crisis, task, or question that moved the person to seek help. Often the issue involves some type of crisis (e.g., the breakup of a relationship, a transfer to a new city, the loss of a job or roommate, the complexities of single parenting).

The information given in the initial session may be only that which is at the individual's level of conscious awareness, not what's at the root of the problem. The counselor may or may not see at the outset that the issue goes much deeper.

Many clients seek counseling when they are already deep in crisis. The immediate task in crisis counseling is to "put out the fire" so the individual can function. Crisis counseling calls for immediate intervention and requires specific action—what can be done, changed, or said to improve the immediate circumstances. When the crisis is alleviated, the counselee can begin working long-term on personal growth issues.

When working with single people, it is particularly easy for counselors to promote dependency on themselves because the counselee has no one at home on whom he or she can depend. I constantly remind myself that my job is like that of a good parent or teacher—to work myself out of a job. My task is not simply to get people over a bad or broken relationship or to help them deal with a pressing problem of loneliness; it is to support them in their work of becoming whole human beings who are able to make wise choices on their own.

The work of counselors is threefold:

1. To care for individuals in crisis and assist them in becoming functional
2. To teach individuals to nurture and care for themselves
3. To support individuals as they achieve health through reaching out appropriately to nurture others

No matter what specific issue a single is dealing with, it is important for the counselor to keep in mind those three tasks.

Some Common Single Adult Issues

The issues I experience most frequently in my practice with single adults involve the following:

- Loneliness
- Frustration
- Grief over broken relationships
- Boundaries
- Destructive relationships/relationship dependency
- Addictive behaviors

- Fear of not having a relationship/mate
- Unresolved family matters
- Ghosts of relationships past
- Single parenting
- Divorce and child custody
- Careers
- Spirituality
- Sexuality
- Life transitions

We will look at each of these issues in more depth.

Loneliness

In her book *Alone in America,* Louise Bernikow states that one of the most difficult things for any human to admit is loneliness. Bernikow traveled across America talking to people and found that they would talk freely about the most intimate experiences of life yet be unable to admit that they were lonely. This is good to remember when working with singles—for underneath most of the stated issues and fears is one feeling— loneliness.

Frustration

Many of the frustrations of singleness have to do with ingrained life expectations and societal and church norms. The single counselor or the counselor who has lived a significant number of years as a single adult has the advantage of a personal understanding of the issues and frustrations of singleness. The counselor who has limited experience as a single adult needs to recognize, validate, and move into those frustrations. They are real. They do not go away. Individuals who have been taught since birth to expect to marry at a certain age and to live out their remaining years with one partner must re-think, re-image, and re-visualize themselves as whole, healthy, and content human beings without marriage.

This issue is integrally related to loneliness, and the two are ongoing in singles counseling.

Giving clients material to read on the subject of society's lack of understanding of the single life and then discussing it with them can be helpful. I recommend *Confronting the Idolatry of Family: A New Vision for the Household of God* by Janet Fishburn. It explains where many of society's ideas came from and will help singles realize that the problem lies with society, not with them as single individuals.

Books can provide valuable head knowledge, but the information needs to move from the head to the heart. Information alone does not change people. Change does not occur until knowledge is internalized and becomes a part of the very essence of a person's being.

Information can, however, help singles realize that there is nothing wrong with them and also help them see that society, including the church, is living in a world that no longer exists. And singles have been living in the new reality for some time. This simple information seems to boost sagging self-esteem.

I also recommend *Single Adult Passages* by Carolyn Koons as a reference for single adults. The statistics help them realize that they are not alone.

It is also important for counselors to help clients develop a way of clearly identifying the emotion they are experiencing as well as the origin of that emotion. For example, the counselor may ask, "On a one-to-ten scale of emotional health, what has been your highest number since we were last together? Your lowest number? Your number now? What word would you use to describe each number?"

The client may say, "High 6; low 2; now 4," and the associated words may be "6, hope; 2, loneliness; 4, relief to have someone to talk to."

Next, the counselor will want to find out about the situations associated with each number and word.

This identification helps the client recognize that not all frustrations, problems, and loneliness are caused by singleness; many are common to life in general and are experienced by people with mates as well as by singles.

Grief over Broken Relationships

Many single people come for counseling when they are grieving over a broken or painful relationship, whether by death, divorce, or a divorce-like breakup of a non-marital relationship. Counselors who work with single adults must have a working knowledge of grief therapy and a true understanding of the grief process.

Grief takes as long as it takes. It is neither orderly nor easy. While grief differs for those who lose a spouse by death and those who lose one through divorce (and thus suffer the added feelings of rejection), the anger, denial, and other stages of grief are similar in both cases.

Not only are people grieving over the loss of an important individual, they are also grieving the loss of dreams: the dream of a long-term marriage, the dream of grandchildren, the dream of happy retirement years.

The temptation many find almost irresistible is the desire to replace the lost relationship with a new one as quickly as possible. The counselor must be strong in advising the grieving person to take plenty of time to make sure that he or she is whole again before getting into a serious relationship.

In dealing with grief I have established three levels of priorities: (1) internal, spiritual wholeness; (2) functional wholeness; (3) social wholeness. Keep in mind that the single adult will be pressured by society to work in the reverse order, placing highest priority on reestablishing a healthy social life.

Single individuals invest great emotion in pets, a caretaking relationship with an aging parent or other relative or friend, and family-like arrangements with close friends. Loss of any of these relationships must be grieved.

A helpful book for both client and counselor is Ann Kaiser Stearns' *Living Through Personal Crisis*. Another helpful book on grief is *Life Is Good-bye, Life Is Hello* by Alla Bozarth-Campbell.

Boundaries

Many individuals never acknowledge, much less develop, a concept of personal boundaries. Boundaries are personal fences that help an individual define where he or she begins and ends—an intangible but strong line that prevents one human being from becoming enmeshed with or taken over by another. In a society that pushes people toward a coupled state and represents this state as sacrosanct, individuals have a difficult time learning the importance of defining their own boundaries and *choosing* when to open those boundaries to connect with another.

Counselors should assist persons in understanding the concept of boundaries; in seeing how family, friends, employers, children, and dates as well as mates have violated those boundaries either physically, mentally, or emotionally; and in learning how to use boundaries constructively.

Living with a concept of personal boundaries requires a new vocabulary that is not "white gloves and party manners." Individuals need to understand that taking care of self is quite different from living selfishly. Helpful books in this area are *Control Theory* by William Glasser and *Your Perfect Right: A Guide to Assertive Living* by Robert E. Alberti and Michael L. Emmons.

You may want to encourage clients to ask these questions: "Is this good for me?" "What boundaries are being violated?" "What boundaries do I choose to maintain?"

Destructive Relationships/Relationship Dependency

When people are lonely they tend to turn to any relationship they can find to "fix" what ails them. But what they find all too often is an unhealthy, destructive relationship with an unhealthy, needy person. Singles who tend toward these relationships are often inconsistent in therapy. They come for help when the significant other is not treating them well or when the relationship is temporarily or permanently broken. Or they come to individual or group therapy, listen, appear to work on some issues, but continue in the relationship that is causing them pain. The need for a relationship can be strong enough to cause the heart to overrule the head, and the individual who may *understand* what the counselor is saying and even *agree* with the counselor and family and friends who are aware of the dysfunction and destruction may yet be unable to move away from the situation.

Typically, a person receives some form of energy from the relationship and feels depleted of energy without it. He or she perceives this state as one of love and connectedness rather than one of vulnerability and neediness. These relationships often exhibit characteristics of addiction. Blinded to the faults of the other person or the relationship, the individual is not aware that the relationship actually narrows life and interferes in certain aspects of it, such as other friendships.

This kind of dependency is encouraged by a society in which pop songs, movies, and TV programs all promote the idea that other people are the antidote for unhappiness and insecurity.

Individuals who exhibit signs of relationship addiction need to work with counselors accustomed to dealing with addictive behavior, those who can get to the root of the problem (which often is the family of origin). A good book for clients and counselors who wish to learn more about relationship dependency is Howard M. Halpern's *How to Break Your Addiction to a Person.*

Addictive Behaviors

Loneliness leads to many addictive behaviors, including dependency on food, alcohol, tobacco, drugs, spending, exercise, sex. Any activity or substance can be abused. Any activity or substance that is overused or misused can be potentially damaging to the user. Addictive behaviors often begin as constructive efforts to broaden interests and get over loneliness or boredom. When an individual cannot live or function without a substance or activity and plans every other activity in life around that substance or activity, he or she is becoming addicted to it. Again, addictions need professional expertise and major support to break the patterns.

Fear of Not Having a Relationship/Mate

For many single adults, the possibility of never having a family manifests itself in such things as depression, feelings of being "stuck" in a location or in a job, fear of flying, and insomnia. At the root of some of these manifestations is the fear that death will occur before a "family" relationship can occur.

Not every person who fears not having a relationship will have serious manifestations, and not everyone who fears flying or suffers from loss of sleep is suffering from the fear of not having a relationship. It is true, however, that the "norms" of society in terms of lifestyle have serious implications for individuals and their mental and emotional health.

Unresolved Family Matters

Many adults have unresolved issues from the family of origin that affect the way they live and function as adults. Often these issues affect the way an individual responds to friends, business associates, and the opposite sex. These issues may surface in a marriage, but they are most obvious in people who move from relationship to relationship without ever finding a satisfactory or fulfilling situation. John Bradshaw's works are good reading for any person dealing with unresolved family issues.

Ghosts of Relationships Past

Kathy was happily assisting her friend Barry plant window boxes for spring. He told her he was going to get some fertilizer and disappeared into the garage. Kathy, who was enjoying the lovely spring day and the activity, continued about her business, not noticing that he had been gone for more than a few minutes. When she did realize, she called, "Barry?"

From the garage came a distressed answer, "Don't be upset! I'm really sorry!" A frustrated Barry emerged from the garage, a profusion of apologies and excuses rolling off his lips.

Kathy was perplexed. She wasn't upset or angry. Why was he reacting so strongly to such a simple inquiry?

In the past, whenever Barry lost track of time in this manner he was confronted by an upset and angry partner. He expected Kathy to react in a similar manner, so he reacted as if she already had!

For many single adults, problems from previous relationships keep surfacing, and it doesn't seem to matter whether or not the relationship was parental, marital, non-marital, or how long ago it occurred.

Ghosts of relationships past come out to play frequently, and men and women may need assistance in sorting them out, learning from them, and getting rid of them!

Single Parenting

Counseling cannot solve some of the major financial and time problems facing single parents, but it can provide support the single parent does not have at home—a sympathetic ear to hear problems and a caring voice to respond to confused thoughts. Loneliness is seldom stronger than for those who parent alone.

Divorce and Child Custody

Child support, family conflict, remarriage, and new relationships and their effect on children are some of the many issues that singles bring to counseling. Due to the touchy nature of these matters, it is helpful if the counselor is familiar with concepts of mediation or can refer the parties to a trained mediator able to assist in working out healthy, workable agreements, beginning with a style of communication that will be effective for all.

The counselor needs to understand the ongoing nature of these issues, how they intersect with the stages of the grief process, and how to assist in the development of coping skills. This calls for a blending of work on boundaries and communications skills (including Myers-Briggs typology work and mediation concepts) because the issues of loneliness and the frustrations of singleness and single parenting color all interactions. If individuals can be taught to disconnect from the old style of relating to the ex-spouse and learn to approach all communication from the perspective of two adults dealing over a business matter of mutual concern, there will be a more healthy resolution of issues as well as more healthy ongoing interaction.

Careers

Young single adults are generally entering first or second jobs and may be looking for career counseling as opposed to personal growth or crisis counseling. It is important, therefore, that those working in counseling capacities with this age group have career resources available and, if they are not equipped to give vocational testing, be able to direct younger singles to career counseling services.

Those who are suddenly single may find themselves in career re-entry or career transition as a result of a life crisis such as divorce or death of a spouse. Women who have spent much of their adult lives as homemakers may find themselves needing to enter the workforce for financial reasons. Men may need extra employment or need to readjust their thinking about their careers in the light of single parenting.

For the single person who has no mate with whom to discuss vocational issues, the counselor will be an important sounding board. Single adults need a setting where this type of discussion can happen with a caring, informed listener.

Spirituality

Singles are often drawn to people and places that touch them spiritually. This is a natural connection. The state of singleness offers the opportunity for introspection, which, when properly channeled, can lead to the development of a rich and rewarding spiritual life.

Most singles come to realize that there is a void in life which they cannot fill with things, activities, or people. At the same time, they may not be ready for a commitment to any church. They are searching. The counselor must stand ready to support in this search, never to pressure. When a single person indicates an interest in finding a place to deepen his or her relationship with Jesus Christ, or simply acknowledges a void in the spiritual realm, the counselor is in a position to provide direction by asking such questions as: Are you looking for a church where the sermon or message is of primary importance? Where the education is primary? Where the communion and liturgy are primary?

While always ready to welcome and assist singles in my own church, I also consider these questions: Does this person prefer a large or small congregation? Among what mix of people would he or she be most comfortable?

Counselors and single adult leaders are most helpful when they know their counterparts in other denominations and are willing to assist single adults in their search.

Sexuality

High on the agenda for most singles in counseling are issues of sexuality and sexual relationships. Raised in a society where sexual relationships were acceptable and blessed only in a lifelong, monogamous, heterosexual marriage, men and women today are marrying for the first time in their late twenties or early thirties— far past the age when "normal" sexual activity begins. In addition, the average lifespan is longer today than ever before, with the eighty-plus age group growing the fastest. Many in this group are single again, as are those who were divorced or widowed at a younger age. Counselors must be prepared to help men and women of all ages think through decisions regarding sexuality.

This requires thinking that considers these three questions:

1. Who are we as sexual human beings created by God?
2. What is meant by mature, responsible, loving adult relationships?
3. What is God's view of humanity in regard to sexuality?

Individuals need to understand the real and rightful need for affection and touch, which is often confused with sexual desire. The great family therapist Virginia Satir taught that every human being needs a minimum of three hugs a day to survive, seven to maintain, and more to be fully healthy and happy. Teaching people ways to experience safe hugs and touch among caring friends acknowledges this basic need and instinct.

Singles need a safe environment where they can talk about sexual issues with a leader who is trained to facilitate such a discussion, is non-judgmental, and has resources to offer on related issues such as AIDS and birth control. Many denominations are holding forums, and, to that end, have published studies to offer guidance.

Single adult counselors need to be aware of the statistics concerning sexual activity among all single adults, including the Christian singles population, and offer resources for learning about AIDS and other sexually transmitted diseases. While some single adults choose celibacy, and some are moving toward that choice, others choose active sex lives as well as active church lives. Counselors must be prepared to work with each of these persons and their choices.

Life Transitions

Transitions—the times between activities—are not periods of life with which Western society is prepared to cope. Yet many single adults come to counseling in a time of transition—post-college and pre-marriage or pre-job, post-marriage and whatever-comes-next, post-job and pre-move. The list goes on and on. Transitional periods should not be rushed or passed by without intention. What has been must be laid to rest and put into perspective with all that has gone before to prepare the individual for the next phase of life.

Single adults are often tempted to move too quickly from one state to another with no neutral time in between—for that "lonely" word pops up again. Looking at the statistics for divorces after second marriages, a counselor's mind will turn to those individuals who hurried into a new relationship rather than live with the loneliness that follows any period of adjustment. A helpful book on this subject is William Brides's *Transitions: Making Sense of Life's Changes*.

Regardless of the issue the counselor and the single adult are working on, there are important basics to remember:

1. *The counselee must take ownership of the issue.* It is his or her responsibility to create and perpetuate the counseling situation, work on the issue, and let it go.

2. *The counselee must be motivated to change.* Change is difficult. A famous Japanese pedagogue once said that if something has

been done one way ten times, it must be done a new way a minimum of 100 times before any change can take place. To want something to be different and to work to make it different are not the same.

If the counselee is "stuck" and unable to move out of a particular rut, ask, "What's in it for you to change . . . (name the behavior)?" Most will insist that they intensely dislike the rut even while they continue to stay in it. And the reason they stay in it generally is because they find some comfort in it. For example, a person who "works" on loneliness and depression in therapy and support group yet routinely refuses to participate in social activities continues to receive attention from concerned friends. When the attention-getting behavior is named and recognized, the counselee must decide whether to stay "stuck" or move on.

3. *For change to occur, knowledge must move from the head to the heart (i.e, the affective level).* This can be likened to the three stages of learning to ride a bicycle. At the head, or knowledge, level, the bicycle is recognized and perhaps ridden with the help of someone pushing and running alongside the two-wheeled machine. At the ability level, the rider can go for short distances without falling. At the mastery level, the skill is so ingrained that the rider can go for long distances, steer with one hand, talk at the same time, and will never forget how it's done.

New patterns of behavior or coping skills must move from the knowledge level to the internalized level if they are to be maintained outside the therapeutic setting, which is the goal of all good counseling.

What about Group Counseling?

Those *trained* in group dynamics and group counseling can make good use of group therapy situations. Notice that I emphasized the word *trained*. One of the dangers of the support group phenomenon is the lack of trained leadership. Group work that intends to go into any depth on issues needs a leader trained to handle responses that may be triggered through the work of the group. I cannot emphasize this enough. It is also important to interview those who want to join a group prior to accepting them. If you are considering someone who is in individual therapy, I recommend using a confidentiality form that requires a notarized signature of the person's therapist before accepting the person into the group. (There may be times when a therapist has good reasons for withholding consent for his or her client to participate in group therapy. Such a decision needs to be respected.)

Benefits of Group Counseling

Many issues can be dealt with beneficially in a group setting, including relationship dependency, inner child work, divorce and grief recovery, as well as basic issues of personal life and growth.

1. The individual can see that he or she is not the only person with a particular problem.

2. Listening to other people "work" can uncover issues that have been buried or defended in one-on-one work. In a group setting, listeners are more relaxed and less defensive and can recognize pieces of their own issues as other members work.

3. Groups provide both support and accountability for those on a recovery journey. People who understand issues and are committed to each other can encourage one another to continue during times of doubt and despair.

4. Groups working under a trained leader move toward health and resolution and develop new interactive as well as coping skills. Without such leadership, groups run the risk of becoming mired in old issues and not moving forward.

The counseling of single adults is a challenging new area for those in the helping professions. Significant research is being conducted in many areas that are new to professionals as well as to laity, so it is important for anyone working in the area to stay abreast of the findings. The issues are broad, diverse, and complex. And as we approach the turn of the century, these findings will apply to nearly half of the population of the United States.

3
Developing Meaningful Support Groups

Jim Dyke

Support groups are small groups that provide ongoing encouragement for people dealing with specific personal growth issues. Support groups are *not* "therapy" groups. Therapy groups are led by professional counselors and provide therapy for psychosis or neurosis—emotional states or issues that are beyond the parameters of effective support-group dynamics. In fact, psychotic or neurotic individuals have the potential of disrupting support groups and should probably be referred to professionals rather than be allowed to participate in the kind of "low-level" support groups we are talking about here.

Support groups typically are not counseling groups either. Counseling groups provide counseling for specific therapeutic issues and give members direction in growth and development. Counseling groups should be led by trained professionals with appropriate degrees and licensing.

Support groups are small groups intended to provide members with a network of encouraging relationships—an ongoing source of support as they take the advice and direction of professional counselors and put it into practice. The support group is a "cheerleading squad" that encourages members and provides account-ability as each person moves forward in personal growth.

Support groups are typically structured around a particular issue—alcoholism, divorce recovery, adult-child syndromes, spou-sal abuse, childhood neglect or abuse, and the like. Many support groups require individuals to make a commitment to a long-term process of growth and healing. Twelve-step groups are a good example of this. Such groups tend to be static in member-ship once they are filled, since members will be participating for some time.

Some types of support groups have a more fluid membership, however, because they deal with issues of a temporary nature. Groups that provide support for divorce recovery, grief recovery, or career transitions are good examples.

Some support groups provide education. Their purpose is to sup-ply members with information to help them cope with their par-ticular situation. Examples of such groups include caregivers for patients with Alzheimer's disease, diabetes, and multiple sclero-sis as well as groups for the patients themselves, such as those who have received organ transplants.

All support groups share the same general parameters: They pro-vide individual support by drawing on the group dynamic for encouragement and accountability.

The Need for Support Groups

The Reality of Our Culture

The single adult phenomenon in America is a cultural tidal wave that is transforming every level of our society. One often overlooked fact is that the single adult phenomenon is not only a cause of societal problems but also an effect. It is the result of fail-ures in marriage, family, relationships, and values. The small group, in its varied forms and applications, is a laboratory that allows members to acquire the skills and capacities that a healthy family is meant to supply. Good small groups help participants learn to love, relate, trust, communicate, care, encourage, give and receive grace, fail, take risks, and grow.

Sermons alone will not meet the needs of people; teaching is too often a cognitive event, separated from real-life application and practice. The counseling session alone will not provide what is needed for healing and growth; therapy is divorced from the relational dynamic of life (a concept that is well articulated in Paul's "body" metaphor in 1 Corinthians 12). In short, we need support groups because *people* need them.

The Reality of Our Limitations

Single adult ministers cannot possibly schedule enough counseling sessions to meet people's needs. To try to do so would be more than an exercise in futility; it would be a denial of New Testament ecclesiology, a refutation of the body life dynamic so important to the health of the church. In short, support groups are necessary because *we* need them!

The Ingredients of Good Support Groups

Leadership

A support group cannot be effective without good leadership. Participants cannot be counted on to keep the group on track, enforce accountability, provide follow-up, or make referrals. The best support groups are led by facilitators who have experienced growth and healing in the issue involved and have had some training that equips them for the role of facilitation.

Focus

Effective support groups generally use a "rifle shot" rather than a "shotgun" approach. In other words, they usually focus on a specific issue rather than try to deal with many different issues. In one respect, this is a practical matter, since some groups (e.g., twelve-step programs) have guidelines that are specific to the issue they are addressing.

Progress

The intent of a support group is that participants will make progress in their area of difficulty. The danger is that the group will become codependent and patronizing, leaving the recipients "stuck" at some point short of full health. The best support groups support members in their *growth*. Ministry leaders would do well to have a monitoring system of some type in place to make sure groups are indeed making progress. Also needed is a plan ready to be implemented if a group is not making progress.

Integration

The support group must reflect a biblical theology of personhood, relationship, Godhood, sin, forgiveness, and healing. Unless the group dynamic is integrated biblically, it is in danger of leading members to destructive decisions and anti-therapeutic attitudes.

Effective support groups are also integrated with the sponsoring ministry, which provides supervision, administration, follow-up, support, and management. A host of issues arises when support groups become part of a ministry (e.g., promotion and advertising, referral, room use, and encouragement of leaders). Someone on staff must accept the responsibility of keeping the support groups from becoming an "orphaned" ministry.

Finally, the support groups must be integrated with other elements of personal growth and life experience. Support groups must never take the place of individual therapy with a trained counselor, nor should they take the place of normal socialization and relationship in the church. It is up to the leaders to hold group members accountable for seeing a counselor (if necessary) and for participating in regular church activities (always necessary!). Without integration on all levels the support group will become unhealthy and dysfunctional.

How to Get Good Support Groups Going

Sometimes the single adult leader will discern a need and initiate a support group. Other times, people will step forward with a desire to start a group to meet a particular need. In any case, it is the leader's responsibility to help discern the will of God with regard to the ministry (i.e., Is this something the Lord wants us to do?) and it is also his or her responsibility to provide direction and to maintain the quality of the ministry (e.g., to select and affirm the leaders and to give general oversight).

Define the Need

"What do you want to do?" is a simple enough question, yet many leaders fail to ask it. Another way of asking this question is "What need do we want to address?" The answer is crucial to a good beginning, because good support groups are specific about the need they address; they are effective because they are focused.

Look around. Get to know people. Think about their needs. Think about the counseling sessions you have had recently. What patterns are emerging? What common life experiences or challenges are people facing? Think. Reflect. Analyze. Pray for discernment and guidance, and then do your mental and spiritual homework. This is the task of the spiritual leader and it cannot be delegated.

One of two things will probably occur at this point—either you will be impressed by a specific need or someone will emerge with a passion to meet a specific need within a group.

Find a Competent Leader/Facilitator

The right group leader is critical to the success of a support group. When you select (or affirm) a leader, you are looking for someone who has general qualities and meets specific requirements. General qualities include emotional and social maturity and spiritual depth. These are important because the leader will be a role model to the group members. The leader also needs to be able to handle the emotional stress of a support group—he or she must know how to shepherd people without burning out. And, most important, the leader must represent the gospel with integrity—he or she must model biblical values and Christlike spirituality. In short, you need a good leader, a "team player," someone you can work with, administrate, and support to the fullest.

In addition to these general qualities, you need someone who understands the life experience the group will address. There is a curious (and maybe biblical) irony here: The best support group leaders are often those who have experienced the issue they will help others face.

A word of caution is in order, however. A common dysfunction among people who have faced painful life experiences is denial. The worst kind of support group leader is one who denies the effects of a difficult experience and represses the resulting emotional issues, often covering everything with false "coping" skills and simplistic spirituality. This is a person who needs intervention and therapy, not a position of leadership.

Look carefully at those you are considering for group leadership. Find out about their life experiences and make sure they are dealing with their own personal issues honestly, realistically, and therapeutically.

The leader you are looking for also needs to have had some training or equipping experiences. The most basic kind of equipping experience is participation in a good support group. For example, twelve-step groups can equip participants. The well-defined structure, values, and tactics of these groups make it easy for members to learn how to make a twelve-step group "work." Find out if prospective leaders have been part of a good group. Ask about other training they have had which has equipped them for leadership (e.g., schooling, training seminars, workshops, co-leaderships, or internships).

If you have a motivated but untrained prospective leader, consider investing some time and resources in training. Keep in mind that this person will be the major factor in the success of the group—screening potential members, facilitating group participation (you need a good listener, not a talker!), referring members to counseling (when necessary), and shepherding and encouraging the members.

Define the Group

Defining the group is a two-step process that begins with paper and pencil and culminates with people. The first step is to develop a clear statement of purpose that defines the group's focus, term, participation, accountability, structure, and other boundaries. The key is to avoid having people join the group with different expectations because that will lead to conflict and disenchantment.

The second step is to assemble a "critical mass" for the group (i.e., the minimum number of people required to make the group effective). If you have fewer than four people who will commit to consistent attendance for the initial term, the group may not survive. It is also a good idea to have an assistant or co-leader for the group—someone who can help shoulder leadership responsibility (especially follow-up and between-meeting "shepherding") or maybe be a "leader-in-training" who has demonstrated the gifts and potential for leadership in the future.

Market the Group

This may sound a bit crass, but you need to get the word out about the group. Do some promotion and advertising. Start with your own church. Use worship folder inserts, posters, handouts, and parish newsletters to let the congregation know about the group. Work the congregational network by connecting with other leaders in your church (e.g., women's or men's ministry, youth ministry, adult Sunday school, staff counselor, etc.).

The next step of promotion is to work the network outside your own congregation—get information about the group to local counseling centers (they often are looking for good support groups to which they can refer clients), pastors, and single adult ministry leaders.

Finally, target the non-churched community by getting information out to local newspapers, community groups, radio and television community bulletin boards, and any other promotional avenue in your area. Seriously consider paid advertising in your newspaper. (Do what you can to keep your ad off the church page. Put it on the same page as "Ann Landers" or "Dear Abby" instead.)

Be creative! Sometimes the best way to promote a support group is by using a special event as a springboard. For example, launch a divorce recovery support group at a weekend divorce recovery workshop. That way you can say to participants at the end of the conference, "If you want to continue the good things you have begun this weekend, join us next Tuesday night at our weekly divorce recovery support group."

The sad reality is that even if you have a meaningful group experience to offer people it may not survive if it's not promoted well enough.

Manage the Group

The ministry leader's role is critical in the area of management—support groups will not manage themselves. Good management begins with a healthy relationship to the group leader—a relationship of accountability and support. The group leader should be directly accountable to an administrative leader. Part of this accountability is organizational, but the most important aspect of it is personal and spiritual. The small group leader will need much encouragement and support. The ministry leader will be the one with the shoulder to cry on as well as the one to exact moral and spiritual integrity from the group leader. (If there is a problem in this area, there is an obligation to deal with it quickly and unequivocally!)

The ministry leader is also the liaison with the organization. This means dealing with a host of administrative details in order to give support to the ministry, such as making sure the group is on the calendar of events with a room assignment and published meeting times. Organizational support includes the physical resources of budget and equipment and the non-material (but essential) political backing required for any ministry, especially one that has potential controversy. Each group needs a champion who will make sure the church leadership understands the importance of the group and gives it credence and support. How your group leader perceives the ministry is vital: Does he or she see it as an orphan or a family member? A member of the ministry family is accepted, approved, affirmed, supported, and given visibility and resources. An orphan is shuffled into the background, given leftover facilities and equipment, and is unrecognized and unsupported. Make sure that your support group ministry is part of the mainstream of ministry life at your church and is given the same kind of credibility and support that other, more traditional ministries receive (e.g., Sunday school, vacation Bible school, youth camp, nursery).

Support Groups Are Many and Varied

Support groups come in many shapes. Each has distinctive elements and must be understood in the light of its unique purpose and the special needs of its members. The following are a sample of highly sensitive group needs to help you understand how important it is to build each group carefully according to its unique elements.

Note that some groups must be led by trained professionals.

Twelve-Step

Twelve-step groups have well-defined elements, including values, approach, handbooks, and even session structure. The special dynamics of alcoholism (or any addiction, for that matter) give definition to the recovery process and the issues that are addressed. Don't be surprised if more people from *other* churches attend than from your own church—many members will be more comfortable if they can maintain anonymity.

Recommended Resources

McGee, Robert S. *Overcoming Chemical Dependency.* Dallas: Word, 1990.

Meier, Paul, et al. *Love Is a Choice: Recovery for Codependent Relationships.* Nashville: Thomas Nelson, 1989.

Springle, Pat. *Healing and Hope for People Caught in the Web of Dysfunctional Relationships.* Dallas: Word, 1990.

Twelve Steps: A Spiritual Journey. Recovery Publications, 1988.

Twelve Steps for Christians. Recovery Publications, 1988.

Adult Children

The experiences of adult children of alcoholics create definite parameters for recovery and healing—their personal growth odyssey is often complicated by codependent relationships, addictions, compulsive behavior patterns, and denial. They often need to confront abusive parents as a part of their recovery. Many times their struggles are wrapped up in divorce recovery and parenting issues.

People in this category comprise a big part of our population, especially if you include childhood abuse (psychological, emotional, and physical) as well as family alcoholism in the childhood experience. The childhood rules that these kids grow up with (according to Friel and Friel, they are "don't feel; don't talk; don't trust") make communication and transparency difficult for them as adults.

Recommended Resources

Carder, Dave, et al. *Secrets of Your Family Tree: Healing for Adult Children of Dysfunctional Families.* Chicago: Moody, 1991.

Ells, Alfred H. *One-Way Relationships Workbook: The 12-week, step-by-step interactive plan for recovery from codependent relationships.* Nashville: Thomas Nelson, 1992.

Farmer, Steven. *Adult Children of Abusive Parents: A Healing Program for Those Who Have Been Physically, Sexually, or Emotionally Abused.* Los Angeles: Lowell House, 1989.

Field, David. *Family Personalities.* Eugene, Ore.: Harvest House, 1988.

Friel, John and Linda. *Adult Children: The Secrets of Dysfunctional Families.* Minneapolis: Interhealth Publications, 1988.

Stoop, David, and James Masteller. *Forgiving Our Parents, Forgiving Ourselves: Healing Adult Children of Dysfunctional Families.* Ann Arbor, Mich.: Servant, 1991.

Woititz, Janet. *Adult Children of Alcoholics.* Pompano Beach, Fla.: Health Communications, Inc., 1983.

Incest and Molestation Survivors

These experiences have lifelong effects on people. Yet the memories of such experiences have often been buried by the victim, sometimes coming to the surface via disturbing images and "flashbacks." The healing process is further complicated by the psychological and emotional barriers erected by survivors. The fragile nature of growth and healing under these circumstances creates unique demands on a support group. Members need individual counseling and specialized facilitation (survivors often confront perpetrators as a part of their healing). Don't try a group like this unless you have help from a counseling professional who deals specifically with this kind of need.

Recommended Resources

Allender, Dan. *The Wounded Heart: Hope for Adult Victims of Childhood Sexual Abuse.* Colorado Springs: NavPress, 1990.

Benner, David G. *Healing Emotional Wounds.* Grand Rapids: Baker, 1990.

Frank, Jan. *Door of Hope.* San Bernardino, Calif.: Here's Life, 1987.

Heitritter, Lynn, and Jeanette Vought. *Helping Victims of Sexual Abuse: A Sensitive, Biblical Guide for Counselors, Victims and Families.* Minneapolis: Bethany, 1989.

Skrip, Cathy, and Kristin Kunzman. *Women with Secrets: Dealing with Domestic Abuse and Childhood Sexual Abuse in Treatment.* Minneapolis: The Hazelden Foundation, 1991.

Religious Abuse

This category is difficult to address because it requires a delicate process of "reprogramming" a victim's theological framework and re-establishing a relationship of trust. This requires commitment and selfless compassion on the part of the group leader. Christian counselors are accustomed to using Scripture in a therapeutic way to address personal issues, but these victims have experienced Scripture as a controlling and exploiting force. A further irony is that many conservative Christian churches, in their legalism, practice a form of the same spiritual control and abuse, even though they profess to be thoroughly biblical.

Recommended Resources

Smedes, Lewis. *Shame and Grace: Healing the Shame We Don't Deserve.* New York: HarperCollins, 1993.

VanVonderen, Jeff. *The Subtle Power of Spiritual Abuse.* Minneapolis: Bethany, 1993.

———. *Tired of Trying to Measure Up: Getting Free from the Demands, Expectations, and Intimidations of Well-Meaning People.* Minneapolis: Bethany, 1989.

Ritual Abuse

This is a new and disturbing form of abuse that has been getting attention in the secular press and therapeutic community. The healing process of these survivors is complicated by their experience of abuse—the very symbols and elements of the church that we associate with the love, grace, and protection of God have been used as instruments of sexual and physical abuse. As a result, many survivors cannot even walk into a church without experiencing disturbing feelings of victimization and pain. To complicate the situation, this experience has been associated with multiple personality disorder (MPD). Don't attempt an MPD group without a strong connection with a professional who has had specialized training.

Recommended Resources

Friesen, J. *Uncovering the Mystery of Multiple Personality Disorder.*

Additional Resources

The Zondervan Lifelines for Recovery Series. Grand Rapids: Zondervan. This series of resources covers the gamut of topics, including incest, eating disorders, sexual addiction, codependency, divorce recovery, and post-abortion trauma.

Life Recovery Guides. Downers Grove, Ill.: InterVarsity. These studies deal with addiction and codependency.

Know Your Limits:
Referring to God and Others

Jerry Schreur

David, help!" It was a normally hectic day at my office and I found myself facing a counseling situation that was over my head. I picked up the phone, as I had done many times before when I didn't know what to do, and dialed the number of one of my referral sources.

Even though I have nearly twenty years of experience as a pastoral counselor and am a Ph.D. candidate in family studies, I often find myself in situations that I am not qualified to handle. Counselees with problems such as anorexia, bulimia, chemical addiction, or clinical depression are beyond my expertise. It took me more years than I care to admit to realize that although I am a good counselor, some people need the help of someone with more specialized skills. I like to believe that I can fix any problem, but the truth is, I can't. I don't know it all and I haven't seen it all. I need to know my own limits and know when to turn my clients over to someone else.

All of us get involved in situations that require a "multitude of counselors" (Prov. 11:14; 15:22 KJV). Some realize it and do not hesitate to ask for help. Others try to do it all themselves. In the process they rob others of the help they need and burn themselves out trying to deal with situations they are not equipped to handle.

Anita came to me at the end of her rope. She was convinced that she was beyond hope, beyond help, and that even God had given up on her. Anita confessed that she suffered from sexual addiction. She had been in counseling with her pastor for many months. After she admitted to him her sin of sexual immorality and asked God for forgiveness, he told her that she was "cured" and that she could go on with her life. Her problem persisted, however, and each failure was followed by a tearful episode with her pastor and another prayer for forgiveness. After many attempts to fix her problem in this way her pastor told her that God was not forgiving her because she did not belong to God. Her continued sin, he said, was the sign of an unrepentant heart. This drove Anita even deeper into sexual immorality, culminating in clinical depression and multiple suicide attempts.

When she came into my office she was a broken, despairing woman. I immediately called a friend who was trained and experienced in counseling those with addictive behaviors, and I referred Anita to her. I wondered why her pastor had failed to do the same thing. What kept him from asking for help with a problem that was so far outside his area of expertise? And I wondered what would have happened to Anita had she not finally found someone who could help her.

How do we know when we are over our heads? When should we refer to others? How do we build referral sources? Why do we find it so difficult to let go? How can we refer counselees to God and His help and providence?

Even after all these years it bothers me to refer my clients to others. Not because I think I'm superman, but because it can seem that by referring I'm admitting that I have failed, that I am not good enough or smart enough to handle this person's problems.

I have seen many counselors refuse to refer their clients even when their counseling is going nowhere and they have no clue as to where it should be going. Often these counselors and pastors blame counselees to rationalize their lack of progress. "He doesn't want to get better" or "She's not following my advice." The real truth may be much simpler. As simple as this, in fact. The counselee has gone as far as possible with the counselor and now needs to be referred to someone else. Someone with different skills and abilities.

It is natural to feel some reluctance to refer a person who has come to you for help. That person trusts you and has honored you with his or her confidence. It is difficult to say, "I can't help you, but I know someone who can." If you refuse to do so, however, you run the risk of becoming bogged down, frustrated, and ineffective.

Discomfort with referral isn't always due to pride or feelings of failure. Some people distrust psychologists and psychology. Pastor Bill refuses to refer any member of his congregation to any psychologist, Christian or not. He believes that psychology has its roots in "godless atheism and secular humanism" and that nothing good can come of it. If prayer, confession, and Bible reading won't help, nothing will.

This pastor is a godly man, but he is guilty of throwing the baby out with the bath water. Not all of psychology is good, but psychology held up to the light of Scripture can be a valuable tool for the pastoral counselor. This pastor's closed mind hurts his congregation and denies many the help they need.

If you struggle with psychology and therapy from a philosophical point of view read books by Christian counselors. Talk to some Christian men and women who use psychology as a tool to help people find God's joy in life. Let these professionals tell you about their own faith so that you will be secure in referring clients to them. Getting to know a godly counselor may relieve some of your fears and help you change your perspective on psychological counseling.

Other people don't refer because they can't let go. A good friend of mine was nearly driven from the ministry by divorces that occurred among the leaders of his church over a concentrated period of time. He wore himself out trying to keep these families together. He couldn't bear to let them go to another counselor because he believed that only he could help them. This man had an unhealthy need to fix everything, and he very nearly lost his own family and his ministry trying to do it. The technical, though overused, term for this is *codependence.* It can devastate both the counselor and the client.

Whatever reasons you have for refusing to refer, honestly acknowledge them and get on with the business of helping hurting people. And sometimes helping them means helping them find someone else to walk with on the next leg of their journey toward healing.

When to Refer

To decide whether or not to refer a client, ask yourself these questions:

- Do I have the time to help this person?
- Do I have the training necessary to help this person?
- Do I want to get involved (or get further involved) in this situation?
- Could someone else do a better job with this person?
- Have I helped this person as much as I can?

The first question is very important, especially for leaders whose responsibilities reach beyond counseling: *Do I have the time to help this person?*

Counseling is about half of my workload, and many times I have to refer counselees simply because I don't have the time available to help them. Some people need to see a counselor three times a week. Do you have time to help such a person? Are you prepared to work with someone over months and years?

Amy came into my office with her head so low I couldn't see the features on her face. Her hair hung limply over her eyes. Every move seemed to take great effort. Although Amy's struggles reached back to her early childhood, I was sure I could help her find the love and strength from God that she had lacked her entire life. I never dreamed that I would be involved in Amy's life for almost three years on a regular basis. Every time we made progress in one area, another problem would rear its head. I should have referred Amy after the first few sessions, certainly after the first year. I didn't have the time to help her. But I didn't refer her; I invested much time and energy into a situation that someone else should have been handling.

Pastor Stockman was a good and godly man who made others feel comfortable. He was in great demand as a counselor, and he was a good one. Word spread quickly throughout the community that Pastor Stockman was available and that his counseling was not only helpful but free. Soon his schedule was so jammed with counseling that he found it hard to meet with people from his own church, and his job performance suffered badly. The situation came to a head at an impromptu personnel committee meeting that turned into a shouting match.

Pastor Stockman could have avoided this hostile encounter with his church leaders if he had acknowledged his own limitations and learned to refer to other counselors those he didn't have the time to help.

The second question is often more difficult to answer: *Do I have the training necessary to help this person?* This does not mean that you need an earned doctorate to be an effective pastoral counselor. Nor does it mean that specialized training is always necessary. It simply means that not everyone is equipped to help every person who needs it. For instance, I refer everyone with an eating disorder or a problem with substance abuse. I simply don't know enough about these issues to be effective. And most adolescents who come to me I refer to my son. Why? Because he's better with them than I am. As a youth pastor and speaker, he has made teenagers his specialty and lifework.

Oh, I could bluff it, but that wouldn't be in my client's best interest, nor in the long run would it be in mine. Another counselor friend refers some of his marriage counseling to me. It is one of the areas in which I am most experienced and well trained.

The answer to this question demands honesty. Keep asking yourself, Is this an area I am familiar with? Can I really shed light on this subject? Am I able to help here or does this person need someone else?

Specialized problems often require specialized help, and the best you can do to help your client is to find a counselor with the appropriate skills and training.

Other areas that send up red flags for me are long-term clinical depression, extreme sexual abuse, and homosexuality. Your list will be different from mine, so take the time to make one of your own.

The third question may seem strange: *Do I really want to get involved in this situation?*

Is it even fair for a counselor to ask such a question? Yes, and not only is it fair, it's necessary as well. Sometimes we don't have the emotional reserves to effectively counsel in certain situations. Sometimes our own struggles interfere with our helping. Before taking on a long-term client, ask yourself, *Do I want to get in this for the long haul? Do I want to spend the hours necessary to help this person?* Sometimes my answer is no. Sometimes I doubt my client's seriousness and don't want to get bogged down with someone who wants to talk about problems but not work on them. Sometimes people are too close to me for me to counsel them effectively. To all these situations I answer, *No, I really don't want to get involved in that situation.*

Could someone else do a better job with this person? If we are honest with ourselves the answer to this question almost always will be yes. There is always someone somewhere with better education, training, or skills. But that's not what I'm talking about.

What I mean is, taking all things into consideration (including a person's financial resources), are you qualified to do the job or could someone you trust do it better?

Another factor to consider is trust. People come to you because they are comfortable with you. Perhaps you've helped a friend or family member, so they trust you. Often that trust is more important than a better education or more experience.

A word of caution here: Just because you haven't dealt with a particular problem before doesn't mean you are incapable of helping a person with it. In the majority of cases you will be able to provide help and hope to your client. This guideline isn't meant to erode your confidence in your skills or your education; it's simply to encourage you to be honest and realistic about your abilities and your experience.

The last question to ask yourself is: *Have I helped this person as much as I can?*

Sometimes counseling relationships reach a point where sessions are no longer productive and your resources and guidance have been exhausted. Then it is time to gently help the person find another counselor. People with deep struggles often need more than one individual to help them sort out their lives. When you have done all you can, let go. It is tempting to stay involved, to think that maybe next week you'll reach that breakthrough. But more often the stalemate will continue, and sometimes clients lose hope if the counselor doesn't say, "I think we've gone as far together as we can. You need someone else for the next step of your journey."

From your answers to the questions above, you can conclude that you should refer in the following situations:

- When you have neither the time nor the training to really help
- When for various reasons you don't feel comfortable getting involved
- When someone else could be of greater help
- When you have given all you can give

It is okay to admit that you can't help everybody, that some people will benefit from another's counsel. It is okay to reach a stalemate and advise your client to seek help elsewhere. "Margie, I know we've spent a great deal of time together and you have been remarkably honest with me. But we're not making the progress we should be making. My friend Tom Williams is a great counselor, and I believe that right now he can help you more."

How Do You Find a Good Referral Source?

Finding good referral sources isn't as simple as opening a phone book and flipping through the yellow pages. Some counselors do everything right: They know their limits, let go of their clients, refer them when they need specialized or continued help, but they don't follow through well. They refer to someone they don't know and maybe don't even trust. One pastor told me that he doesn't refer his counselees because he doesn't know any psychologists he can trust.

How do you find qualified people whom you can trust to guide your counselees through their struggles? How do you find people with the specialized knowledge that is often required? How do you really know that your referral source is doing a good job?

There are no easy answers to those questions. Finding good referral sources is often hard work, and it uses up a precious resource: time.

The first avenue to explore when looking for qualified referral sources is local pastors. Find out whom they recommend.

Another good place to get names is by calling the major Christian counseling clinics. Yes, you can call Minirth-Meier, Rapha, and New Life Treatment Centers. Ask for recommendations in your area. These clinics have relationships with many counselors across the country.

Next, go to local hospitals and talk to the mental health directors. They often have good leads.

If the names of one or two people keep coming up, call and set up a time to meet them individually, maybe over lunch or breakfast.

Then ask direct questions. First, of course, is "Are you a Christian committed to biblical truth?" Some other questions to ask are, "What is your view of mental illness?" (You'll want to be sure it is similar to your own.) "What do you believe about divorce?"

Express your concerns and be forthright. Explain that you are looking for referral sources and that they have been recommended to you. Tell them that you want to find out about them as a person as well as about their counseling skills and areas of expertise.

Once you have a list of potential referral sources, it is up to you to get to know them individually and to make your own judgments. An important thing to remember when looking for referrals is that you have to be comfortable with them. If you are not comfortable with them, chances are you won't refer, or you'll wait too long before doing so. Spend the time necessary to find good, qualified, caring people. In the last two months I've added two names to my list of referral sources and removed one.

I also recommend having more than one or two sources. Find people who are specialists, especially in such areas as eating disorders, sexual addiction and dysfunction, substance abuse, and sexual abuse. I also suggest working out an arrangement whereby busy counselors will see your referrals fairly quickly. Referring counselees and then watching them struggle as they wait for two months for an appointment may cause you to think twice before referring again. Ask your new sources if they have a backlog of clients (many of the best ones do). You want to be sure they can handle the people you send to them.

How Do You Refer People to God?

Perhaps the most difficult task of helpers is to get people to look to God for help. Many clients are despairing and have lost hope. Abusive backgrounds or horrible circumstances have caused them to see God as someone who is uncaring, punitive, or vengeful, not as a loving Father.

Entire books have been written on this subject, so all I want to do here is stress that real healing and growth do not occur outside of a relationship with God. The first and often biggest step toward healing is accomplished when counselees lift their eyes heavenward and ask for healing and forgiveness from God.

The responsibility of Christian counselors is to help people come to a biblical understanding of the God of all comfort (2 Cor. 1:3–7) and to see Jesus as the man of sorrows, acquainted with grief (even theirs) (Isa. 53). They need to see His power in their lives and to feel His healing hand and His comforting embrace. Hurting people need to experience God's presence to know that He is there and that they are loved by the One who made them.

Finally we need to show them God's providence. They need to see that the world is not spinning out of control, that the Creator and Sustainer of the universe is there and that He has the final say. Pointing people to God is an important task, and it is necessary for most psychological growth to take place. We cannot create a complete dichotomy between the spiritual and the emotional. They are intertwined.

Referring counselees to God, therefore—to get them to see His love and healing hand and to feel His presence in their lives—must be one of our primary objectives and responsibilities.

Dos and Don'ts for Counselors

Do refer to Christian counselors when possible. Shared personal and spiritual values make for a better referral relationship and for better counseling.

Do refer clients as soon as you know you cannot adequately deal with the issues.

Do know your limitations. No one knows it all; it is okay to refer.

Do be aware of your strengths and use them. You are better at some things than licensed counselors and psychologists. Don't shortchange yourself.

Don't wait until clients are in a crisis before referring. In some cases they could hurt themselves or others if you do not refer them at the appropriate time.

Don't think because you lack a Ph.D. you cannot be effective.

Don't assume all non-Christian counselors are evil and cannot be helpful. Many non-Christian counselors are well trained and are not biased against Christianity.

Don't believe everything you hear about a particular counselor, especially if your source of information is a disgruntled former client. Talk to the referral source directly and get the other side of the story. Remember, because of confidentiality the counselor may be unable to tell you very much. Talk in generalities rather than specifics.

Don't assume credentials make a good counselor. There are some great counselors without the sheepskin. And there are some people whose walls are covered with academic honors and degrees who are not helpful counselors.

Part 2

Helping with Difficult Feelings and Emotions

5

Low Self-Esteem and Self-Worth: Am I Valuable?

Dennis Franck

One of the most common struggles of single adults today is low self-esteem, and the problem is not limited to any particular economic, social, spiritual, cultural, racial, political, or ethnic background.

Webster defines esteem this way: "to value highly" or "to have a great regard for." Consequently, persons with low self-esteem do not regard themselves very highly and do not think they are valuable. Other phrases that describe low self-esteem include "not feeling worthwhile or important," "feeling inferior," "having a low perspective of oneself," and "not loving oneself in a wholesome and healthy way."

People with low self-esteem are like those who use crutches. They can function, but their mobility is hampered. Feelings of low self-worth keep them from functioning freely.

The results of not conquering low self-esteem are seen and felt in all aspects of life.

Spiritual—growth slows down and may even cease for periods of time.

Relational—relationships grow slowly and with difficulty.

Social—growth slows down or becomes non-existent for a period of time; social situations are tense and the single adult feels awkward.

Emotional—frequent discouragements and occasional despair.

Physical—appearance and health may be affected in one of two ways: undercompensation or overcompensation.

Vocational—work habits are affected in one of two ways: undercompensation, meaning little or no effort is put into a vocation, or overcompensation, meaning the person becomes a workaholic.

Symptoms and Struggles

Spiritual

Single adults with low self-esteem may have trouble accepting God's love because they feel unloved and may think of themselves as unlovable. The question "Why would God want to love me?" sometimes persists. They think they must earn God's love by being "good enough" to deserve it and are frustrated because they don't seem to measure up. They may have trouble believing the promises in God's Word because they see them through their perspective of low self-worth. People with low self-esteem may have difficulty desiring to pray or even believing that God would answer prayer. Consequently, they may not pray very much.

Relational

People who believe they are inferior to others have trouble believing anyone can truly enjoy their company. This makes it difficult for them to make friends and keeps them from having confidence when relating to others.

Too often they play the dangerous game of comparison. I call it dangerous because people with low self-esteem usually compare themselves to those who have more ability, money, talents, friends, or confidence. As a result they may think even less of themselves than before. Comparison only reinforces low self-esteem.

People with low self-esteem make little effort to relate to others because they feel they have little to offer. And when they do seek a relationship the person on the other end, perhaps sensing that he or she will have to do most of the giving, shows little interest. As a result, interpersonal relationships are many times strained and shallow.

Those with low self-esteem seek approval and affirmation from other people. This may show up in "doing and giving" in order to evoke feelings of self-worth or commendation and approval from others.

Social

Single adults with low self-esteem may appear awkward, nervous, and tense. Consequently, they may avoid social functions where many people will be present. Feeling as if they do not measure up, they become shy and timid.

On the other hand, single adults with an outgoing temperament may become boisterous and talkative as a way to cover up their lack of confidence. They fear having others discover their weakness of low self-worth. (I have known a few who wanted someone to discover their pain, but they admitted this only after it had been uncovered.)

Emotional

People who long to conquer their inferiority complex but have been unable to do so often become discouraged. Discouragement sometimes leads to jealousy of those who seem to be confident, poised, and self-assured. They wish for the same confidence and self-reliance they see in others. Feelings of despair and hopelessness may persist for quite a while.

If anyone senses the need and offers encouraging comments, people with low self-esteem may become even more despondent, thinking "He's just saying that to be nice" or "She doesn't really believe those good things about me."

Physical

The constant struggle with low self-worth may reveal itself in sloppy and unkempt dress. Low self-esteem often causes people to do little or nothing to try to look physically attractive. Taking a defeatist attitude, they reason, "What's the use? I'm not going to be attractive no matter what I do."

In addition to apathy toward grooming, low self-esteem may show up in lack of concern for nutrition and health. Overeating and lack of exercise could also be a symptom of a poor self-image.

On the other hand, some people with low self-esteem over-compensate in all of these areas. They spend an excessive amount of time and money on expensive clothing to convince themselves and others that they are "somebody." They may go overboard in the categories of food and exercise as well, being overly picky about food and excessively concerned with exercise.

Vocational

Symptoms in this area may be laziness, apathy, and slothful-ness toward finding and/or retaining employment. A low self-con-cept drains motivation and self-discipline. Many single adults find this to be true when it pertains to a job or career. The opposite, however, may also be true. Some people may overcompensate by working a lot of overtime and becoming workaholics. This makes them feel productive and, as a result, feel good about themselves.

Counseling Suggestions

Your choice of counseling strategies will depend on the length of the person's struggle, the severity of the problem, and the extent to which the person recognizes and understands the situation. Use discretion regarding these suggestions.

Help Counselees Recognize and Admit Their Poor Self-Image

Most counselees will have little difficulty expressing their prob-lem to you. Some, however, do not recognize it due to confusion, depression, or comparison to others. If you recognize the problem first and try to discuss it, they may hesitate to admit their struggle. Suggest that low self-esteem is a problem and ask if they agree. In a few cases, counselees may not want to admit their struggle due to embarrassment, possible humiliation, fear of rejection, or misunderstanding. In these cases, assure the person of your total acceptance and concern.

Help Counselees Discover the Causes of Low Self-Esteem

Most causes of low self-esteem can be traced to a specific time period in life. And often there is more than one cause.

Childhood

- Perceived lack of parental love and affection
- Long-lasting hurt resulting from parents' separation or divorce
- Unhealthy step-parent relationship
- Painful memories from a workaholic or alcoholic parent
- Death of a parent
- Lack of healthy peer friendships
- Perceived rejection from significant people (parents, grandparents, siblings, etc.)
- Ongoing ridicule
- Misunderstanding of the difference between wholesome and arrogant pride
- Perceived inferiority due to race, lack of education, physical or mental handicap, poverty, etc.

Adulthood

- Breakup of a long or close relationship
- Separation or divorce
- Loss of a job
- Acceptance of distorted media influence[1]
- Failure
- Pride, anger, envy, or greed

- Lack of healthy peer friendships (possibly due to schedule, job transfers, etc.)
- Chemical imbalance
- Dysfunctional relationship (maybe abusive)
- Perceived inferiority due to race, lack of education, physical or mental handicap, poverty, etc.

Start out by asking counselees if they know what is causing their poor self-image. If they do, you've got a head start. If they don't, begin asking questions to find out. Here are some to get you started:

- "When did you begin to feel this way? Was it as a child or as an adult?"
- "Is this a continuous or an occasional struggle?"
- "When do you notice it the most?"
- "Is there anything in particular that triggers these feelings?"

Help Counselees See What Can and Cannot Be Done

What happened in the past cannot be changed. The neglect of parents or the pain of being fired from a job are incidents that no one can undo. However, the feelings, reactions, and responses to those situations can change.

If there is lingering anger or resentment toward a parent, friend, or boss, help the person see the need to forgive. Lead the person through the steps of forgiveness and toward reconciliation when possible and appropriate.

Lead Counselees to a Personal Relationship with God

Experiencing Christ's forgiveness in a personal way lifts guilt and confusion from a person's life and replaces it with peace and joy. This alone may restore a healthy self-concept for the counselee. It is difficult to have a healthy relationship with yourself if you do not have one with your Creator.

Help Counselees Develop a Healthy View of Singleness

Many single adults struggle with low self-esteem because of a distorted view of singleness. They may think, "If I am not part of a couple, I must be unlovable." They are influenced many times by the implication in some churches and religious organizations that people are incomplete or immature until they are married.

A single person must develop a sense of wholeness in his/her singleness. Traditionally, this has been extremely difficult to accomplish, since our society puts a high premium on marriage as an indicator of one's worth.[2] Scripture says, "in [Christ] dwells all the fullness of the Godhead bodily; and you are complete in Him" (Col. 2:9–10 NKJV).

The season of singleness is usually temporary and is not fatal. God knows the single person's needs concerning the opposite sex and is capable of meeting those needs in His time. Until then, we must learn to accept singleness along with its advantages and disadvantages.

Jason Towner wrote the following:

> I am alone!
> I have accepted my aloneness.
> I have not cursed it,
> nor have I welcomed it for a prolonged visit.
> At this point I choose to be hospitable
> rather than face a duel.
> Aloneness is an abstraction,
> a coloring-book word,
> and the coloration I choose to grant it,
> will define whether I become
> a warden to aloneness
> or merely a prisoner.[3]

Help Counselees See and Understand What God Says about Them

Use Scripture to support the truth of what God thinks about people. God's Word is full of affirmations and statements of His unconditional love for human beings, His highest creation. Following is a partial list of relevant Scripture passages:

Genesis 1:26—We are made in the image of God.

Ephesians 2:10—We are a product of God's workmanship.

Psalm 139:13–15—We are wonderfully made.

John 3:16—God gave His only Son's life for us.

Romans 5:8—Even as sinners, God loves us.

Matthew 6:24ff—We are God's most valuable possession.

Note in particular Romans 12:3, which reminds us not to think of ourselves more highly than we ought to think. Some people say this means we are not to think highly of ourselves. Help counselees to understand that their problem may be that they are thinking *less* of themselves than God desires them to think. They may not even be thinking as they ought to think—"soberly, as God has dealt to each one a measure of faith" (Rom. 12:3 NKJV). Continuing to think defeating, depressing thoughts about ourselves will defeat and depress anyone!

Help Counselees See God's Work in Their Lives

While in your presence, have counselees make a list of their strengths, talents, and abilities. Add to the list if you can. Encourage them to think about the good in their lives the next time they begin to feel of little value. (See Phil. 4:8.)

Have them make a second list of everything they can think of to be thankful for, including emotions, people, and possessions. Pointing out the good in their lives tends to make them feel good about themselves and their circumstances.

Help Counselees Understand the Difference between Acceptance Based on Performance and Acceptance Based on Personhood

The world conditions us to get our self-worth from our performance. We know that if we don't produce and perform well on the job, we may be fired. If we don't please the boss we may be demoted.

It's the same in most relationships, whether they involve family, friends, or someone with whom we are romantically involved. If we don't please the other person with our thoughts, words, and actions, he or she may do something to make us feel unacceptable. This is the principle of "acceptance based on performance" at work. People who believe they are valuable because of what they can do are setting themselves up for failure and low self-esteem. No one is able to please everyone all of the time. Self-worth should not be measured by performance because we all ultimately fail.

Counselees need to understand that even though people may judge them by this principle, it is not a true test of their value. Opinions will vary, based on many different circumstances. We should not look to others for approval and self-esteem, but to the One who created us.

God's method of granting worth is far different, far more liberating, and far more refreshing than that of the world! God bases our value on our personhood, not our performance. The fact that He made us and loves us as we are speaks volumes concerning self-worth. To God, we are worth everything, whether we perform to His standards or not. And we cannot. But He loves us, period. In response to His love, out of thankfulness and desire, we live to please Him, but not to earn His love. This is the relationship from which we should draw a correct understanding of our own self-worth.

Help Counselees Develop Interests and Goals

Many times single adults with low self-esteem do not develop their personal interests and goals. Because they do not think too highly of themselves, they may tend to put life on hold and live in a state of limbo.

Janice Harayda speaks about this in her book *The Joy of Being Single.*

Most single people, however, find subtler ways of passing up a rich, fulfilling life. Instead of losing themselves in compulsive activity, they lose themselves in compulsive inactivity. They live in a state of existential drift, denying themselves the very real joys available to them in the present. Many are victims of what a minister I know refers to as the "can't do everything so I won't do anything" syndrome. They can't make the big changes in their lives, such as getting married and having children, so they don't make any little changes either. The catch is that making a lot of small modifications might add up to a much larger one: they would be living in the present instead of in the future.[4]

Help counselees see the benefit of discovering activities that excite and refresh them emotionally, mentally, and socially. Stress the importance of finding interests and pursuing growth through involvement with people who have the same interests and desires. Even though they may be reluctant to become involved because they think they may not be accepted, assure them that the risk is worth taking and that the joy and excitement of the experience will outweigh the fear. Poor self-image will also begin to change as they realize they are capable of making changes and developing new interests.

Help Counselees to Minister to Others

It is important for people who suffer from low self-worth to be involved in the lives of others by giving, helping, or ministering in some way. For single adults attending church, there will be several areas of possible involvement. Make an effort to help counselees discover these ministries. Even the least involvement in simple, manual tasks can bring a sense of worth and being needed.

Becoming involved in the lives of people will bring a much deeper sense of personal satisfaction and healing. Helping to meet the emotional needs of acceptance, love, appreciation, and healing in others will bring the same benefits to the person who is giving. The Bible says that what we sow, we will reap (Gal. 6:7).

Have counselees contact someone they know on the church staff to find out what areas of ministry need workers. Give counselees the responsibility of making the connection and reporting back to you the outcome.

Help Counselees Become Part
of a Christian Fellowship or Support Group

People with low self-esteem can be greatly helped by joining a group of people with similar hopes, interests, and hurts, where there is opportunity for giving, receiving, supporting, listening, laughing, playing, and working together. It is in this setting that the healing of Christian fellowship, acceptance, and nurture can flow into the lives of people.

Counselees who are not part of such a group should be steered in that direction. Refer them to a community group and give out any information you have about these groups. Ask counselees to visit one of the groups and call you with a report. To reduce fears, it may be necessary to meet with the counselee and a group member before an actual group meeting.

Introduce Counselees to Someone of the Same Sex
Who Is Having Victory over Low Self-Esteem

Helping the single adult establish a relationship with someone who experienced the same struggles is encouraging in that:

- it gives counselees an example of hope.
- it gives counselees the opportunity to see that they aren't the only ones with this struggle.
- it gives counselees a potential ongoing relationship of support.
- it gives another person an opportunity to minister.

Dos and Don'ts for Counselors

Do schedule a definite time and place to meet. Author and counselor Clyde Narramore wrote, "A counseling session is worthy of a definite appointment. Even though a fee may not be involved, the help that is received is valuable, and the time spent should be established in a professional manner. Making a definite appointment tends to increase your counselee's respect for you. He knows that you are efficient and orderly, and that you are taking his care seriously."[5]

Do pray about the upcoming session. When appropriate, either before the counselee arrives or as soon as you are ready to begin, commit the session to God in prayer. I believe God will guide the counseling process and give insight to both the counselor and the counselee. I believe God will help you sort out the sometimes difficult and complex issues of life as you give Him opportunity. Prayer will help counselees see that you realize, even as counselor, that you don't have all the answers and that you depend on God's insight, wisdom, and guidance.

Do assure counselees of confidentiality. People dealing with low self-image may be suspicious of your motives for spending time with them. It is risky to share innermost concerns and struggles, especially when it involves personal problems and weaknesses. If you are not well known to them, they may wonder if you can be trusted to keep their stories confidential. They need assurance that you won't use the information in any way that will add to their hurt.

Do ask direct questions about the perceived problem (if needed). People often hesitate to divulge their problems when they first talk to a counselor. They may begin with one thing, when actually they came to talk about something else. There are several reasons people begin by talking about issues that are not the real problem. For example, they may:

- not know how to begin.
- not know what the problem really is.
- be unsure whether you are competent to handle their particular difficulty.
- find it too painful to discuss.
- want to be certain that the session is confidential.
- be unsure of your attitude.

A wise counselor will listen closely for the real issue to surface. If after a reasonable amount of time the major problem has not been disclosed, you may need to say something like, "This is all very interesting, Joe, but is this the real issue you came to tell me about?" Other direct questions you might want to use are:

- "Tell me, what is your real struggle?"
- "What brought you here today?"
- "What is most troubling in your life right now?"
- "What are some of your fears?"

Do listen intently to counselees. It is very important for counselors to listen intently to counselees and concentrate solely on what they are saying. Maintain eye contact. Observe facial expressions, body gestures, and voice inflections. These are often clues as to what counselees are trying to say and indicators as to how they really feel. Counselors need to observe as much of the interaction as possible to be able to best assess the needs and issues of counselees. Counselees involved with counselors who know how to listen perceive that the counselor:

- is interested in their struggles.
- cares about them.
- thinks what they have to say is important.
- thinks they are important.

Do show counselees that you care about them. People with low self-esteem believe others don't care about them. Many have lived with this belief for some time and may subconsciously look for signs to confirm it. This is why everyone who works with people suffering from this problem has heard a phrase like, "You didn't even acknowledge me when we passed in the hallway." Counselees struggling with this issue are overly sensitive. They frequently misinterpret such seemingly small things as a missed "hello" when someone doesn't see them. Therefore, it is important for counselors to show that they care about their counselees. Listening closely is one way to accomplish this. A timely word of encouragement during the session (e.g., "I do care about you") is appropriate. A nod of agreement and appropriate facial responses to what is being said also convey affirmation and understanding.

Do record a few notes of the session. It is easy to confuse the details of one person's case with another, no matter how good your memory is. More than once I have made a comment to a counselee based on what I thought I remembered, and he or she looked at me with a confused stare as if to say, "Where did you get that information?" Believe me, this does nothing to build your credibility as a counselor. Some counselors advise against taking notes out of concern that clients may not feel free to divulge certain information if the counselor is taking copious notes. I believe this can be true in many cases. However, if you fear you may not be able to recall the details following the session, simply ask the counselee for permission to take a few notes. Usually he or she won't mind and may even express joy over the fact that you are interested enough to do so.

Do pray with counselees about their needs. One of the best things counselors can do to bring hope and direction to people's lives is to pray with them. Depending on the person's spiritual condition and background, you may want to ask permission. Usually you will get a positive response; some will be enthusiastic.

If possible, have counselees pray aloud about their situation. Some will feel uncomfortable doing this, but encourage the practice with those who show no signs of discomfort. They may never have prayed with anyone about this need.

Do give counselees homework. Depending on the number of times you meet and on the severity of the problem assign some sort of appropriate homework, such as:

- Read a chapter from the Bible (recommend Ephesians 1, Psalm 139, or Philippians 4)
- Read some other book (choose carefully)
- Listen to a tape (sermon tapes from your church may be appropriate)
- Complete a worksheet (ask other counselors for samples)
- Visit a group
- Speak with a particular person

By giving counselees something to do after they leave your office, you are saying:

- "I care about you enough to give you further help."
- "I realize that it took time to develop this feeling of low self-worth, and it will probably take time to overcome it."
- "I want to see how serious you are about getting through this."

Ask counselees to bring the homework assignment when they return for their next visit so you can review it together. If you do not plan on meeting again, arrange to talk by phone about the results of the assignment.

Do refer counselees to another counselor when necessary. In some instances, you may not feel qualified to deal with the issues that are causing the low self-esteem or you may not have enough available time to bring the person to a point of healing. In these situations it is best to refer the person to someone you trust who is capable of handling the case. Be sure to offer an honest explanation to the counselee.

Don't tell counselees not to feel sorry for themselves. People with low self-esteem already feel sorry for themselves. By telling them not to, you only make them feel more guilty. Low self-esteem naturally produces personal feelings of sorrow and sometimes pity.

Acknowledge your own tendency to feel sorry for yourself (showing that you understand), and suggest ways you use to limit the number of times per day/week that you give in to your feelings. Refer to the list of interests and opportunities the counselee has created and make suggestions that will lead to personal maturity and will help prevent self-pity, which is the fuel of low self-worth.

Don't expect counselees to feel better in a short period of time. Low self-esteem does not develop over a short period of time, and people tend to ignore it until it creates other problems they can't ignore. Promising a "quick fix" will not help. Overcoming low self-esteem takes time, and you will need to evaluate your role and commitment of time to this process.

Suggested Scripture

Psalm 63:7–8; 139:13–14
Jeremiah 29:11; 31:9b
Matthew 7:11
John 1:12; 3:16; 10:10b
Romans 8:15–16, 38–39
2 Corinthians 5:17
Ephesians 1:3–6
1 Peter 2:9

Prayer

Heavenly Father, I come to You today with an honest and open heart. I admit to You that I do not think very highly of myself. I want to see myself as You see me. I know that Your Word says that You love me as I am. I want to believe and experience the security of Your love and allow it to affect the image that I have of myself. Please help me to do this in any way You think is good for me. Help me to overcome my insecurities and feelings of inferiority. Teach me to look less toward other people and more toward You for my self-worth and identity. I desire to fully believe what You think of me. Help me to see my value in You as Your son/daughter. I love You, Lord, and thank You for Your love, acceptance, and help. In Jesus' name, Amen.

Resources for Counselees

Fagerstrom, Douglas, ed. *Singles Ministry Handbook*. Wheaton: Victor, 1988.

Larson, Ray. *A Season of Singleness*. Springfield, Mo.: Radiant Books, Gospel Publishing House, 1984.

McAllaster, Elva. *Free to Be Single*. Christian Herald Books, 1978.

McDowell, John. *Unlocking the Secrets of Being Loved, Accepted, and Secure*. Dallas: Word, 1984.

McDowell, Josh. *His Image . . . My Image.* San Bernardino, Calif.: Here's Life, 1985.

Narramore, Bruce. *You're Someone Special.* Grand Rapids: Zondervan, 1980.

Schuller, Robert. *Self Love.* Old Tappan, N.J.: Revell, 1969.

Seamands, David A. *Putting Away Childish Things.* Wheaton: Victor, 1982.

Smith, Harold Ivan. *Life-Changing Answers to Depression.* Eugene, Ore.: Harvest House, 1985.

———. *Positively Single.* Wheaton: Victor, 1986.

Smith, M. Blaine. *One of a Kind: A Biblical View of Self-Acceptance.* Downers Grove, Ill.: InterVarsity, 1984.

Sroka, Barbara. *One Is a Whole Number.* Wheaton: Victor, 1978.

Van Note, Gene. *Building Self-Esteem.* Beacon Hill, 1982.

Resources for Counselors

Dobbins, Richard D. *Your Spiritual and Emotional Power.* Old Tappan, N.J.: Revell, 1984.

Narramore, Clyde. *The Psychology of Counseling.* Grand Rapids: Zondervan, 1979.

Schuller, Robert. *Self Love.* Old Tappan, N.J.: Revell, 1969.

Smith, Harold Ivan. *Life-Changing Answers to Depression.* Eugene, Ore.: Harvest House, 1985.

———. *Positively Single.* Wheaton: Victor, 1986.

Smith, M. Blaine. *One of a Kind: A Biblical View of Self-Acceptance.* Downers Grove, Ill.: InterVarsity, 1984.

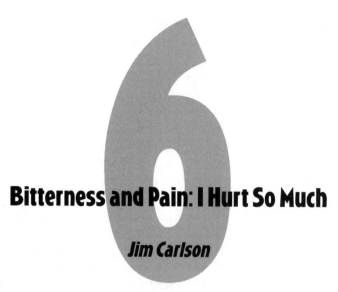

Bitterness and Pain: I Hurt So Much

Jim Carlson

When Cindy walked into my office, I knew that this was not going to be a pretty scene. Her clenched jaw and quivering lip revealed the combination of anger and hurt she was experiencing. The first minutes of conversation brought emotional release and accompanying tears. After only three years of marriage, Cindy's husband had walked out on her, leaving her alone with their one-year-old daughter. Cindy's anger was a response to her husband's infidelity; he had moved in with another woman. Her hurt was a compilation of disappointment, loneliness, and rejection.

Bitterness and Pain Described

Cindy's experience is not unique. Life is filled with pain and bitterness, and help must begin with an understanding and an acknowledgement of their existence.

The all-too-frequent responses of "It doesn't bother me," "I don't really care," "That's his problem," "Who? Me? Bitter? Never!" are indications that hurting people don't understand their own feelings and often deny that negative or hard-to-handle feelings even exist.

Pain and bitterness camp on the doorstep of our lives, waiting for the door to open . . . and open it does. In fact, it flies open when common life experiences such as these occur:

Loss—death of a child or marriage partner; divorce; loss of position in a company; loss of property due to a botched real estate negotiation; loss of money due to a bad investment.

Illness—debilitating disease; pain or permanent injury due to an accident; the uncertainty of cancer; inconvenience of endless pain clinics, hospital bills, and doctor appointments.

Violence—fear that accompanies war; hurt and bitterness stemming from emotional or physical abuse; rape.

Failure—the realization in parenting that honest attempts to be a conscientious mom or dad have ended in disaster; the termination of employment because services are no longer needed.

The list could be much longer. With all the potential for pain and bitterness, it is no wonder that so many people hurt so much.

Daniel lashed out at nearly everyone. According to him, his 19-year-old son was "irresponsible, irrational, and lacked any respect for authority." Daniel's wife "lacked discipline and sympathy." He accused his pastor of becoming "hard-nosed and insensitive," and he described his boss as a "demanding tyrant." The neighbor children were "unruly," and "the dog barked too loud, slept too much, and cost more to keep healthy than he was worth."

During our third session together, Daniel's anger turned to sadness as he revealed that he never felt his dad loved him. There were no hugs, no "well dones," no cheers at the ball game (or even fatherly instruction) because dad seldom attended. Under all the angry outbursts was the pain imposed by an absent father who had physically abused his son during a six-year period of his childhood and early adolescent years.

Anger is only one evidence of pain. Withdrawal and addictive behaviors like overeating, drugs, and drinking can also be indicators that the hurt is too great to handle. Professional counselor Paul Welter notes that "bitterness in people sometimes goes with coldness and is marked by intensity, regret, animosity and unpleasantness. The bitter person is abrasive to anyone who happens to be around, but most abrasive to people who are close . . . the kind of person who strokes a cat from the tail to the head."[1] Welter also notes that predicaments, crises, and the tendency to alienate others also are typical of the bitter person.

Guidelines for Those Who Hurt

Coming alongside a person in pain is a challenging experience. Pat answers or magic formulas just won't cut it, but the following guidelines will help.

Encourage Counselees to Admit Their Pain

Denial is a monumental obstacle in dealing with hurt and bitterness. People don't like to admit pain and in fact have been taught mechanical responses for avoiding it: "I don't feel bad." "It's okay, I can handle it." "It's just one of those things." "That's life."

Kind of hollow, aren't they?

Dale's daughter was a talented, attractive young woman of eighteen. The trauma of her first year away from home was lessened by the joy of her success during that year of college. A bright student and a gifted musician, she was the kind of person many sought out for friendship. But a quick trip home to surprise her family brought tragedy. Alone in her car, she lost control, crashed, and died instantly.

Dale appeared to take it in stride. With some sadness, he greeted friends at the funeral home and assisted in the memorial service. His demeanor was so upbeat that he was able to comfort many grieving family members and friends. But one year later Dale was a withdrawn, non-functioning, suffering person. For months he had denied the feelings of sadness, anger, and disappointment that were lying just beneath the veneer of the "Christian" response that "all things work together for good."

Counselors need to encourage people in pain to admit their hurt. It may stem from disappointment due to shattered dreams, grief due to deceit or betrayal, anger due to undeserved loss, or paralyzing fear due to uncertainty. Cover-ups in any form will cause ultimate destruction.

Help Counselees Understand the Nature of Pain

Misconceptions about pain and suffering often hinder hurting people from dealing honestly with their feelings. Consider several:

Pain is a mistake. Something went wrong. Bad things should never happen to good people. Such thinking is simply not true!

Pain is to be avoided. No one likes to suffer, but to run or hide from pain at all costs is unrealistic! Happiness binges sound great, but real life says some pain is inevitable.

Pain is a punishment. Theology that says all pain is God's penalty to straighten people out is a lie about God. God is not a cosmic law enforcement officer waiting to pounce on every offender. Nor is He the judge, jury, and executioner rolled into one. Yes, He disciplines, but with love, mercy, and justice.

Pain is a detractor from life. Pain is not always negative. The discomfort of touching a hot stove warns us of catastrophe. Pain can be the means by which changes in life occur for the good . . . for good! If an individual is able to grasp the idea that emotional pain is not an unusual experience and can have positive results, progress won't be far behind.

Help Counselees Differentiate between Deserved and Undeserved Pain

Proverbs 14:12 teaches that "there is a way that seems right to a man, but in the end it leads to death." Peter emphasized the principle that pain is at times the result of our bad choices or foolish actions. "But how is it to your credit if you receive a beating for doing wrong and endure it?" Peter asked (1 Peter 2:20). The obvious answer is, it's not to our credit; it's what we deserve!

In analyzing hurt, it is imperative to understand natural consequences. Drinking alcohol may cause violence or death; promiscuous sex may result in an unwanted pregnancy or AIDS; guilt over deceiving a mate or a friend may take its toll with stress and anxiety, which in turn may bring about major physical problems. If one ignores prayer or Bible study and claims a personal relationship with God, the incongruity will eventually result in malice, bitterness, and anger.

When suffering is deserved, the cause needs to be identified, acknowledged, and confessed. Then the consequences can be understood and appropriate actions taken.

On the other hand, suffering people need to see that pain is often undeserved. Realizing this doesn't eliminate the pain, but it can help an individual deal with it and avoid bitterness.

Floods and earthquakes cause lots of trouble. So do death, accidents, and economic collapse. But humans don't have much (if any) control over such calamities. The tragedy of injury caused by a drunken driver or the crushed self-esteem brought on by job loss due to a company's demise is tough to cope with. But in such instances, guilt can be eliminated.

Joseph is an example of someone who suffered undeservedly (Gen. 37:4ff). His brothers' hatred for him resulted in abandonment, alienation, and even imprisonment. His pain and suffering were real, but he was able to avoid bitterness because he knew he was not responsible.

Help Counselees Gain Perspective on the Pain

"No pain, no gain!" is true in many circumstances. Knowing that gain can come from pain doesn't make pain welcome, but it can make it easier to bear if the person can learn to focus on the gain that is possible.

As I finished writing the above paragraph, a young couple stopped in to see me. I'd met with them twice the previous week. They had been dating for several months, but the relationship had not been healthy. Sinful sexual involvement, jealousy, mind games, and insensitivity had become routine. The hurt they were both experiencing was turning to anger, and they were striking out at one another. After the second meeting, I suggested they both make a specific list of how they had hurt the other person. Then we agreed to meet today to discuss their lists and determine future direction.

At our meeting today each confessed to a long list of hurtful actions, some intentional, others unintentional. Each asked forgiveness. Tears flowed freely. After each had expressed a willingness to forgive the other, they determined to spend one month apart . . . no dates, phone conversations, or letters. The thirty-day focus was to allow each of them to deepen their personal relationship with Christ. The "separation" would be painful, but it could result in great gain. Time would tell.

In helping people deal with pain, the following perspectives are useful:

Pain can produce a greater appreciation for pleasure. A major league baseball team suffered through one horrible season and ended up last in their league, but the following year they went from worst to first! The joy of their "top o' the heap" finish was accentuated due to the agony of the previous season.

The apostle Paul was especially thankful for his salvation when he reflected on the fact that he was "the least of all God's people" (Eph. 3:8).

Real joy is not determined by circumstances. Individuals handle pain more effectively when they comprehend this truth. Joy comes from a relationship to Jesus Christ, which remains secure even when the events of life are chaotic and discouraging. We are in His hands (John 10:28); the Holy Spirit lives within us (1 Cor. 6:19–20); we are members of one body (1 Cor. 12:12–13); we have access to God (Rom. 5:2); and we are acceptable to Him because of Christ (Eph. 1:5).

Joy doesn't need to disappear when we experience the loss of money, property, or position; the absence or death of a family member or friend; a broken relationship; or unfulfilled ambitions.

Pain is not always Satan's weapon of destruction; it can be God's tool for construction. If allowed, Satan can turn deserved and undeserved hurt into questioning, bitterness, discouragement, and a ruined testimony. God, on the other hand, can use that same difficulty and build patience, steadfastness, and resiliency (Rom. 5:3–4).

When Eva's husband died unexpectedly, she shut herself up in her home and lay on her living room couch for six months. Then she died! Even though she expressed confidence that his eternal destiny was heaven, she allowed disappointment and sadness to overwhelm her.

Hugh, on the other hand, when his son was killed in an automobile accident, stood at his son's funeral and remarked, "My son and I were very close, and we enjoyed our years together. But I have no regrets." Sadness, yes! Bitterness, no!

Identifying positive outcomes will help make pain bearable. God shows Himself in our suffering. "[Trials] have come so that your faith . . . may be proved genuine and may result in praise, glory and honor when Jesus Christ is revealed" (1 Peter 1:7).

God shapes, molds, and remakes us in pain. Paul's thorn in the flesh was not a punishment, but a protector, "to keep me from becoming conceited. . . . Therefore . . . I delight in weaknesses. . . . For when I am weak, then I am strong" (2 Cor. 12:7, 9–10).

Just as pain plays a significant role in guarding the cells of our physical bodies, it also allows God to protect His body, the church, because emotional pain alerts members to a spiritual problem that needs their attention, that needs brothers and sisters to care for each other.

- Sorrow? We comfort one another (2 Cor. 1:3).
- Rebellion? We confront one another (2 Thess. 3:15).
- Sin? We restore one another (Gal. 6:1).
- Confusion? We support one another (Rom. 15:1).
- Alienation? We promote reconciliation (Phil. 4:2).

The way believers handle pain can be a powerful witness to the world that God is real and alive. On the other hand, the failure to deal with pain can bring reproach to Christ. When the church of Jesus Christ is at work forgiving, healing, and restoring it speaks volumes about God's greatness.

Dos and Don'ts for Counselors

Do provide guidance for spiritual development.
Do encourage realistic doses of Bible study and prayer.
Do look for evidence of pain even when words do not express it.
Do allow counselees to identify what they believe is the source of their suffering.
Do verify that the feelings are not right or wrong; they just are.

Do guide counselees through ways of dealing with the pain.

Do encourage the development of a specific plan to handle the hurt.

Do make referrals if the issues become too great for you to handle.

Do help counselees develop relationships with others who have been through similar circumstances.

Don't imply that you have all the answers.

Don't indicate that you "know exactly" how the person feels.

Don't judge an individual's responses. Instead, listen to the responses and acknowledge them. Then help the person work through them.

Don't handle the situation for the person.

Don't let "pity parties" dominate the agenda meeting after meeting.

Suggested Scripture

Genesis 37

Jeremiah 11:18–23; 12:6; 20:1–6

Job 1:13–20; 2:5–7

Matthew 10:16–20

John 19–20

Acts 5:41; 7:55; 9:15–16

Romans 8:17–18

2 Corinthians 4:17–18; 11:23–25; 12:7, 10

Philippians 1:29

2 Timothy 3:12

1 Peter 1:6–7; 2:18–21; 4:19

Prayer

Father, though I don't like or understand the pain, thank You for the promise that You will carry me through it and put me down on the other side as a stronger person. May I see Christ through the tears. May He see me through the fears. And may all see *Him.* Amen.

Resources for Counselees

Allender, Dan. *The Wounded Heart.* Colorado Springs: NavPress, 1990.
Backus, William, and Marie Chapian. *Telling Yourself the Truth.* Minneapolis: Bethany, 1980.
Crabb, Larry. *Inside Out.* Colorado Springs: NavPress, 1988.
Seamands, David. *Healing for Damaged Emotions.* Wheaton: Victor, 1984.
Strauss, Lehman. *In God's Waiting Room.* Grand Rapids: Radio Bible Class, 1984.
Swindoll, Charles. *Encourage Me.* Portland: Multnomah, 1982.
Yancey, Philip. *Where Is God When It Hurts?* Grand Rapids: Zondervan, 1977.

Resources for Counselors

Allender, Dan. *Bold Love.* Colorado Springs: NavPress, 1992.
Benner, David. *Strategic Pastoral Counseling: A Short-Term Structured Model.* Grand Rapids: Baker, 1992.
Crabb, Larry. *Effective Biblical Counseling.* Grand Rapids: Zondervan, 1979.
Watson, Jeffrey. *The Courage to Care: Helping the Aging, Grieving, and Dying.* Grand Rapids: Baker, 1992.
Welter, Paul. *How to Help a Friend.* Wheaton: Tyndale, 1981.
Worthington, Everett Jr. *How to Help the Hurting.* Downers Grove, Ill.: InterVarsity, 1985.
———. *When Someone Asks for Help.* Downers Grove, Ill.: InterVarsity, 1982.
Wright, Norman. *Making Peace with Your Past.* Old Tappan, N.J.: Revell, 1985.

7

Depression and Anger: Down and Dangerous

Jacquelyn R. Meurs

Julie is a 26-year-old single woman. She's been coming to your church for about five years and has been active in many ministries. Over the last year, however, Julie is rarely seen in church, and she hasn't attended a single adult activity for months. When she does come, she seems distant and isolated, and she is never with her old friends. Julie's appearance has deteriorated as well. Her clothes are disheveled and even her hair seems to have lost its luster. She has lost quite a few pounds, and she walks with stooped shoulders, hangs her head, and drags her feet.

Out of concern you call her aside and ask if you can help. Immediately, Julie begins to cry, telling you that her troubles began after the death of her father nearly two years ago. Since then she has felt discouraged, hopeless, and alone. None of her friends can relate to her heartache, and one by one they have abandoned her. She admits that sometimes she is even angry at God for allowing her loving father to be taken away from her. Life should be fair, she says, and God just isn't playing by the rules. And if life isn't going to be fair, she doesn't want to live it.

Julie is being sucked into the whirlpool of depression.

Depression, perhaps the most common emotional problem in America, is certainly the most frequent problem counselors encounter. Many believe depression has reached epidemic proportions as nearly 10 percent of people could be diagnosed as depressed at any given time.

Everyone feels down and "blue" sometimes. Such things as stress, anxiety, worry, trying circumstances, and difficult decisions lead even the most stable of people to feel sad and discouraged. Depression, however, is more serious than this. The duration and severity of the struggle is the fundamental difference between normal stress-related problems and depression. Discouragement due to normal but troublesome circumstances may last several hours or even a couple of weeks. Depression like Julie's can last for years.

Depressed people may have a history of unresolved difficulties dating back as far as childhood. They may never have received any kind of treatment, and so depression became a part of their pattern of living and relating.

Granted, some mildly depressed people seem to "come out of it" naturally and continue with their lives. Others, however, continue in this negative coping style, and depression-related problems permeate their lives. Many lose jobs, loved ones, and all ties to the outside world. But they continue to "pull in," immersed in their own misery and pain.

Though isolation is certainly harmful, by far the greatest danger to the depressed person is suicide. In fact, depression is the leading cause of suicide for people at all age levels. Depressed people are the most likely to attempt suicide and to succeed, especially if they are not receiving any kind of treatment. This is why intervention is crucial. It can truly be a matter of life and death.

Unfortunately, the biggest obstacle to effective treatment has to do with the coping style of depressed people: isolation. As depression becomes more severe, they move further and further from the outside world. It may take a great deal of effort for them to get out of bed in the morning, let alone meet with someone or build a relationship with a helper. They may feel they do not have the emotional or physical energy to deal with the magnitude of the situation. Because depression often carries with it feelings of hopelessness, helplessness, and worthlessness, those who are depressed may feel that they are not able to get better, that the problem is totally out of their control, or that they are not worth "fixing."

Symptoms and Struggles

As no two people are alike, neither are their depressions. We all have unique personalities and coping styles on which we rely to deal with life's situations. However, some common symptoms weave through the lives of the depressed. Following are the most common.

The most obvious sign of depression is a downcast countenance. Depressed people look sad. They smile infrequently, and when they do, their smile has an empty, almost forced look. They may also cry easily.

The "body language" of depressed people is also downcast. They evidence what is known as "psychomotor retardation"—the slowing of body movements.[1] For the severely depressed, every movement seems to take Herculean effort. Everything they do seems to be in slow motion.[2] Mildly depressed people may walk slowly or shuffle their feet, thus appearing considerably older than they are. Julie displayed a classic bodily sign of depression—stooped posture and rounded shoulders—almost as though she were truly carrying the "weight of the world."

Depressed people have difficulty making and maintaining eye contact. They may spend an entire conversation looking at the floor. Even when prompted, they may be unable to hold the gaze of another person. They may wring their hands (also a sign of anxiety), and bite or pick at their fingernails.

Depressed people will report problems in many areas of their lives. Biological symptoms seem to be particularly distressing. Sleep disturbances are common, especially an inability to fall asleep (insomnia). They may also wake at a very early hour and be unable to fall back asleep ("terminal insomnia"), or wake several times during the night ("late insomnia"). Another frequent problem is excessive sleeping ("hypersomnia"), often interpreted not only as a sign of depression but also a method to avoid dealing with problems. Depressed people frequently report feeling worse in the morning and slightly better by evening. This is known as "diurnal mood variation."[3] Other common biological signs are loss of appetite and sex drive, feelings of fatigue, constipation, and vague physical complaints.

The social functioning of depressed individuals is usually impaired as well. Due to their loss of interest in what were once pleasurable activities, they may drop out of clubs, sports teams, church groups and classes, or other social activities. Their social circle then decreases, leading to isolation. The nature of their emotional distress causes them to easily become engrossed in themselves and in their own problems, often to the neglect of friends and loved ones. As a consequence, they can be rejected by the people they most need, as Julie experienced, causing further isolation and alienation. Others may reject them simply because they are not fun to be around.

Depressed people invariably engage in negative thought patterns, which lead to negative emotions. They see the world and their circumstances as hopeless and often believe they are powerless to improve their lot in life. Social psychological research has shed an interesting light on this phenomenon. It appears that a more realistic appraisal of life's events leads to depression.[4] In other words, people who are depressed may be that way because they see themselves and their circumstances more accurately than those who are not depressed![5] It may be that the fabled "rose-colored glasses" serve to ward off discouragement and, thus, depression.

Notwithstanding, depressed people do tend to be overly negative and critical. Their focus is narrow. They see few options, and none looks promising.

"Masked depression," a variant form of depression, carries a different set of symptoms than the "classic" depression described above. The case of Mark, a 25-year-old single male, illustrates this phenomenon. Due to a long history of vague health problems, Mark never kept a job for more than three months. At the insistence of his fiancée (in fact, his fourth fiancée), Mark went for counseling. During the initial session, he seemed unable to discuss anything about himself other than his health problems. The counselor discovered that all of Mark's other engagements had been broken due to his "illnesses." When asked how he felt, he responded with a complaint about a bodily ache, not a description of an emotion. This, in fact, is the hallmark of this disorder: a physical preoccupation to the exclusion of emotions. In other words, the "mask" of depression is physical problems. Mark may have been taught that men don't have any emotional struggles, that "real men" don't feel. Therefore, since he cannot directly deal with his emotional pain, it comes out in his body.

Though not considered "masked depression," certain other behaviors should be seen as a sign of depression. These self-destructive patterns seem to represent a kind of death wish. Foremost of these is substance abuse. Depression is one of the most common correlates of substance abuse. Depressed people will attempt to numb their emotional pain by the misuse of alcohol and prescription and illegal drugs.

Other behaviors that signal depression include physical recklessness, an affinity for daredevil activities, sexual promiscuity, excessive fatigue, and workaholism. In all these, those who are depressed are attempting to get rid of or avoid feelings by acting out. Chances are good that unless they realize their self-destructive pattern and its root cause, they will continue to engage in the behavior, often with mortal consequences.

A unifying theme in the symptoms of depression is anger. Unlikely as it may seem, most, if not all, depressed people are angry, very angry. But why? When asked, this question yields a multiplicity of answers.

One likely cause of anger is unrealistic expectations. Like Julie, people prone to depression are perfectionistic. They have high expectations for themselves and others. They live under the domination of what is known as "the tyranny of the should." Their lives are controlled by thoughts of how things "ought" to be or "should" be. And since life is never how it should be (to them this would mean perfection), they are constantly disappointed and frustrated. They become angry that neither they nor others can live up to how they believe life "must" be. Hence they become bitter, angry, and resentful. Life does not match up to their demands. To compound the problem, these people tend to see reality more clearly and consequently realize just how unfair and imperfect the world is. Their high expectations and accurate assessment of reality become a double curse.

With this knowledge, then, why don't people just get angry instead of depressed? The answer to this question is not completely clear, but several factors are evident.

Many Christians have the faulty belief that Christians are never supposed to get angry. When trouble comes, they are either to smile and deny it with a "God is blessing me" attitude, or to stoically bear the burden, accepting it without emotion as their lot in life.

However, the biggest cause of depression by far, especially among Christian women, is the fallacy of "niceness." Many have been taught that "nice" people, especially nice Christian girls, don't get angry; that anger is not an acceptable emotion. Some, through the misinterpretation of Ephesians 4:26 ("In your anger do not sin"), have even been taught that anger is a sin. So how is a nice person to react when confronted with the inevitable failings of life?

Nice people find a more acceptable feeling—hurt, disappointment, depression. It is far more "Christian" to be hurt than to be angry. Unfortunately the anger is still there; it is just mislabeled and consequently never dealt with. Over time, it grows and festers, infecting family, work, and social life.

Counseling Suggestions

The diversity of causes of depression calls for diversity of approach, and a skilled counselor will not look for *the* cause of depression, but for the many possible causes that may exist.

Look for Possible Physical Causes

Certain medical conditions (e.g., hypoglycemia, hypothyroidism, strokes) can cause depression. It is, therefore, helpful in the first interview to get a basic medical history. If you have any further questions regarding the counselee's physical problems, ask permission to consult with his or her doctor. It is possible that the depressive symptoms can be alleviated with proper medical care.

Another physical factor that may cause depression is a chemical imbalance. Some people, severely depressed over a long period of time, develop a biochemical imbalance in their brains that requires medical treatment. These people are prescribed various drugs in order to restore the proper balance of mood-influencing brain chemicals. For this treatment, counselees will need to be evaluated and monitored by a psychiatrist.

The psychological effects of any physical trauma, either recent or remote, also need to be evaluated as a possible cause of depression. Loss of limbs, paralysis, cancer, AIDS, strokes, heart attacks, and other such traumatic experiences can lead to discouragement and depression. It is then the task of the counselor to determine if the counselee's reaction is appropriate to the degree of physical distress or if it is unusually long or severe. Though either conclusion could necessitate counseling, the duration, intensity, and focus would vary depending on the "normalcy" of the counselee's response to the circumstances.

Determine the Duration of the Depression

Ask counselees how long they have felt this way, when the problem first started, and whether the depression has become better or worse lately. By finding out the severity of the depression and how long it has lasted, you will be able to assess more accurately your ability to serve this person. In general, the longer the feelings have persisted and the greater the number of symptoms, the more severe the depression. Don't discredit your own abilities, but don't hesitate to get a second opinion or to refer the person to another counselor when in doubt. It is the counselor's ethical obligation to help counselees obtain the best treatment possible.

Assess the Symptoms

Using the list above, or any other, formulate questions that will cover the major problem areas: sleep patterns, social interactions, negative thought patterns, perfectionism, physical symptoms (e.g., recent appetite changes), substance abuse, etc. Speak frankly, but tactfully. Do not be afraid to ask for clarifications or further information.

Related to the inventory of symptoms is the assessment of suicide potential. This is another area where frankness is crucial. If counselees sense that you are afraid to bring up the subject they too will be afraid. An easy lead into the suicide assessment is to say, "You know, almost everyone has thought of committing suicide at some point. Have you ever thought of trying it?"

There is not room in this chapter to fully cover suicide assessment, but the following list will help you assess your counselees. Be sure to cover every point and to use the follow-up questions. (Even if counselees answer the question "no," ask the follow-up questions anyway, using the "What if you were thinking of it . . ." tack.)

- How long ago did you last think of trying suicide?
- Have you ever attempted it? When? What happened?
- How lethal were past attempts? (Overdoses, lateral wrist-slitting, and superficial wounds are generally not considered lethal attempts; shooting, hanging, wrist-to-elbow slitting, multiple substance overdosing, etc. are considered more lethal and thus more serious. Keep in mind that women are twice as likely to attempt suicide, but men are two to three times more likely to succeed due to their choice of methods. Men who attempt suicide use far more lethal means than women, thus greatly decreasing their chances of rescue.)
- How lethal would a future attempt be? (If you were going to try it again, what method would you use?)
- How accessible are the weapons you would use? (Do you have loaded guns in your possession or access to them?)
- If you were feeling suicidal, would you tell me?
- Would you contract with me that if you ever feel suicidal you will call me and two or three other support people and continue calling until you reach someone?

These are the basics of suicide assessment. If you believe your counselee is suicidal it is imperative that you contact the authorities and your local crisis center to obtain a professional assessment.

Counseling Intervention

Through regular contacts you can walk counselees out of their deep hole of isolation, anger, and despair. Keeping in mind the probable causes of their distress, begin to focus on the following areas:

Realistic Thinking

Perfectionism and unrealistic expectations go hand in hand with depression. It is the task of the counselor to gently challenge counselees' assumptions of how the world "ought" to be. Grieve with them over the unfairness of life, but model acceptance of imperfection, particularly theirs. Help them examine their expectations in light of reality and the Bible. (Many counselees will point to Christ's admonition in Matthew 5:48, "Be perfect, therefore, as your heavenly Father is perfect," to justify their perfectionism. It will bring them great comfort and freedom when you explain that "perfect" in this verse means "complete."[6])

Ask counselees to write down their irrational and unrealistic expectations (e.g., "I must do everything right the first time or I'm a failure"). Then help them formulate new and attainable expectations. Later, have them analyze their perfectionistic tendencies in other areas. For example, in relationships are they always testing their friends for signs of betrayal or other misdeeds? Do they have a history of short-term relationships? Are family members never quite good enough or loving enough? In the area of self-discipline do they have an all-or-nothing mentality? For example, if they eat one Oreo cookie, do they start binging because they believe one snack ruins six months of total self-control? In regard to jobs and careers are their aspirations realistic? For example, do they believe they can work eighty to ninety hours a week indefinitely in order to someday impress the boss? Do they believe the only successful person in the company is the CEO and that attaining anything short of that position is failure?

Creating new, realistic expectations is the final task in the battle against perfectionism. Help counselees determine first and foremost what God's expectations are for their lives. Then help them make a realistic assessment of their strengths and weaknesses, with the emphasis not on self-criticism but on growth and change where needed. Reality-based goals and expectations will help counselees overcome "the tyranny of the shoulds." State these as reaffirming phrases that counselees can say to themselves. For example, "I don't have to do everything right the first time." To increase the impact of these new goals, have counselees write them on notecards and place them in prominent places around their home (e.g., above the kitchen sink, on the bathroom mirror, near the telephone). Reinforce these expectations by repeating them to counselees during your meetings. This shows counselees that you believe them, too.

Exercise

The phenomenon called "runner's high" is caused by mood-elevating hormones (endorphins) that are released into the bloodstream during strenuous exercise. Those who exercise regularly know the feeling of elation and relaxation that follows an aerobics class or tennis game. What is not well-known is the positive effect this has on people who are depressed. Depressed people who begin a regimen of regular exercise will very likely experience, at the least, temporary relief of their symptoms. Not only will the endorphins act as natural antidepressants, but regular exercise can improve the quality of their sleep, increase energy levels, decrease appetite, tone muscles (thereby relieving aches and pains), and improve self-esteem by promoting a sense of accomplishment and efficiency. Going to a health club or an aerobics class will also serve to pull the depressed person out of seclusion and isolation.

The importance of frequent, consistent exercise in the treatment of depression cannot be stressed enough. Though it is very difficult for depressed counselees to consider the possibility of expending such a great deal of effort, the benefits for those who do will be clear.

The best strategy may be to explain in detail all the good that comes from exercise and then make a "try it and see" contract. Encourage counselees to conduct an experiment by agreeing to exercise at least three times per week for two or three weeks. Before and after each period of exercise, have them write down how they feel and whether they experienced any lifting of the depression. Each week, have them evaluate success in other problem areas, such as overeating, sleep disturbances, etcetera. Chances are good that positive changes will have occurred. It is your job then to help counselees see that exercise is good not only for physical health but for emotional health as well. (If you are not involved in a regular program of exercise, it will be difficult for you to persuade counselees to commit to it. Successful counseling has much to do with "selling" counselees on an idea, and the best salesperson is a satisfied customer. Testimonials are powerful.)

Forgiveness

For many depressed people, a boiling pot of anger is at the crux of their suffering. They are mad at everything and everyone. Life is unfair. People have let them down. God seems silent. They have been neglected, abandoned, rejected, abused. And they are mad, really, really mad.

The biggest obstacle in the treatment of anger is denial. Most depressed people cannot fathom that they could be angry; that anger is, in fact, one of their primary problems. Consequently, the bulk of the work here entails challenging counselees' assumptions about their own anger and then helping them recognize, process, and release it.

Because anger is energy, coming to terms with how mad they really are will greatly increase the amount of energy counselees have. Properly channeled, the anger energy can significantly boost the counselee's commitment to growth. Counselees working on anger issues should decide on productive activities to engage in during the flow of their fury. Such activities could include creative endeavors such as drawing, journaling, playing or composing music, crafts, house- or closet-cleaning, or vigorous exercise.

Spiritual issues are especially important in the processing of anger. Christians must realize that the Bible is replete with references to God being angry (Num. 11:1; Deut. 6:15). Even Jesus became angry (Mark 3:5), yet never sinned. Anger is a natural, God-given emotion. However, if it is not released, it will destroy the one it occupies. The process of anger realization must necessarily include forgiveness, the releasing of the responsible party (Eph. 4:31–32).

To make this work, counselors should explain the harmful effects of unresolved anger (e.g., depression, physical problems, emotional struggles, relationship instability, spiritual blockage) and make it known that forgiveness is the only answer. Emphasize that forgiveness is a gift given to the self, not to the other person. We forgive in order to release ourselves from the power the offending party has over us. Once truly forgiven and released, that person or situation can no longer hurt us.

Once counselees understand the freeing power of this action, they must work diligently, not falling into the old anger habit. Real forgiveness is the only thing that will eliminate the destruction anger produces, and hence, the grip of depression.

Positive Thinking

Closely tied to anger are negative thought patterns. Without fail, depressed people engage in pessimistic, critical, and destructive thoughts often related to events that are the cause of their anger. And because life is never completely positive the process of negative thinking can be refueled daily.

Depressed people need to learn new thoughts and ways of thinking. To do this, however, they must first learn what they are saying to themselves. All of us spend our days in a constant inner conversation. Though largely unaware of it, we talk to ourselves about our perceptions of ourselves, others, our future, etc. Sadly, few of us really know *what* we are saying to ourselves. To change negative thinking, depressed people must stop and listen to what they are telling themselves about the world, paying careful attention to negative messages and irrational ideas.

To accomplish this, counselees may want to carry a small notebook and record what they hear themselves say each day. During counseling sessions, the counselor and the counselee can examine the thoughts and evaluate their accuracy.

Although many of the negative thoughts may indeed be true (e.g., "It's going to rain all day today"), some negative thoughts (e.g., "I'm going to have a lousy day today" or "I'm never going to find a husband") come true due to a phenomenon called "self-fulfilling prophecy." As the name implies, these things come true due to the actions of the "prophet." People who say they are going to have a bad day generally do just that! And a woman who tells herself she'll never find a husband may pass up many prospects and opportunities due to her firmly entrenched belief.

Help counselees look for negative self-fulfilling prophecies; we all have them. As with perfectionism, counselees must create new, positive thoughts. The key here, however, is balance. For counselees to create only positive thoughts would cause the pendulum to swing too far in the opposite direction, creating a whole new set of problems. Counselors, therefore, must help counselees choose reality-based thoughts, thoughts that take into consideration both positive and negative outcomes.

Along this same line, it is helpful to spend some time discussing with counselees the positive effects any negative experiences may have had on them. Far too often counselors overlook the value of suffering. Christians, however, know that God can and will turn all our experiences into good (Rom. 8:28).

Talking to counselees about the growth that has occurred due to events they consider negative can lead them to reevaluate many of their "woes" and to become thankful to God for their lot in life. Incidentally, there are few greater blessings for the Christian counselor than to see counselees seek out and find the goodness of God amid their trials and to be able to rejoice together over the treasure discovered there.

Counseling the depressed is both challenging and rewarding. Though the causes and symptoms of depression can be overwhelming, knowing and believing that in Christ "all things are possible . . ." (Mark 9:23 KJV) will lead even those in the deepest despair to hope and victory.

Dos and Don'ts for Counselors

Do reach out and enter the pain of counselees.

Do model healthy, productive behavior.

Do express faith in the healing power of God.

Do pray with and for counselees.

Do tell counselees often that you believe they can overcome their struggles in and through the Holy Spirit.

Do seek out supervision, consultation, and second opinions.

Do motivate counselees to take action to stop the destruction of negative thoughts and behaviors.

Do give practical, relevant "homework" assignments.

Do listen more than you talk.

Do engage other supportive people in the helping process (e.g., friends, family, church members, pastors).

Do take care of yourself, making sure your emotional and spiritual needs are adequately met.

Don't give up—even if the counselees do or tell you to.

Don't judge counselees' spirituality based upon how well they handle their emotional struggles.

Don't assume you know what the counselees' problems are and how to fix them—inevitably, you'll be surprised.

Don't let yourself get sucked into the whirlpool of negativism and eventually your own depression.

Don't take credit for the healing. (Some studies show that about 75 percent of depression "cures" itself, spontaneously disappearing without the intervention of counseling!)

Don't be afraid to confront when necessary.

Don't use labels for feelings that the counselees do not also use. For example, when counselees call themselves "discouraged," don't refer to them as "depressed" or you may lose the rapport you are working to build.

Suggested Scripture

Deuteronomy 31:8
Psalm 13; 35:19; 40:1–3; 42; 55:1–2, 22–23; 103
Isaiah 41:10
Matthew 11:28–30
John 15:7
2 Corinthians 2:3–5; 4:17–18
Ephesians 4:26, 31–32
Philippians 1:6; 2:13–15; 4:13
Colossians 3:8, 13–14
James 1:2–6

Prayer

Heavenly Father, You are Abba, Daddy. You know me inside
and out, yet You love me and accept me just as I am. I believe that
You want to bring healing in my life and hope to my soul. Holy
God, You know my struggles and pain, how I have agonized in the
pit of despair. I come to You now for help, knowing that You alone
are able to bring the peace and comfort I need.

I know some, but not all of the reasons I feel this way. I recognize my responsibility for my pain, and my own sinfulness and
inability to relieve my suffering. I confess to You my perfectionism and unrealistic expectations of others. I know I have used these
traits as a way to hold grudges against people. I also confess the
anger I hold against people, and even You sometimes. I choose to
turn away from these sins, believing that by Your grace I will commit them no more. I place in Your hands all the people and circumstances that have hurt me. I will not hang on to them any
longer, trusting that Your justice will prevail.

Take control of my thoughts, too, Lord. I have a destructive habit
of dwelling on the negative. Break this pattern and give me a bal-
anced perspective. Show me the positive aspects of Your work in me.

I am depressed/discouraged/in despair. My life seems hopeless and bleak. Sometimes, in my darkest moments, I wonder why You even created me. But from today forward, I will choose to believe that You have created me with a special purpose in mind. Therefore, You will bring healing to my life as I surrender it to You and wait expectantly for You to unfold Your will for me. I give You complete control of my life. In Jesus' name, Amen.

Resources for Counselees

Backus, William, and Marie Chapian. *Telling Yourself the Truth.* Minneapolis: Bethany, 1980.

Baker, Don, and Emery Nester. *Depression: Finding Hope and Meaning in Life's Darkest Moments.* Portland: Multnomah, 1983.

Carter, Les, and Frank Minirth. *The Anger Workbook.* Nashville: Thomas Nelson, 1993.

Carter, Les. *Good 'n' Angry.* Grand Rapids: Baker, 1992.

———. *Mind Over Emotions.* Grand Rapids: Baker, 1985.

Minirth, Frank B., and Paul D. Meier. *Happiness Is a Choice.* Grand Rapids: Baker, 1978.

Papolos, Demitri and Janice. *Overcoming Depression,* rev. ed. New York: HarperCollins, 1992.

Resources for Counselors

Backus, William. *Telling the Truth to Troubled People.* Minneapolis: Bethany, 1985.

Cosgrove, Mark P. *Counseling for Anger.* Resources for Christian Counseling. Dallas: Word, 1988.

Hart, Archibald D. *Counseling the Depressed.* Resources for Christian Counseling. Dallas: Word, 1987.

Hunter, Robert L. *Helping When It Hurts: A Practical Guide to Helping Relationships.* Philadelphia: Fortress Press, 1985.

Minirth, Frank B., and Paul D. Meier. *Happiness Is a Choice.* Grand Rapids: Baker, 1978.

Worthington, Everett L., Jr. *How to Help the Hurting.* Downers Grove, Ill.: InterVarsity, 1985.

Guilt and Rejection: I Blew It; Now Nobody Wants Me

Phyllis Alderman

For sin shall not be your master, because you are not under law, but under grace.

—Romans 6:14

God pardons like a mother who kisses the offense into everlasting forgiveness.

—Harriet Ward Beecher

feel like a part of me is dead." "I can't believe there is any hope for my future." "I've failed again!" "I can't ever forget." "God could never forgive me because I can't even forgive myself."

These and other painful words are common expressions of single adults who are struggling with guilt due to mistakes involving physical and spiritual thoughts, decisions, and behaviors. They are torn by the futility of trying to eliminate "feelings" of guilt while struggling to define the causes, a task that is much like trying to unscramble eggs!

Definition

Guilt is an emotion that stems from a real or perceived violation of a person's conscience, resulting in a sense of shame or remorse that is consuming. These feelings are symptomatic of two types of guilt: earned and unearned. Both types lead to a sense of separation from God and a loss of peace. They also activate sorrow which some people use constructively and others deny, leading to further destructive consequences.

Guilt is an invitation—even a calling—to come to Jesus for forgiveness, healing, and restoration through confession (1 John 1:9). When people deny guilt and refuse to accept personal responsibility, they are rejecting this invitation, and doing so may cause the conscience to trigger physical reactions (e.g., anxiety, allergies, asthma, high blood pressure, and a myriad of stress-related symptoms). Continued lack of attention to guilt is like ignoring warning lights on the dashboard of a car.

Shortly after the odometer of my vehicle reached 50,000 miles, the "maintenance required" light came on. With a sense of anxiety, I opened the operator's manual and discovered that the purpose of the light was to draw my attention to a need for maintenance which, if not done, could result in serious damage. The manual stated that the light would not go out until I had the car serviced by a professional.

How similar is the warning signal of guilt. It is a pervading, nagging call to pay attention to our spiritual condition or risk spiritual breakdown. Jesus made provision for release from guilt and, in His Word, said that He came "to set captives free." Everyone struggling with guilt need only run to Him to appropriate the "professional" care and grace He offers.

Symptoms and Struggles

Unresolved guilt shows up in a myriad of symptoms, many of which are addictive behaviors involving such things as alcohol, drugs, food, sex, money, and even religion. These addictions serve as an anesthetic in that they numb feelings of guilt.

As the use of desensitizing alternatives increases, guilt-producing behavior becomes more complex, and withdrawal and isolation soon follow. One guilt-producing behavior leads to another, and self-justification adds more weight to the already heavy load of guilt. When people succumb to the temptation to avoid the pain of guilt, they only postpone it because the result is diminished self-worth and spiritual strength complicated by increased destructive behavior.

Anger is another common symptom of guilt because blame is a convenient way for people to cover up their guilt. In most broken relationships, anger is used to hold others accountable and to avoid self-examination and personal discovery. Anger keeps people from accepting personal responsibility and, ultimately, it keeps them from resolving their guilt through confession, forgiveness, and restoration.

One young single woman came to the end of her "blame game" when she yielded her right to remain angry at a young man who had rejected her after she became pregnant with his child. Guilt had fostered anger in the young woman, and anger had fostered self-justification. She wound up at the threshold of an abortion clinic, but before going inside she surrendered her burden of guilt and discovered God's strength. As she turned away from the clinic, God's mercy flooded her soul. Later, she came to understand that the life within her was not the "consequence" of her sin; the consequence of her sin was the struggle waged at the threshold of the abortion clinic. The enemy tried to defeat her by offering a tempting "choice" that appealed to her self-centeredness. Sin had placed her on the front line of the battle between self and God.

The symptoms of guilt experienced by Christians require careful listening, empathy, and analysis. A relationship of trust and encouragement between the counselor and counselee is essential for identifying the root causes of guilt. The symptoms often evolve when the person lives out unhealthy responses to loneliness, broken relationships, compromised values, unfulfilled expectations, or lack of meaningful support systems in families.

The symptoms and struggles of unbelievers differ from those of believers. Those outside a relationship with God are indeed guilty, as Romans 3:23 declares: "For all have sinned and fall short of the glory of God." Although unbelievers may indeed be struggling with guilt concerning thoughts, issues, actions, and behaviors, their guilt is deeper and their need more desperate!

Release from guilt comes only through forgiveness, and forgiveness comes only from God through His Son, Jesus. In order for people to have victory over the powerful force of sin, they must accept God's forgiveness and be cleansed and reconciled to Him. This comes only by believing that Christ is indeed the Son of God and that He has power to forgive and overcome sin. Only when people accept this truth and submit to God's authority can they claim God's forgiveness and His promise of freedom from sin and guilt.

Counseling Suggestions

Victory over guilt comes only with an accurate understanding of God. Those who do not understand His forgiving nature and His everlasting love cannot fathom, nor appropriate, His forgiveness. In addition to being holy, just, and merciful, God is also committed to forgiveness. He is not soft toward sin, but He stands ready to forgive, despite the extent or enormity of a person's sin.

To successfully deal with guilt, counselees may need a counselor's help to:

Become familiar with the attributes of God and to claim His forgiveness.

Examine their behavior. Are they living out the truth of God's Word, the pre-conditioned behavior of their childhood, or the behavioral patterns of people in their lives who have modeled their own shortcomings or dysfunctions? Are they relying on God's promise that "You will know the truth, and the truth will set you free" (John 8:32)?

Take personal responsibility (but *only* personal responsibility) *for their share of the guilt.* Counselees need to accept that they are responsible only for their own guilt, no one else's. They cannot change others, but they can change themselves with God's intervention.

Honestly define the guilt. David sought God's perspective when he prayed, "Search me, O God, and know my heart; test me and know my anxious thoughts. See if there is any offensive way in me, and lead me in the way everlasting" (Ps. 139:23–24). Help counselees to be transparent with God and to accept the conviction He filters through His loving hands.

Appropriate God's resource for anxiety, guilt, and rejection. This can be accomplished through simple obedience to the command to "Humble yourselves, therefore, under God's mighty hand, that [H]e may lift you up in due time. Cast all your anxiety [including worry, doubt, fear, guilt, rejection] on [H]im because [H]e cares for you" (1 Peter 5:6–7).

Humility is the gateway to the liberation of God's unconditional love and forgiveness. Relief from the burden of guilt becomes a reality only when people surrender their own rights to God. This "humbling" is a recognition that they cannot live victoriously through their own efforts. Victory is accomplished only by taking God at His Word, believing that He forgives and removes confessed sin as far away as the east is from the west. As a child once explained, "God has a big eraser." God forgives; therefore we can forgive ourselves, others, and God.

The struggle with failure remains active in human memory because the most difficult things to forget are the things people want to forget. Tim Timmons, author and lecturer, likens memory to a rearview mirror. Compared to the front window of the car, he says, the rearview mirror is small, narrow, and defined. Seeing what is behind enables us to make better decisions about the future. However, we must only glance into the rearview mirror, and then fasten our gaze once again through the front window to watch where we are headed.

Seen in this way, every mistake or failure is an opportunity to appropriate God's grace and mercy and to profit from discipline, experience, and growth.

Some singles struggle with unearned guilt that has been passed on to them by people who have not accepted their own responsibility. These singles generally fall into two categories: those who excuse others from accountability and those who have been so conditioned by childhood experiences that they accept blame without question. The dysfunctions of others heap guilt upon them without resistance.

Satan loves to make people feel like failures, thus robbing them of joy, hope, and the opportunity to be salt and light to the world.

To turn the tables and make Satan the failure, counselors and counselees alike must learn to be "self-controlled and alert," for our enemy, the devil, is prowling "around like a roaring lion looking for someone to devour" (1 Peter 5:8).

Dos and Don'ts for Counselors

Do encourage counselees to go directly to God's Word.

Do show counselees how to take all failure to Jesus. Then they can *confess* responsibility for earned guilt, *receive* God's forgiveness, and *forgive* God, self, and others.

Do make sure counselees have a correct biblical understanding of guilt. If they refuse to honestly face the causes of earned guilt or the behavior patterns of unearned guilt, refer them to another counselor or pastor.

Do help counselees develop a "front window" approach to life. Show them how to use wisdom gained from past failures to make good decisions concerning the future.

Do remind counselees to remain alert to the adversary. Single adults need to put on the whole armor of God every day and refuse to listen to spiritual pride when it says, "You have arrived."

Do help counselees maintain a "learner's permit" mentality that causes them to depend on the Lord for constant direction.

Do encourage counselees to never give up! Paul said, "Brothers, I do not consider myself yet to have taken hold of it. But one thing I do: Forgetting what is behind and straining toward what is ahead, I press on toward the goal to win the prize for which God has called me heavenward in Christ Jesus" (Phil. 3:13–14). Failure is the practical experience upon which to build the future. "The glory is not in never failing, but in rising every time you fall" (unknown).

Don't offer pat answers.

Don't minimize the root cause of guilt. Minimizing the cause of guilt easily turns into rationalizing "why" rather than dealing with "what."

Don't magnify the root cause of guilt. In the beginning stages of recovery singles often take on more blame than belongs to them. Phrases such as "If I had been more loving, my spouse would have stayed" or "I failed because I didn't express my love sufficiently" avoid placing responsibility with others, where it is earned and deserved. Facing the facts honestly is the quickest and surest way to repentance and release from guilt.

Suggested Scripture

Psalm 119:105
Micah 7:18
Matthew 11:28–30
John 8:11
1 Corinthians 13:5
Galatians 6:1
1 John 1:7

Prayer

Father, my troubles and guilt are never greater than Your grace. Your provision for forgiveness and cleansing is never lacking. Thank You, Jesus, for intervening in my life by giving Your life in exchange for what I deserved. Your love is higher than any human understanding. Thank You for defeating the sin, worry, anxiety, and guilt that would surely defeat me. I am humbled that You faithfully cast all my sin and guilt into the deepest sea, and when I come back to You and cast my burdens once again upon You, You never grow weary. You are my Comforter, my Deliverer, my Fortress. Thank You for making all things work for good for me, and for turning my trials and failures into wisdom and experience. Lord Jesus, as I count my blessings from the past, I am confident of Your provision for the future. Lord, I commit my burdens and my life to You. Thank You for the victory. Your will be done. To God be the glory forever and ever! Amen!

Resources for Counselees

Crossland, Don. *A Journey Toward Wholeness.* Starson Communications, 1991.

Littauer, Fred, and Florence. *Freeing Your Mind from Memories that Bind.* San Bernardino, Calif.: Here's Life, 1988.

Solomon, Charles R. *Handbook of Happiness.* Wheaton: Tyndale, 1971.

Splinter, John P. *The Complete Divorce Recovery Handbook.* Grand Rapids: Zondervan, 1991.

Wallace, Joanne, and Deanna Wallace Early. *Starting Over Again.* Nashville: Thomas Nelson, 1991.

Wright, H. Norman. *Chosen for Blessing.* Eugene, Ore.: Harvest House, 1992.

Resources for Counselors

Backus, William. *Find the Freedom of Self-Control.* Minneapolis: Bethany, 1987.

Sala, Harold. *Coffee Cup Counseling.* Nashville: Thomas Nelson, 1989.

Seamands, David A. *Healing of Damaged Emotions.* Wheaton: Victor, 1985.

Wilson, Earl D. *Counseling and Guilt.* Resources for Christian Counseling Series, vol. 8. Dallas: Word, 1987.

Wright, H. Norman. *Crisis Counseling.* San Bernardino, Calif.: Here's Life, 1985.

Stress and Anxiety:
Burned Out and Worried Sick

Larry Kent

The intensity of Tom's expression matched the desperation of his voice. The words came out like a confession, an admonition, a plea for help. "I can't take it anymore," he said. "I feel swallowed up by too many things to do. There isn't enough of me to go around. No matter where I turn I'm letting someone down."

Mounting stress had caved in on him. His work with an insurance agency was requiring more and more hours and attention, leaving no time for hobbies, little time for friendships, and hardly any time for dating. Wherever Tom turned there was a hassle. His car had been in for repair, he was behind on bills, and three out of four weekends of the month his two sons came to visit. Having two growing boys in his one-bedroom apartment was becoming increasingly difficult, and finding things to do with them added even more activities to his already over-scheduled life.

"I'm always tired," he said. "And I'm not having fun at anything. I just want to stop the world and get off for awhile." Adding to his stress was a preoccupation with tasks he couldn't complete and a waning of spiritual vitality. "I believe the Lord put me here for more than this. I'm missing something somewhere. I'm often annoyed by something as minor as a headache or a cold I can't seem to shake. I'm just not feeling good. I need some help before I go down for the third time!"

Trying to be present in so many places that he failed to feel present in any of them was taking its toll on Tom.

But Tom is not alone in this struggle. Many people get to the point of being unable to renew their life because they can't live up to personal expectations. Some of these expectations are self-imposed, others are imposed by family, friends, employers, and society.

The sense of inadequacy for the tasks at hand and the inability to find time for rest or renewal often leave people feeling as if they have no options.

Definition

The word *stress* as we are using it is actually "distress," and it refers to the challenges and pressures of life that deplete physical and emotional energy, leaving people feeling spent, uptight, and discouraged. Everyday hassles, disappointments, and high expectations all create stress.

Left unchecked, stress causes numerous levels of suffering. In addition to emotional effects such as apathy, depression, and anxiety, stress also causes physiological symptoms such as headaches, high blood pressure, stomach disorders, restlessness, and weakened immunity.

Rather than embrace a life filled with opportunities for joy and enrichment, people suffering from stress lead a one-track existence. They yearn for self-worth, but their life is in such chaos they have no reason to believe they are important. Having lost perspective on what is important, they are overwhelmed by each new problem because they believe it requires their entire attention.

The accumulation of stress can lead to a condition known as burnout in which people feel emotionally, physically, and spiritually debilitated. People in this condition feel overwhelmed, incapacitated, and without adequate knowledge or resources to make life better.

The closer people move to burnout, the more difficulty they have in establishing priorities. Troubles magnify, distress intensifies, expectations seem more important, personal resources seem more limited. If ignored, these symptoms will cause feelings of helplessness and discouragement. Unable to function effectively and creatively any longer, people experiencing burnout may suffer mounting physical symptoms. They may seem desperate and disconnected. Their speech and actions may become increasingly emotional. Although they may find reasons for discontinuing their destructive routine, they may be unable to grant themselves permission to do so. In a moment of intense misery, realizing they are unable to enjoy life any longer, these people may admit their inability to continue life as it is and cry out for help.

Symptoms and Struggles

Burnout is characterized by the continuing and persistent nature of symptoms associated with stress, but it is caused by a combination of factors, not any single one. For example, the strain of commuting, impossible workloads, insufficient training and experience, poor diet, inadequate rest, low pay, and overfilled calendars can combine to bring a person to the breaking point.

It is the cumulative effect of life's demands and frustrations that nudges people closer to burnout. Therefore, it is crucial to rethink the significance of the seemingly little things in life and the impact they ultimately have on health and well-being.

People suffering from burnout are preoccupied with their own pain. Their exhaustion reveals itself in a tendency to be irritable, cynical, and joyless. They have difficulty sleeping or relaxing. Their lack of energy and sense of tiredness make it difficult for them to concentrate, and their sense of scatteredness makes it difficult for them to remember.

Along with being tired, those who are burned out find it difficult to laugh or to pursue depth in even their most treasured relationships. Life may seem to be without feel or focus. In the midst of all this, they feel unable to introduce positive change into their world.

The anxiety of burnout makes people feel as if they have no control. Despite their inability to perform the tasks and responsibilities at hand, they also find it nearly impossible to release them. Unable to choose a more constructive course, they hang on to familiar routines even though they are being consumed by them. The depth of their discouragement often leaves them unwilling or unable to ask for help.

People tend to view their life and experience in fragments rather than as a whole. But the truth is, what people do in one area of life affects all other areas. For example, what they spend their time doing or not doing determines what they will or will not accomplish in another area. To deal with one area of stress effectively, it is helpful to do so against the backdrop of what is going on in the person's whole life.

People are more complex than they generally realize, and sooner or later their ongoing problems, worries, frustrations, hassles, disappointments, and mounting pressures will have an effect.

Counseling Suggestions

Open the Door

When people take the initiative to request a meeting with you to discuss an area of struggle, it indicates a desire to tackle the problem. Meet this request with an open door. Remind them that they have taken the most crucial step in the counseling process by deciding to *begin* the process. Some people will feel relief and improvement simply because they have been able to make an appointment with you.

Your willingness to meet them and be their partner in that venture will encourage them to pursue the counseling process. It tells them they won't be alone in the process, and it also honors their desire to move forward.

Identify the Problem

People frequently seek permission to unpack some troubling area of their life without recognizing the specific nature of the problem. So your next task is to find out what brought them to see you. It is possible that the stated reason may not be the reason at all. Those complaining about being overworked and having too much to do may in fact be asking for help in bolstering self-esteem and learning to define boundaries by saying "no." Those who feel victimized by the attitudes and actions of friends, colleagues, or family members may in fact be asking for help in taking control of their lives. Those who have experienced failure at work or in relationships may be looking for "meaning therapy" to determine what gives life meaning and purpose and hope.

Two things happen when the nature of the problem is identified. First, people are better able to understand and define some of the core issues of their life. And second, such knowledge frees their subconscious to generate insight for solving the problem at hand. The simple act of naming the problem encourages counselees to believe that the solution can be known as well.

Encourage Counselees to Set Short-Term Goals

Most problems are not created overnight. To expect immediate solutions is unrealistic. However, short-term goals and objectives can help make the problem more manageable. Counselees are energized by even a few positive changes because they indicate progress and create hope.

Some possible short-term goals are:

- Begin a modest exercise regimen.
- Schedule a three-hour block of time for personal enjoyment and recreation.
- Say "no" to at least one unmanageable expectation imposed by someone during the next week.
- Agree to a deadline for leaving work.
- Commit to a five-minute period of prayer and devotional reading each day.

The fact that the counselee is able to do something, and do something new, indicates the ability to not only change behavior but circumstances as well.

Assure Counselees That "This Too Will Pass"

Few feelings are permanent. The feelings of today are not necessarily the feelings of tomorrow, next week, or next month. Pain today does not mean pain for a lifetime. Encourage counselees to trust that their situation will get better. The accomplishment of each short-term objective validates that possibility. God does not abandon people in their suffering and struggle. Rather, He promises to meet them in the midst of it.

Encourage Active Participation in Problem Solving

During times of stress and anxiety encourage counselees to answer the following questions:

- What is contributing to the intensity of my feelings this moment?
- Is all of my concern justified, or is some of it in response to things that might not happen?
- Have I intentionally/unintentionally isolated myself from the comfort and support of others?
- What does my present emotional state say about what is going on inside of me?
- Am I using all my resources or have I overlooked some possibility of healing and help?
- Have I been willing to express my struggle and frustration so that others know?
- Have I spent time praying and reading Scripture so that God might guide me?
- Is there an area of my life that I am trying to avoid?
- Am I positioning myself to face the darkness and my own limitations or to face the light and God's promised help and care?

Encourage Counselees to Make Decisions about Their Health and Well-Being

Being decisive brings comfort because it gives a feeling of control. Help counselees understand and accept that health comes only when they allow Christ to change their attitudes and aspirations to coincide with His. Also point out that inner peace comes not from their environment, but from their attitude toward their environment.

Help Counselees Construct a "Worst Case" Scenario

Counselees who are preoccupied with a particular worry or concern might benefit from imagining the worst that could happen. Would it mean the end of a relationship, the loss of a job, or a need for transition? Might it mean that money would be depleted, the future temporarily darkened, that they would reach a dead end?

Once counselees have indeed imagined the worst, ask what would happen then. Would they have to start over, look for new work, develop a new relationship, learn a new behavior, apologize for being late?

Then ask, If the bottom really dropped what would still be intact? Would they still have the ability to position themselves for growth and a fresh start? Probably so. Would they still have the support of loved ones and friends? Probably so. Would the vitalizing power of Christ continue to exist? Absolutely!

It is always good for counselees to see that the final word has nothing to do with situations or circumstances. The final word belongs to God, and it is always a word of hope and help. It is a word they can trust . . . no matter what.

Encourage Praise as a Means of Affirming Hope

Counselees are all startled to discover that God is more present in their circumstances than they are. Praising God reminds them that God is God and that God can do anything. Praise reminds them that God knows their needs even better than they do. Praise frees them to receive what God wants to give. Praise keeps them from being consumed by self-pity. Praise helps them realize that God has already heard their plea and that He will meet their need. It helps them say with trust and confidence, "Into Your hands I commit my spirit."

The following promises are among those for which counselees can praise God:

- "When you pass through the waters, I will be with you" (Isa. 43:2).
- "I am making everything new!" (Rev. 21:5).

Help Counselees Discover an Arena for Service

Coming face-to-face with the trials and tribulations of others often gives counselees a new perspective on their own situation. Furthermore, counselees can lessen their own pain by helping to relieve the pain of others. Serving others causes people to put their own problems on a back burner for a time. It also underscores the critical and important web of human relationships. Helping others frees counselees to receive the blessing of others' efforts, because they learn how important it is to give and share.

Point Counselees to the All-Sufficient Christ

Creative alternatives narrow when people look at their own insufficiency, but they widen immeasurably when people recognize Christ's sufficiency. Prayers of affirmation are especially helpful. For example:

- "I thank You, God, for always meeting me at my point of need."
- "Gracious God, help me to sense Your power seeking me."
- "Abide with me, O Christ, with a healing power that will never fade or fail."
- "I praise You, O God, for the light You are bringing into my darkness."
- "Help me to sense even now that underneath me are Your everlasting arms."
- "Gracious God, in my time of trial, help me to look beyond myself until I see You."

Dos and Don'ts for Counselors

Do communicate in a way that recognizes the counselees' struggle. Those affected by stress and burnout may bring with them an array of problems and needs. Some of these that seem inconsequential or insignificant may be evidence of a deeper level of anxiety. Counselees appreciate and respond to communication that indicates you are aware of their struggle.

Do remind counselees of the importance of taking time. Encourage counselees to take the necessary time to sort out their issues and recognize them for what they are before trying to adopt coping strategies or expecting too much progress.

Do help counselees to see that they are not alone in their struggle. Assure counselees that other people have come up against these challenges and have found ways to emerge victorious.

Do, when appropriate, use humor. Humor can help you establish rapport with counselees. There may be times when it is appropriate to make a light-hearted comment such as, "You must have been in great shape after that one!" "Did you believe that God appointed you alone to run the universe?" "Would you say that you have refined the art of worrying?"

Do be quick to affirm counselees' insights. The road to effective living and self-management is long and complex. Counselees readily respond to feedback that says they are making progress.

Do encourage counselees to cultivate faith by participating in worship, Scripture reading, and prayer.

Do assure counselees that you will continue praying for them.

Do suggest specific resources that might be helpful. Many people are not aware of the wide array of support groups and activities that are available. Such recommendations also communicate the scope of your sincerity and continuing helpfulness.

Do call into question unrealistic expectations and agendas.

Do be a role model of how to live effectively and sanely. Show your willingness to acknowledge your limitations and give evidence of the type of organization and pacing which lessens the potential for stress.

Don't make your experience normative for counselees. Each person has particular needs, possibilities, histories, and desires which must be addressed uniquely. Well-intended personal illustrations usually provide limited help.

Don't respond to any expectation that places you in the position of being the fix-it person. Your role is to help counselees find positive solutions for themselves. You cannot do it for them.

Don't respond to the compulsive tendencies of counselees by making yourself too available. It is important to maintain the boundaries of actual counseling appointments. To encourage or give permission for people to call you at home (except for emergencies) or see you with increasing frequency violates the counseling focus and places unmanageable burdens and expectations on you.

Don't mislead counselees with the reassurance that everything will work out well and quickly. Although you definitely want to give counselees hope, you want to avoid giving them unrealistic expectations. Give a perception of reality which recognizes that problems created over a period of time need an extended period of time for resolution.

Don't discourage counselees who desire in-depth therapy. Some counselees may have particular needs that call for the physiological and diagnostic expertise of a psychiatrist or the skilled awareness of a practicing clinician. Just because you cannot provide everything for your counselees does not invalidate what you can provide.

Don't think of yourself as the healer; you are an instrument for the Great Healer to use.

Suggested Scripture

Psalm 4:8; 29:11; 32:7; 62:5–6
Proverbs 2:3–5
Isaiah 43:1
Jeremiah 31:3
Matthew 6:30
John 16:33

Ephesians 3:12
Colossians 2:10
1 John 3:1

Prayer

Lord, the pace of my life is out of my control. Even when I have time I can't seem to slow down. I am carried along by a lifestyle I can no longer control. I have forgotten how to play, how to sing, how to dance, how to sit in silence. Remind me that to serve You with a life that is less than whole is to fail in offering You my best. Bring me back together, O God, through Jesus Christ our Lord. Amen.

Lord, the Psalmist writes that You neither slumber nor sleep. Sometimes I work as if You are sleeping and that everything rests on me. Teach me the joy of letting go and lying down to pleasant dreams, in Jesus Christ our Lord. Amen.

Recommended Resources

Foster, Richard. *A Celebration of Discipline: The Path to Spiritual Growth.* San Francisco: HarperSanFrancisco, 1988.

Frankl, Viktor. *Man's Search for Meaning.* New York: Pocket Books, 1984.

Freudenberger, Herbert, and Geraldine Richelson. *Burn-Out.* New York: Bantam, 1984.

Hart, Archibald. *Adrenalin and Stress.* Dallas: Word, 1988.

Kelly, Thomas. *A Testament of Devotion.* New York: Harper and Row, 1941.

Nouwen, Henri. *Making All Things New: An Invitation to Life in the Spirit.* San Francisco: HarperSanFrancisco, 1981.

Oates, Wayne. *Your Right to Rest.* Louisville: Westminster, 1984.

Weatherhead, Leslie. *Prescription for Anxiety: How You Can Overcome Fear and Despair.* Nashville: Abingdon, 1979.

Death and Dying:
The Loss Is Too Great to Bear

Richard Krieger

Death mocks all our pretensions at being the possessor of life.
—John Timmer

Of the two certainties of life—death and taxes—death is the one least talked about but the one that has the most profound effect on our lives. Sooner or later we all come face-to-face with it. Death is the reason I am a single adult.

God created us to need each other. We find evidence of this in God's own account of creation. He said, "It is not good for the man to be alone" (Gen. 2:18). All of us need the fellowship of other people. Death diminishes us because it takes away relationships.

Many single adults have no immediate family, so the death of a close friend can affect them in much the same way the death of a spouse or close relative would.

Grief Defined

Grief is the emotional and psychological response to the death of a loved one, and the intensity of grief is related to the closeness of the relationship. The death of a spouse leaves a person alone. There is an emptiness in the person's house but also in his or her life. With the death of a relative or friend, on the other hand, the loss has less effect because usually the person was not a part of daily life.

Grief is normal. In fact, it is abnormal to experience a significant loss and not grieve. The Bible does not condemn grief. In 1 Thessalonians 4:13, Christians are encouraged not "to grieve like . . . men, who have no hope." We also know that grief is normal by the behavior of Jesus. In John 11 we see that Jesus was deeply moved at the tomb of His friend Lazarus. The response of the crowd was, "See how He loved him" (John 11:36 NKJV).

Grief is a process, not an event.[1] It is the process of giving up that which we no longer have; it is adjusting emotionally to what we know intellectually. It is a process that takes time, sometimes a very long time, and the amount varies for each person.

The process of grief is seen in *A Grief Observed* by C. S. Lewis. Near the beginning of the book Lewis struggles to deal with God during his grief:

> Meanwhile, where is God? . . . go to Him when your need is desperate, when all other help is in vain, and what do you find? A door slammed in your face, and a sound of bolting and double bolting on the inside. After that, silence.

But toward the end of the book, we see a more mellow Lewis. Having dealt with some of his grief, he is able to write,

> When I lay these [previous] questions before God I get no answer. But a rather special sort of "no answer." It is not the locked door. It is more like a silent, certainly not uncompassionate, gaze. As though He shook His head not in refusal but in waiving the question. Like, "Peace, child; you don't understand."

Grief is an emotion. Expressions of grief therefore are not always logical. For example, when a grieving wife sees people laughing or having fun, she may think, "How can other people be having fun when I hurt so much?" Or when a grieving husband hears about a man who is divorcing his wife, he may think, "Why didn't his wife die instead of mine? I wanted mine."

Grief is a tribute to the one who has died. It is an expression of love.[2] People grieve because the person they have loved has been torn away without the benefit of anesthesia or pain medication. There is no emotional medication to relieve the pain of a loved one's death.

Grief is inward. Grief often makes people seem self-centered. Sometimes all a bereaved person can do is just take care of basic personal needs. The intensity of grief ranges from struggling for emotional stability to struggling for emotional survival. While self-centeredness is not something grieving people want to feel, it is a way of protecting themselves from additional hurt at a vulnerable time. This reaction may last for weeks or for months. But as the issues of grief are resolved, a healthy self-centeredness will return. It's part of the process.

Grief is loneliness. This is especially true when a spouse dies. Married people are used to "aloneness," but not to loneliness. Aloneness is being by yourself but knowing it's only temporary. It is being alone in a house or in a room but knowing your spouse will return. Aloneness is a fact, not a feeling. Loneliness, on the other hand, is a feeling that something is missing that should be there. Lonely people *feel the absence,* and it's frightening because they know it is permanent.

How to Comfort Grieving People

Grief is largely an emotional experience. Yet in times of grief people generally turn to ministers whose area of expertise is spiritual. Assuming that grieving people need spiritual counsel, many ministers make the mistake of offering spiritual advice. However, what many grieving people need most at a time of loss is simply comfort.

A friend whose sister died in a plane crash recalled that the family's pastor spoke very little when he was with them. He simply sat with them and cried with them. He was there to share their grief, not talk.

Many people want so badly to comfort grieving people that they try to say something that will help. They find a verse or passage of Scripture that seems appropriate—usually something about the promises of God. Although this would seem helpful, or at least harmless, grieving people may see it differently. To them it is like putting a Band-Aid over a gaping wound.

This in no way denies or nullifies the ability of God's Word to comfort. But promises are not necessarily comforting. Most Christians are well aware of the promises of God. They know their loved ones are with the Lord. But knowledge does not diminish their feelings of loss. As mentioned before, grief is emotional, and it needs to be treated emotionally.

(For those who do not know God's promises, such passages may be helpful at the appropriate time. For example, John 14:1–3; 1 Cor. 15:51–57; 1 Thess. 4:13–15.)

For believers, grief has little to do with where the deceased person is and everything to do with where the grieving person is. The grieving person is here, and he or she is alone. The issue at hand is death and separation. The "homegoing" belongs to the deceased. *Grief and loss belong to the survivor.* He or she has come face-to-face with the cessation of physical life and the stark reality of separation and loss.

If you want to truly comfort those who are grieving, be there for the long term. Many people expect a person to bounce back in a couple of months. But in two months the grieving person may be just beginning to feel the full impact of the pain.

What Not to Say to Grieving People

Perhaps the most common phrase people say to those who have lost a loved one is, "I know how you feel."

In truth, no one knows how another person feels. Even though I am widowed, I would not say this to another widowed person. No two people are emotionally the same. No two marriages are the same. Therefore two widowed people will not experience the same grief.

One young woman was at the funeral home after the death of her husband when a well-meaning friend hugged her and said, "I know how you feel. This may sound funny, but I lost someone special too. My dog died this week. I know it's not the same, but I feel your loss and pain."

This is an extreme example of insensitivity, but such remarks are not as uncommon as you might think.

What to Do for People Who Grieve

Let grieving people feel their grief. Grief needs to be expressed, and tears are part of the expression. It is normal to cry. Crying is an emotional release. "A psychological response of the whole body to the experience of loss is involved in the shedding of tears. The person who does not cry . . . is often the person generally regarded as the 'king-pin' of the family. . . . Such persons are said to 'hold up' so well. They are often reinforced in this by those around them. Religion is often invoked as the force which enables people to bear pain and emotional loss stoically, with no expression of emotion. Sometimes this ability is even extolled as a religious virtue. Not so! Sooner or later such emotions will come out, if not in one form then in another."[3]

Dr. John Canine states that people who cry are physically healthier than those who don't cry.[4] And Haddon Robinson put it beautifully when he wrote that "weeping is the language of the soul."[5]

Let grieving people speak. In other words, listen! This may mean hearing the same things over and over. Grief wants to be heard; it *needs* to be heard.[6] Grieving people tend to repeat things because they are trying to process what happened, trying to make sense out of the loss, trying to grasp the reality of it.

Many people ask a grieving person, "Is there anything I can do for you?" Or they say, "If there is anything I can do for you please let me know."

Most grieving people do not want or need any additional things to think about, so few of them will ever accept such an offer. To be truly helpful, friends must see what needs to be done and offer to do it. For example, if the lawn isn't getting mowed, offer to cut it.

The Stages of Grief

According to Dr. Elisabeth Kübler-Ross, grief has five stages (other authors cite as many as ten). Although she studied grief with people who were terminally ill, not with surviving loved ones, her conclusions are generally considered applicable to all types of grief. I use her stages because they seem to be the most widely known.

Not every person goes through all the stages, and some stages may blend together. Also, there is no certain order.

Denial

Usually denial is the first stage. "I can't believe it." "I can't believe this is happening to me." "I can't believe this is real." "Other people's spouses might die in their forties, but not mine."

Depending on the type of death, shock might be part of the denial stage, and denial may include numbness in which the bereaved walks around as if in a daze.

Denial can be a first line of defense in that it lets a person grasp what has happened.[7] It is usually a short stage, and it comes in several types: (1) denial that refuses to acknowledge what has happened; (2) denial that avoids talking about the loss; and (3) denial that escapes in a flurry of activity such as over-involvement in work or hobbies.[8] Many people who are alone try to keep busy after a death or divorce in order to keep from facing their loss.

Viewing the body helps some grieving people get through denial. It allows them to "see for themselves" that the loss is real. If the body is not considered "viewable," discuss other options with the funeral director.

Some people believe that viewing a body is pagan because the real person is no longer there. However, life consists of spiritual, emotional, intellectual, and physical aspects, and each one of these is a part of who we are. When life departs from the body, and the soul goes to heaven, there is still the physical part of the person left, and seeing it sometimes makes it easier to say good-bye.

Anger

Anger, another part of the grieving process, comes from a feeling of powerlessness, and it may be directed at numerous people.

For some grieving people, God becomes the object of their anger. Ironically, people become angry at God because they have faith in Him, not because they don't. Anger actually acknowledges the survivor's belief in the sovereignty of God. The person reasons, "Since God is all powerful, He could have healed and sustained life, but He didn't, so He either allowed my loved one to die or caused the death."

Anger at God sometimes leads to feelings of guilt. The survivor may think, "Since God did not answer my prayer to heal my loved one, perhaps it was because I did not have enough faith."

My purpose here is not to debate the theological correctness of such statements; it is only to explain why grieving people feel the way they do.

Grieving people often feel anger at themselves, too, especially if the loved one was killed in an accident in which they were involved or if they failed to give the loved one proper care during the last stages of illness.

Even the deceased person can be a target of anger. Grieving people often feel as if they have been abandoned. In the case of suicide this feeling may be particularly strong, and there may be feelings of rejection as well. People grieving a suicide victim often feel tremendous guilt. Suicide leaves survivors in the worst of all worlds.

Others toward whom a grieving person may be angry are:

- A doctor who had poor bedside manners
- A funeral director who committed some offense during the visitation
- A minister who said something wrong or failed to say something right during the service

People are very sensitive, maybe overly sensitive, during this stage of grief.

Anger needs to be resolved because it affects behavior and relationships. But before it can be resolved, people need to determine the reason for and the object of their anger.

Some anger can be resolved by using a friend as a sounding board. If you are the sounding board, the best thing to do is to allow it to happen. Let it pass, and do not take it personally.

Anger can also be released through exercise or by finding a place of solitude to yell, shout, or cry. (See chapters 7 and 24 on anger and crisis counseling for additional help.)

Bargaining

Another stage of grief involves bargaining. Bargaining contains "if . . . then" propositions. For example, "If only I had . . . then" or "If only I hadn't . . . then." This is when the grieving person experiences the regrets of the relationship and thinks of all the things he or she should have done differently.

No one goes through grief without dealing with guilt and shame.[9] No human being is perfect and every relationship is a complex mixture of actions and reactions.[10]

People may feel guilty for things they did or did not do. For example, they could have watched television programs the loved one liked rather than gone upstairs and watched their own favorite program.

God's way of dealing with the "If onlys" is called forgiveness. Those who are grieving need forgiveness from God, and they need to feel forgiveness from the deceased loved one.

Even if you believe that past offenses no longer matter to the deceased, you may be called on to help someone who doesn't have that assurance.

One psychologist advises bereaved counselees to place a picture of the loved one in a chair, tell that person their regrets, and then ask for forgiveness. Another method is to write a letter requesting forgiveness.

In addition to needing forgiveness, grieving people also need to forgive.

Some may need to forgive God. If they believe He had a part—either active or passive—in the loved one's death, forgiveness is in order. To forgive God is to recognize His sovereignty. When people come to the place of letting "God be God," they are able to accept life despite the unanswered questions that surround death.

Grieving people must also forgive themselves. To forgive themselves, they must accept that they were not a perfect mate or friend. No one is. People who beat themselves for their mistakes are trying to atone for them. But only one person can do that: Jesus Christ. And He's already done it. Since that is the case, there is no reason for anyone to deny themselves forgiveness.

What good can come from mistakes? Mistakes can be turned into wisdom for the future.[11] The process of grieving causes people to examine their relationship with deceased loved ones and come to terms with their behavior. With the lessons of the past in mind, the next relationship or marriage can be better.

Depression

Depression, another stage of the grieving process, has been defined as "anger turned inward." Dr. Bill Greenman calls depression "constipated anger." It surrounds people, breaks down their defenses, and can dominate and crush them.[12] It is normal in the first few months following death,[13] and usually passes in time. However, if it continues for an extended period of time, or seems unusually severe, refer the person to a counselor with expertise in this area.

Some signs of depression are loss of appetite, insomnia, and fatigue.

Increased responsibilities and financial burdens often add fuel to the fire of depression. One way to help grieving people deal with depression is to do things that ease their mind. Spend time with them, listen to them, invite them to activities, and explore options for getting their life back together.[14]

The thought of living without the person to whom they have had strong emotional ties can be overwhelming, so it is common for grieving people to think about suicide after a significant loss.

These thoughts range from a flash across the mind to serious planning. When faced with no option but to begin a new, unknown life, depressed people may ask themselves, "Would I rather face it here alone or in eternity with my loved one?"[15] Whenever thoughts of suicide are more than fleeting, immediate intervention of some type is called for.

Acceptance

The last stage of grief is acceptance. I say it is last, but actually it is the first stage of "beginning again." Acceptance is the stage in which emotions begin to catch up with intellect. Acceptance is to stop fighting, to be willing to live with the pain, and to realize that not all questions will be answered in this life.[16]

With acceptance comes a gradual lessening of the pain and a willingness to start enjoying life. There is wholeness in marriage, and there is wholeness in being single. It's just a different kind of wholeness. Grieving people were whole before the relationship, and they need to be assured that one day they will feel whole again. Time permits God to heal, and this He does. It took me fifteen months before I was able to say, "It's okay to be single."

Such are the things that newly widowed and divorced single adults face.

Dos and Don'ts for Counselors

Do make yourself available.
Do be willing to listen, in silence.
Do be patient.
Do share your own experiences if they are relevant to the grieving person.
Do provide help with day-to-day tasks (cooking, cleaning, yard work).
Do send cards.
Don't say, "I know how you feel."
Don't quote Scripture casually.

Don't worry if you feel awkward and don't know what to say.
Don't be afraid of tears. They help cleanse and release. They
are not a sign of weakness.
Don't be afraid to discuss the loss.

Suggested Scripture

(The following list is adapted from *Growing Through Grief* by
James E. Townes, 82–86.)

Facing grief
Romans 8:26–28
2 Corinthians 1:3–5
Loss of self-worth
Psalm 139
Feeling inadequate
2 Corinthians 12:9–10
Philippians 4:13
Depression
Psalm 23
Hebrews 13:5
Inner peace
Isaiah 26:3
John 14:27
Philippians 4:6–7

Guidance
Proverbs 3:5–6
James 1:5
Courage
Psalm 138:3
Ephesians 6:10–13
Protection
Psalm 23
Psalm 91
Psalm 121
God's keeping power
Romans 8:38–39
Philippians 1:6

Recommended Resources

Kolf, June. *When Will I Stop Hurting?* Grand Rapids: Baker, 1987.
Lewis, C. S. *A Grief Observed.* New York: Bantam, 1976.
Townes, James E. *Growing Through Grief.* Anderson, Ind.: Warner
Press, 1976.

Part **3**

Helping with Difficult Backgrounds and Circumstances

The Dysfunctional Family Background

Michael Platter

The term *dysfunction* has become a catchword in pop psychological literature. You find it in the paperback section of your local bookstore, you hear it frequently on radio, and you see its many faces on talk shows. And it probably merits the attention it receives. An understanding of the impact of dysfunctional family background is an important tool in the counseling profession.

Counselors have come to understand dysfunction to mean the living out of unhealthy patterns of behavior—particularly those that hinder positive growth and wholesome relationships. Seen in this light, dysfunction is understood as behaviors to which persons or families resort to manage daily life, doing so repeatedly, even though the behaviors result in harm or pain. For example, take John's dysfunctional pattern of relating to women. He likes to date, and claims he wants an ongoing relationship with a woman, yet he is continually driving his girlfriends away because he becomes extremely possessive after only one or two dates. Counselors describe his dating pattern as dysfunctional because it produces pain and hurt for himself (and others) over and over again. In general, then, we understand dysfunctional behavior to exist when *behaviors* (or *thoughts*) in a person's life tend to cause *harm* rather than positive *growth* in a *pattern* that seems to be *repetitive.*

147

Dysfunction usually has yet another dimension. It is not simply a present problem; it often has a long and deeply rooted history in a person's family background. In fact, counselors must be able to look beyond their client's dysfunctional behavior to find its roots. Often they will find that the dysfunctional behavior (such as John's dating problem) is merely one episode in a long history of hurtful patterns that began in childhood.

If behavior is rooted in dysfunctional family backgrounds, it is difficult for people to prevent the negative effects of the behavior. They may learn a new set of behaviors and put them into practice when encountering a problem, and that may help for a while. Eventually, however, many people discover that simply changing a behavior does not end the negative results of dysfunction. Dysfunctional patterns then tend to show themselves in other aspects of their lives. A dysfunctional family background is somewhat like an inflated balloon. If you put pressure on one side, the pressure in the entire balloon is increased, and the other sides experience the pressure too.

Without counseling or some form of intervention, people tend to repeat the dysfunctional patterns. A single adult may experience some relief by changing specific behaviors. But usually deep-rooted dysfunction will find another behavior or attitude through which it rears its ugly head. A counselee has to invest real effort, searching, and wisdom to get to the root of family dysfunction and heal the damaged *pattern* rather than simply change the behavior.

Symptoms and Struggles

Single adults may request counseling for any one of numerous issues, but seldom will they ask your help in dealing with a dysfunctional family background. Most likely, it will be another problem—one that is stressful *now*—that will send them to see you. The issue that is distressing is the surface manifestation of the underlying dysfunction. Counselors refer to such a surface issue as the *presenting problem* (or *presenting symptom*).

Presenting problems take all forms. The single adult may want to talk about poor self-esteem, depression, phobias, memories of abuse, homosexuality, alcoholism, codependency, relationship struggles, and so on. These presenting symptoms should not be ignored. Other chapters in this book discuss these problems.

But how do you determine if the presenting problem is actually the outgrowth of a deeper dysfunction? Here are four signs that can help you recognize whether the presenting symptom is rooted within a dysfunctional family background.

First, persons with dysfunctional backgrounds tend to experience relationship difficulties that follow persistent patterns. Of course, not all relationship problems indicate family dysfunction. To determine if they do, listen for references to the identical problem in other relationships and ask questions about prior attempts to handle the problem. Does a pattern emerge? If so, help clients trace the history of their behaviors regarding this type of relationship struggle. When family dysfunction is the root, single adults will be able to see that the basic script of this relational play was acted out repeatedly by their families.

Second, persons with dysfunctional backgrounds tend to be locked into certain unhealthy and damaging belief systems. This becomes evident after carefully listening to the person's feelings about the presenting problem. People from damaged families tend to have strong, unhealthy beliefs about key issues such as self-esteem, sexuality, guilt, forgiveness, male-female roles, and anger. For example, a college girl named Carla feels tremendous guilt each time she gets angry with a friend, roommate, or boyfriend. So she seeks out a place of privacy and, with her long fingernails, begins to pinch her sides until she sees a bit of blood. As soon as this occurs, the intense guilt sharply subsides. A counselor might label her presenting symptom as an obsessive-compulsive anxiety disorder. But a good counselor will get to the root of these powerful guilt tendencies to discover why she feels the need to punish herself.

Third, persons with dysfunctional backgrounds tend to be resistant to "cure." As most counselors have experienced, it is easy to cure a client of the presenting problem only to find that the client later experiences the same problem with a different "face." For example, persons who are overweight may be able to get control of their bad eating habits. Two or three months later, however, the same persons may be smoking or be hooked on sexually explicit magazines. When counselors see these patterns, they understand that the client has a deeply rooted problem that surfaces in different forms and in different "life locations." It is similar to underground pressures that erupt into geysers on the earth's surface. You can cap off one geyser, but the pressure will eventually find another route to the surface. If you see that a single adult shows this pattern, know that your search will eventually take you below the surface. Long-term family dysfunction may be the fire from which the steam rises.

Fourth, persons with dysfunctional backgrounds tend to have difficulty dealing with their parents or their primary caretakers—sometimes even with the memories of these relationships. Of the four tendencies, this is probably the most obvious sign of family dysfunction. God intended the family unit to be a safe place for children to be raised. It was within the walls of our family of origin that God intended us to learn the values of respect, honesty, security, patience, forgiveness, laughter, friendship, and the essential concept of unconditional love. Family relationships were intended to be the template on which children patterned their understanding of future relationships with friends, authority figures, spouses, offspring, and with God Himself. In a dysfunctional family system, the safe haven of the family is destroyed, and the relational template is warped or incomplete. When the child becomes an adult, he or she is likely to experience difficulty relating to the authority figures of that home. If abuse of any kind was allowed in that home, the difficulty may be more pronounced, and intense emotions such as anger, guilt, or fear may be experienced frequently between this now-grown child and one or both of the parents.

A word of caution is in order here: The presence of one or all four of these tendencies does not prove that a client has a dysfunctional family background. However, the guidelines are good to keep in mind as you listen to single adults talk through some of the issues surrounding their presenting problems.

Counseling Suggestions

Once you have determined that the counselee is dealing with issues from a dysfunctional background, evaluate your readiness to progress toward healing. The effects of family dysfunction are deeply ingrained in people and are highly resistant to change. A dysfunctional background colors a vast and varied landscape of life—self-esteem, relationships to the opposite sex, relationships to authority figures, relationships to children, sense of initiative, optimistic/pessimistic outlooks, work ethics, beliefs about God, and even attitudes about counseling. The point is: Counselors must realize that healing from a dysfunctional background is a long and tedious process, often requiring months if not years of counseling. Unless you are a full-time therapist or counselor, you will not be able to make that sort of time commitment. The issues also become very complicated, requiring training in such aspects of family relations as communication and structural theory, the development of family rules, techniques for memory healing, systems theory, and techniques for restructuring, among others. Therefore, it is wise to begin the counseling process knowing that you may eventually have to refer your client elsewhere (see chapter 4). Counselees should know up front that referral could be essential to complete the journey.

Your role is to help single adults begin the journey. Let them know that you can help them get started and perhaps even map out the healing journey. But let them also know that for the process to be thorough and satisfactory, extended time and skilled counselors will be needed. As you can imagine, this is generally not what counselees want to hear. But to be fair, you must tell them that the issues involved have taken years to develop and cannot be completely healed in a short time. Assure counselees that you will refer them to qualified Christians and that you will help ease the transition by personally introducing the therapist if necessary. To keep counselees from becoming discouraged, assure them that you are not recommending referral because the case is hopeless. You are doing so because they have the right to thorough and satisfactory attention.

Counseling procedures will be affected by the issues that underlie the presenting problem. Hopefully, you will be able to relieve the stress of the symptoms while directing counselees toward the issues of their dysfunctional past. Your goal is to help counselees gain insight into the role of their dysfunctional past and its negative effects on their attitudes, relationships, and particularly their presenting symptom(s). The following suggestions will help you accomplish this task.

Listen Actively

To be a good guide for counselees, you must let them tell the story of their dysfunctional pasts. Speaker and writer Doug Manning once made an interesting observation about the healing power of listening. He said something like this: "Many of our churches believe in healing by the 'laying on of hands.' I believe in healing by the laying on of ears!" When people truly know they are being listened to, they are empowered to talk about their past. You need to have counselees talk about their journeys. Active listening means that the counselor takes the initiative in spurring clients on in the disclosing process. Ask leading questions to let them know you are interested and to help them dig deeper. Paraphrase their statements and repeat them so they will know you are paying attention and are understanding. Use body language to express your attentiveness: smile, lean forward at times, keep good eye contact, and nod your head. This will encourage counselees to express themselves in nonverbal ways as well. Remember, aside from your prayer of faith, the most important thing you can do is listen: steadily, patiently, actively, sincerely, and lovingly.

Look for the Links

As you listen, remain aware of three major ways of mapping the terrain of family dysfunction: (1) The *structure* of family interaction—particularly the boundaries and bonds formed among family members (and sometimes among family and outsiders)—often reveals the effects of dysfunction; (2) the effects of dysfunction also can be seen in the *communication* patterns and rules the family followed; (3) the effects of dysfunction can sometimes be understood by looking at the *roles* played by family members.

Vast amounts of research and numerous books have been produced on each of these theories, and it would be valuable to further acquaint yourself with some of the unique and helpful concepts in these areas of family analysis. For now, though, it is important to know how the maps can help you interpret your counselee's story and see where the roads are leading. Look for patterns of behavior in the family's past and try to link those with present problems. For example, if in one female client's family, females were to be seen but not heard, you may suspect a link between that "family rule" and the client's inability to speak up for herself in her male-female friendships. If you follow *structural theory* you will likely understand that boundaries between males and females in her family were rigid and impenetrable. Therefore, she still perceives those boundaries in her relationships with men. If you use the map of *communication theory,* you may see that she never learned to communicate with males. Therefore she needs to get used to applying her already established verbal skills to conversations with the opposite sex. If you analyze families from the *role theory,* you may conclude that she reverts to a role of servant or maid in the presence of males. Therefore she will need to be taught a new role (that of equal or partner) in her relationships with males. This may require ongoing counseling (or perhaps forms of psychodrama or gestalt therapy) to assist her in learning new roles.

For the purpose of this chapter, it is not important which theory you use to analyze stories. What is important is that you have an understanding of individual development within the context of a dysfunctional family and that you try to look for the links between the family's behavior patterns and the counselee's current problems.

(Note: There is neither time nor space in this brief chapter to give a more thorough picture of family dysfunction. But it is important to note that the vast majority of dysfunctional family issues involve the parents as key figures who perpetuate the hurt and pass it on to their children. Be especially sensitive to parent-child issues; the parent-child relationship is the foundational pattern for perceptions of unconditional love, self-esteem, authority figures, and even our image of God. In Western civilization, the father [or sometimes the grandfather] seems to be psychologically empowered to mold much of a person's sense of self-respect and worthiness of love.]

Bring the Links to Light

Develop the map as your understanding of your counselee's story increases. Then begin to share with him or her some of the *possible* links you see. Do this cautiously and appropriately, and only after you have listened patiently and consistently. By doing this, you give the counselee an opportunity to gain insight into why he or she has often felt certain ways or has repeatedly experienced certain things. If your insights are correct, they will help define significant opportunities for healing and growth. If your map is incomplete or incorrect, ask the client to help you adjust your perceptions as you continue to look for clues.

Actively Plan to Overcome Negative Patterns

When you help clients gain insight into the ways that family wounds affect and influence their behavior, that insight alone is an effective tool for change. A little knowledge is a powerful thing, and God may use the insight to set them free. But the roots of dysfunction extend deeply and spread into hidden areas of life, so it takes hard work and lots of time to get rid of them.

Help clients create an action plan for dealing with negative patterns. The following are elements of a good action plan that will help counselees let go of old behaviors or attitudes.

- Make sure a support system is in place. Lasting change is difficult in a vacuum.
- Set goals that are attainable. Instead of "I will not lose my temper anymore," try "I will attempt to speak slowly and take deep breaths when I get angry."
- Replace the behavior or attitude that needs to be changed with something positive and productive. Most behaviors are

changed not by ignoring them but by making them incompatible with a new behavior.

- Give counselees room for failure. If dysfunctional family issues are at the core, healing will take time.
- Practice with counselees new ways of thinking or relating to family members or friends if the conflict is relational. It makes the tasks less formidable.

Planning Private Funerals

The task of dealing with family dysfunction and successfully moving beyond it is formidable. There is no way to right all the wrongs or undo all the hurt that began in infancy and has continued well into adulthood. At some point, counselors need to lead clients to forgive the injustices of the past. This is not easy. If rushed, the forgiving act will lack its full power. You want to help them release the past and move forward. As Melody Beattie has said: One of the most important tasks of life is to learn the "language of letting go."

When a friend or loved one dies, one of the most difficult emotional tasks for those still living is that of letting go. By nature, humans resist accepting the death of a loved one until we acknowledge that person's existence, legacy, and what he or she meant to us. Then we can say good-bye. At some point during the counseling process, clients need to let go of the pain of the past. Help them to acknowledge the memories, the persons, and the relationships one by one. Help them to see the legacies—especially the positive ones—that have been left by those persons or events. Then help them name the pain and hurt that resulted from those legacies. Help counselees grieve the losses and acknowledge the pain, and let the past truly slip into the past. Lead them to forgive the injustices and to say good-bye.

The effects of a dysfunctional background can take a long time to heal, and for some people healing may never be complete until they reach heaven. But single adults can reach a place where the past is largely behind and where they are daily pressing ahead in newness of life. My goal in counseling is to help clients blend optimism and realism. This is illustrated in the answer of a handicapped man who was asked, "Doesn't your disability color your life?" His response: "Yes. Yes, it does. But God and I decide the color."

Dos and Don'ts for Counselors

Do keep in mind the distinct differences that are inherent in the single adult lifestyle. However, the issues of single adulthood *do not* demand a different counseling approach than you would use for any other adult—regardless of marital status. Therefore, good literature on this issue applies regardless of marital status.

Do keep in mind the ramifications of the client's age, socioeconomic status, desire for companionship, and living situation. These factors can complicate the counseling process because the same dysfunctional relationships or patterns that caused the initial problems may still be in place, especially if the client is living at home. This subjects your counselee to ongoing exposure to the problems instead of allowing an opportunity to deal with them from a safe distance. It may be necessary to include the family in some of the counseling sessions (an experienced family therapist should handle this), or perhaps to see the family members once or twice in counseling to help set boundaries for your counselee. Counselees may need to move out of the family home if the environment is hindering the counseling process.

Do emphasize to counselees the importance of good relationships. Since it is in the context of relationships that dysfunctional patterns begin, it is generally believed that it is in the context of relationships that they must find healing. But the single adult lifestyle tends to exclude two types of relationships—engagement and marriage—in which healing is often facilitated. Also, single adults may have been prevented from developing good relationships because of the dysfunction of their pasts—a likely scenario since it is in the arena of relationships that dysfunctional patterns often do their most damage. Therefore, encourage counselees to spend more time with friends, get into a support group, or become active in a program at church or in a singles ministry that will help them develop a relationship safety net.

Don't push marriage as the answer to the problems of a dysfunctional family background, although a healthy marriage can be a place in which to heal. Single adults live in a society where they are often viewed as being out of the mainstream of adulthood. Sometimes they are labeled oddballs, leftovers, sexually promiscuous or deviate, poor in relationship skills, and a variety of other names most people would not want to be saddled with. Although many single adults wish they were married, and hope to marry eventually, they need to feel as if their current marital status is okay. The type of counseling covered in this chapter often pushes a person toward relationships in an attempt to overcome the effects of past family dysfunction. Exercise caution here. The real answers to dysfunction lie in God's love, Christ's new family, love of friends, and the work of letting go with a caring counselor and guide for the journey.

Suggested Scripture

2 Kings 20:5
Psalm 42:11; 68:5
Isaiah 43:18–19; 49:15–16; 50:4
Romans 8:14–17
2 Timothy 4:7–8

Prayer

Heavenly Father, You have promised that You would be a Father greater than any earthly father. You have assured us that Your love goes beyond the love of any mother for her children. You have called us to forget the things that are behind, so that You can do a new thing. Thank You for Your faithfulness and unfailing love.

We pray for those who need Your special fatherly care and attention. We pray for those who long to feel a love that makes up for the lack of love from their parents. We pray for those for whom family life was a desert and a wasteland—with pains and hurts and unquenched thirsts. Would You do a new thing for these our brothers and sisters? Would You heal the memories and convince them of their right to "forget the former things"? Lead them forth in newness of life and love, as wounded healers in a world of hurt people.

Thank You for the confidence we have in You. You are a God who kept His promise in Christ to our forefathers—You are a God who hears and answers prayer. In Jesus' name, Amen.

Recommended Resources for Counselees

Hemfelt, Robert, and Paul Warren. *Kids Who Carry Our Pain.* Nashville: Thomas Nelson, 1990.

Hendrix, Harville. *Getting the Love You Want: A Guide for Couples.* New York: Holt, 1988.

———. *Keeping the Love You Find: A Guide for Singles.* New York: HarperCollins, 1990.

Koons, Carolyn. *Unstuck: Risking Change in Adult Life Passages.* Ann Arbor, Mich.: Servant, 1993.

McGee, Robert S. *The Search for Significance.* Waco: Word, 1985.

Okum, Barbara, and Louis Rappaport. *Working with Families: An Introduction to Family Therapy.* Belmont, Calif.: Wadsworth, 1980.

Reed, Bobbie. *Learn to Risk: Finding Joy as a Single Adult.* Grand Rapids: Zondervan, 1990.

Satir, Virginia. *Peoplemaking.* Palo Alto, Calif.: Science and Behavior Books, 1972.

Seamands, David A. *Healing of the Memories.* Wheaton: Victor, 1985.

Abused and Feeling Used

Norm Yukers

There are many forms of abuse in our society and countless books on the subject. One form of it seems to be forcing its ugly way to the front, presenting itself to pastors and counselors and almost challenging them to deal with it. I am referring, of course, to the sexual abuse of children.

Initial Understanding

Sexual abuse of children is any sexual act between an adult and a child. This includes incest, assault, rape, molestation, and victimization. It is *not* normal physical affection between parents and children such as hand-holding, hugs, kisses, and healthy physical play—all essential ingredients of a loving family. Abuse is fondling, molestation, exhibitionism, and sexual intercourse between adult and child.

Some estimates report that as many as 40 percent of all women in the United States have had at least one experience of sexual abuse during childhood. *Psychology Today* reports that as many as 40 million Americans (approximately one in six) may have been sexually victimized as children. The statistics are indeed grim.

Some studies indicate that 70 percent of prison inmates and 90 percent of known prostitutes were molested as children. In a seminar, Bill Hybels stated that the average age of the victim is seven and a half. Last Days Ministries reports that the average length of abuse is seven years. Twenty percent of the victims are under the age of seven. It is imperative that church leaders come to grips with the magnitude of the problem.

It is a sad fact that the majority of abusers of children are members of the children's own families or are close friends of the families. It is estimated that 75 percent of the abusers are the children's parents, and a stepfather is five times more likely to be the abuser than is a biological father. In light of the rising number of blended families, this is alarming.

Personal Testimonies

"On the outside we looked like your everyday family, but behind those doors we were not. My dad started fondling me when I was nine. The reason he did not do it earlier was because he was messing around with my older sister. He molested me for four years. My mother knew but denied it. My dad would be real nice to me if I cooperated, but would be real mean and often choke me if I did not. There was a lot of fear in my life! I could have gone to the police, but I was afraid of what my dad might do. Also, I didn't want to break up my parents' marriage, and I sure didn't want people to know!"

"I am part of a family secret. I played a part in a secret sin. I'm in my twenties now and all this occurred between the time I was seven and eleven, but I still carry the emotional scars. I really don't think those scars will ever leave. You may wonder what this family secret is. Well, my uncle is a child molester and I was his victim. The thing that hurts the most is that I feel like the guilty party! I should have stopped him. As an adult, and now as a Christian, I know this is false guilt, but I spent a lot of years in a private torture chamber. Right now the biggest thing I feel is hurt. A deep aching hurt that never goes away. When I was younger I was much more angry. I used to have nightmares, but they are less frequent now. However, they will probably never go away completely. I never let anyone touch me anywhere! Maybe someday I'll get over that. I get real nervous when we are at family gatherings and my uncle steps up to kiss me good-bye."

"The incest I experienced was at the hands of my father, whose alcoholism was secondary to that of his severe mental illness. My mother knew but was afraid and would not seek help. The only nurturing I ever remember was that of a sexual nature with my father. It must have been too painful for my mother, and the only way she knew how to deal with that was simply to not acknowledge my presence at all in our home. That rejection penetrated my heart at a young age and so I clung to a father who abused me."

"Pastor, please don't ask me to climb up in my heavenly Father's lap like I used to do in my earthly father's. You see, pastor, my father used to abuse me when I did that. I can't even picture God as a male, and if I could He surely wouldn't have a lap!"

Symptoms and Significant Results of Abuse

Hatred toward the Offender

Some children are abused several times a week for years. Try picturing yourself in that plight. Why do they allow it to continue? The answer is fear, threats, shame, and often guilt. Those who abuse are experts at controlling the emotions of their victims. One woman shared that she had been abused by her grandfather for years. At ten years of age she told her mom that she didn't want to go visit her grandparents because of abuse. Her mother would not believe her and made her continue the visits. The abuse continued for another three years. "How do I keep from hating my family for this?" she asks.

Mistrust

A much too familiar theme from an abused female is, "I'll never trust again." This often manifests itself in a problem with male authority figures. They do not want to submit to men because every time they did they were abused. They associate submission with abuse; and submission is one thing Christians teach—submission to the headship of the male. Many survivors of abuse, especially incest, tell this type of story: "I believed the lie that men only wanted one thing from me—my body. I hated them for that and I used my body as a weapon against them. I'd attract them through action or dress and then cut them off so they could experience the pain I had felt. In an effort to keep my past from affecting me, I allowed it to completely control me."

Guilt

Ironically, victims feel as if they were at fault. They often describe themselves as being stained or dirty. Amy Grant sings a song, "Ask Me," dedicated to a friend of hers who was a survivor of sexual abuse. In that song she describes her friend taking baths to try to clean the dirt away.

Poor Self-Esteem

The survivor feels she is not worth anything to anyone. Some may refer to this as the damaged-goods syndrome. Who would want damaged goods? This is not poor self-esteem; it is lack of self-esteem. The enemy convinces many survivors that if others knew their secret, they would hate them or at least shun them. So they keep it a secret and others wonder what is wrong with the person who is angry, mistrustful, and rebellious against male authority.

Diminished Desire for Sex

This applies to sex within marriage. If during childhood every touch was like a hot poker against your skin, it is natural to shy away from it as an adult. However, some survivors who feel guilt use promiscuity as a form of self-punishment. Others use sex as a weapon against those they perceive as the enemy. Still others cannot set proper boundaries because theirs were violated as a child.

Escape

Escape often takes the form of dependency on drugs and alcohol. Those who are living a twenty-four-hour nightmare will often do anything to block it out—even if only for a while. Many sexually abused people chase euphoria to ease the pain. For them relief is spelled H-I-G-H.

Second Generation Abuse

The previous six results lead to the conclusion that children of abused parents stand to be abused themselves if their parents have not been healed of their own emotional and often physical hurt.

Other Symptoms

Some of the other signs and symptoms of adults who were abused as children are in the areas of:

- *Physical health*—headaches, migraines, insomnia, eating disorders, asthma, reaction to smells, odors, and, in women, painful PMS
- *Relationships*—poor boundaries, inappropriate touch, affairs, multiple marriages, isolation
- *Sexuality*—sexual dysfunction, addictions and promiscuity, confused sexual identity, confusion between affection and sexuality, sexual abuse of others
- *Emotional health*—depression, agoraphobia, obsessions, compulsions, alcoholism, substance abuse, nightmares, disassociation (Multiple Personality Disorder [MPD]), memory gaps, doubt, despair, hatred, resentment, loss of hope, distortion, denial, ambivalence, suspiciousness

Most of the data presented thus far deals with survivors of childhood sexual abuse. Other forms of childhood abuse are:

- *Physical*—any of several forms of treatment or punishment including, but not limited to, whipping, cutting, bruising, burning, failure to feed and clothe, and beating
- *Emotional*—any of several forms of verbal or emotional treatment or punishment by caretakers (including parents) such as intimidation, berating, abandonment, chronic anger, and persistent comparison and evaluation

There are varying degrees of sexual abuse that may result in different degrees of punishment if the abuser is arrested, tried, and convicted. However, any degree of sexual abuse may bring on any degree of the aforementioned signs and symptoms.

Let me restate the enormity of this situation. There are nearly one-half million *reported* cases (most are not reported) of sexual abuse each year. One in ten families becomes involved in incestuous activity (again, only reported cases). Child rape occurs once every forty-five minutes in the United States. The survivor is not alone! Counselors have a big job ahead!

Recommendations for Counselors

Can a person heal from sexual abuse? Absolutely! But there are some steps that must be put into place to bring about that healing.

Encourage Counselees to Talk to God

There is a merciful God in heaven and He provided His Son, Jesus Christ, to overcome sin and its effects and to restore shattered and battered lives. We cannot do it apart from Him. A survivor *must* confide in Christ.

Jesus can help sort real guilt from false guilt. He can take away hatred, mistrust, and false dependencies. He can rebuild destroyed self-esteem. He is a *man* who can be trusted because He was more than a man. He was and is God. Isaiah 43:1–2 says:

But now, this is what the LORD says—[H]e who created you, O Jacob, [H]e who formed you, O Israel: "Fear not, for I have redeemed you; I have summoned you by name; you are [M]ine. When you pass through the waters, I will be with you; and when you pass through the rivers, they will not sweep over you. When you walk through the fire, you will not be burned; the flames will not set you ablaze."

Listen to Counselees Tell Their Story

Become a trusted listener. Counselees will be afraid to share their stories, so a safe person and place is needed. You can be just that.

As they recount the incident or incidents and walk through the feelings, listen and respond with kind, loving acceptance. Those who are confided in must be compassionate and understanding. You will have the opportunity to display the love of Christ in a great way.

Encourage Counselees to Attend a Support Group

Help single adults find a support-group ministry specifically for survivors of sexual abuse. A group experience will provide help and information crucial for healing. It will encourage personal responsibility and reveal to counselees the connection between past experiences and present symptoms and behaviors. It also will remove some of the feelings of isolation.

Assist Counselees in Finding Reputable Christian Counseling

Counselees need answers that a trained counselor is able to provide. Questions like: Why did it happen? What caused those misguided desires in the abuser? Could I have prevented it? are uppermost in a victim's mind. A counselor can help in the area of flare-ups of anger and mistrust. A good counselor can help bridge the communication gap between the abused and the abuser. A counselor can help renew relationships and assist in the rebuilding process with others.

Pray Together

Second Samuel 22:2–7 and 17–20 can encourage and sustain the single adult.

> The LORD is my rock, my fortress and my deliverer; my God is my rock, in whom I take refuge, my shield and the horn of my salvation. He is my stronghold, my refuge and my savior—from violent men you save me. I call to the LORD, who is worthy of praise, and I am saved from my enemies. The waves of death swirled about me; the torrents of destruction overwhelmed me. The cords of the grave coiled around me; the snares of death confronted me. In my distress I called to the LORD; I called out to my God. From [H]is temple [H]e heard my voice; my cry came to [H]is ears. . . . He reached down from on high and took hold of me; [H]e drew me out of deep waters. He rescued me from my powerful enemy, from my foes, who were too strong for me. They confronted me in the day of my disaster, but the LORD was my support. He brought me out into a spacious place; [H]e rescued me because [H]e delighted in me.

Watch for Self-Destructive Behavior

Many single adult ministry leaders may be in situations of being the only ones close enough to survivors to notice self-destructive behavior (i.e., suicide, addiction to drugs or alcohol, or other acts of self-sabotage). As a counselor, you are caught in the dilemma of needing to get help to protect your clients but not wanting to be viewed as a betrayer. If you fear that any of your survivor-counselees are suicidal, let them know how concerned you are about their well-being. Ask them how they are feeling when they act this way. Try to determine what is triggering those feelings. In other words, get beneath the self-destructive act. (Read the chapter in this book on depression.) Tell them that you want to support them, and encourage them to get professional help; even volunteer to go with them. If the destructive behavior is substance abuse, some of the same considerations apply. If there is a long history of abuse, you may suggest a detox or in-residence treatment program. Again, be ready to help in any way.

Dos and Don'ts for Counselors

Do believe your counselees. When survivors take the step toward healing and confide in someone, they need to be believed. If you have doubts, keep them to yourself for now. As survivors begin to reclaim memories, it is important for them to be believed.

Do demonstrate acceptance. Many survivors will have notions about how they were affected by their abuse and will attempt to link current problems with past experiences. Even if these connections seem to be illogical, accept them for the time being and let time be the connector.

Do remind counselees that they are not responsible for the abuse. Survivors need to be reminded that the abuser was responsible for the act, not them. Try to understand what it was like to be growing up under that threat and in that environment. You may not understand, but you can empathize.

Do learn all you can about the subject. It will be important for you to know the issues and long-term effects of abuse. The more you become educated on the subject, the more readily you can empathize. This will put you in a good position to support the survivor.

Do try to understand the feelings of survivors. It is important that you accept the survivors' feelings about their families, which may seem extreme to you, but they lived in a situation where their feelings were negated and now they must reclaim them. When you understand where they are coming from, you can probably help them deal with any wrong feelings later. If you do not have understanding at this stage you probably will not be part of the recovery.

Do give support. Even though you may at times feel uncomfortable giving support, remember that survivors need to be validated as real people. Their road to recovery is long and hard and they have much need for encouragement.

Do confront counselees when necessary. It is important to intervene when survivors engage in any self-destructive behavior. They may resist your efforts but will trust you later because you showed concern. Be wise, go slowly, and be careful. Be advised by a skilled counselor before confrontation.

Do encourage counselees to get more help if necessary. Survivors may need to be encouraged to get the help necessary for recovery. This help may consist of therapists, Alcoholics Anonymous, support groups, or a combination of all of the above.

Do be patient. The amount of recovery time for each individual is different, but it is important that you understand that at every level *time* will be required. Survivors need someone to travel with them, to be their sounding board, to help them through a long, difficult journey.

Don't challenge survivors on the facts of abuse. That must be determined by the survivors.

Don't instruct them as to how they should feel. Give them time to flatten out the peaks and valleys of their emotions.

Don't take the abuser's point of view. Survivors need someone on their side for a change. If you persist with the abuser's view you soon will become the abuser to them.

Don't develop a codependent relationship with them. Make sure you are giving out of genuine concern and not because of something in your own life that needs fulfillment.

Don't treat the survivor like a child. Be honest but not judgmental.[1]

Today's world is an awfully mixed-up place. It is full of hurting people of all sizes and shapes. They come in all colors and with all belief systems. But healing is available through the Great Physician who uses spiritual leaders like you and me.

Suggested Scripture

Psalm 18:6, 16; 27:5; 40:1–3; 86:5–7
Jeremiah 31:25
Romans 8:38–39
Philippians 1:21
Hebrews 3:13; 7:25
Revelation 21:4

Prayer

Lord, Heal Me

Lord, heal my hurts is my request as I pray I look to you, Jehovah Rapha, is all I can say

Please dig deep to the problem within that I might be free from this bondage and sin

Show me the root wherever it lies for only to you and your love do I want to be tied

Help me to be cleansed as I give to you all the hurts, the wounds, and the unforgiveness, too

As I choose through you my fellow man to love, strengthen me through Jesus whom you sent from above

Help me to be patient as you cleanse each spot for only you have the power to remove each blot

And, as I walk in the power of your healing help me not to rely on my own feelings

But take all thoughts captive and trust in you to listen to what you say for me to do.

—Carol Lee Huff

Recommended Resources

Allender, Dan. *The Wounded Heart: Hope for Adult Victims of Childhood Sexual Abuse.* Colorado Springs: NavPress, 1990.

Arthur, Kay. *Lord, Heal My Hurts.* Portland: Multnomah, 1993.

———. *Lord, I Need Grace to Make It.* Portland: Multnomah, 1993.

———. *Lord, Where Are You When Bad Things Happen?* Portland: Multnomah, 1992.

Buhler, Rich. *Pain and Pretending.* Nashville: Thomas Nelson, 1988.

Carlson, Kevin, and Randy Carlson. *Unlocking the Secrets of Your Childhood Memories.* Nashville: Thomas Nelson, 1989.

Edwards, Katherine. *A House Divided: The Secret Betrayal—Incest.* Grand Rapids: Zondervan, 1990.

Forward, Susan. *Toxic Parents.* New York: Bantam, 1989.

Forward, Susan, and Craig Buck. *Betrayal of Innocence: Incest and Its Devastation.* New York: Penguin, 1988.

Frank, Don and Jan. *When Victims Marry: Building a Stronger Marriage by Breaking Destructive Cycles.* San Bernardino, Calif.: Here's Life, 1990.

Frank, Jan. *A Door of Hope.* San Bernardino, Calif.: Here's Life, 1990.

Friesen, James G. *Uncovering the Mystery of MPD: Its Shocking Origins . . . Its Surprising Cure.* Nashville: Thomas Nelson, 1994.

Gil, Eliana. *Outgrowing the Pain: A Book for Adults Abused as Children.* New York: Launch Press, 1984.

Hunter, Mic. *Abused Boys: The Neglected Victims of Sexual Abuse.* Lexington, Mass.: Lexington Books, 1990.

Koons, Carolyn. *Beyond Betrayal.* San Francisco: HarperSanFrancisco, 1986.

Lew, Michael. *Victims No Longer: Men Recovering from Incest and Other Sexual Child Abuse.* New York: HarperCollins, 1990.

Littauer, Florence. *Hope for Hurting Women.* Waco: Word, 1985.

Littauer, Fred. *The Promise of Restoration.* San Bernardino, Calif.: Here's Life, 1990.

Littauer, Fred, and Florence. *Freeing Your Mind from Memories That Bind.* San Bernardino, Calif.: Here's Life, 1990.

McDowell, Josh. *His Image . . . My Image.* San Bernardino, Calif.: Here's Life, 1984.

McGee, Robert. *Search for Significance.* Waco: Word, 1985.

O'Martian, Stormie. *Stormie.* Eugene, Ore.: Harvest House, 1986.

Peters, David. *A Betrayal of Innocence: What Everyone Should Know About Child Sexual Abuse.* Waco: Word, 1986.

Potter-Efron, Ronald and Patricia. *Letting Go of Shame.* San Francisco: HarperSanFrancisco, 1989.

Ritual Abuse, Definitions, Glossary, the Use of Mind Control. Report of Ritual Abuse Task Force, Los Angeles County Commission for Women, September 15, 1989.

Sandford, Paula. *Healing Victims of Sexual Abuse.* Tulsa: Victory House, 1988.

Seamands, David A. *Healing for Damaged Emotions.* Wheaton: Victor, 1981.

———. *Healing of the Memories.* Wheaton: Victor, 1985.

Thomas, T. *Men Surviving Incest: A Male Survivor Shares the Process of Recovery.* New York: Launch Press, 1989.

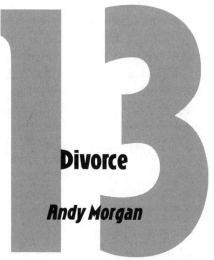

Divorce

Andy Morgan

Divorce is considered by some to be the most traumatic event in a person's life. Many consider it more traumatic than death. Death is final, but the effects of divorce can linger for a lifetime. The scars may remain even if a person remarries, and for many it seems as if something is always opening the wounds of the past. No one can honestly say, "Divorce is a breeze. It didn't bother me at all," or, "The kids are fine and are handling it very well." Research has shown that divorce can have a long-term effect on all those involved. All who go through a divorce need the help of some kind of support system while they are dealing with this transition.

Those who have become single through divorce have had part of their lives cut off. They do not seem to fit into a normal lifestyle. The church has a responsibility to help divorced individuals through transition and recovery.

The realities of the split, the ensuing guilt, anger, helplessness, and loneliness, as well as a long list of unexpected emotions, are just some of the reasons a person will seek out a counselor or pastor for answers to problems.

Divorce is painful and unsettling. From the moment a person realizes that the marriage is over until the divorce is finalized, he or she goes through significant and profound changes in every area of life.

Each divorce is unique in some aspect, and each divorced person has individualized decisions to make. This chapter focuses primarily on the reluctant partner in the divorce, since this is the person who is most inclined to initiate counseling. Along with confusion about what happened and why, individuals who initiate counseling are often hurt, angry, and grieving over the loss. At the same time they may be lonely and uncertain about the future. They need an opportunity to express such feelings in an accepting, sympathetic, forgiving, and safe environment.

Definition

Divorce is the legal dissolution of a marriage. In divorce counseling, the counselor may seek to give the support, guidance, and practical help that people need to get through their crisis.

Christian marriage counseling attempts to keep marriages together by helping couples develop smoother, more fulfilling Christ-centered marital relationships. Divorce counseling is aimed at helping a person separate from a marriage relationship in a way that is consistent with Scripture, with a minimum amount of pain and destruction, and with a maximum amount of growth and recovery.

Counseling the divorced is rarely easy. For many counselors it is difficult to remain objective, listen carefully, understand, or avoid condemning. This can be the result of a counselor's own issues or belief systems as well as an overall resistance to divorce. Whatever the case, it is important for counselors to personally reflect on their own attitude toward divorce and divorced persons. They need to answer this question: What is my responsibility as a representative of Jesus Christ to people who are hurting, confused, frustrated, angry, and despondent due to a marital breakup? Before beginning a counseling situation, counselors should search their own hearts, motives, intentions, and seek God's will in regard to counseling a divorced person.

Practical issues to discuss during counseling include:

- *Establishing a new identity.* Divorce takes formerly married people and throws them into the past to worry about life in the future. This situation provides the counselor with an excellent opportunity to ask them about their insecurities and to talk about life again as a single adult.
- *Assuming responsibility.* Divorced persons need to look realistically at their situations and take responsibility for the direction they are going. Many have relied on someone else to be responsible for their future direction; now they are responsible for choosing their own.
- *Forgiveness.* One of the most difficult issues to deal with in the divorce process is that of forgiveness. Many people do not have a proper understanding of what forgiveness is and what it does for the person who is willing to forgive. People who will not forgive are allowing the other person to continue to control them. Forgiveness performs spiritual surgery on the person who forgives. (See Mark 11:25; Ephesians 4:31–32.)
- *Letting go.* The divorced person who wants to recover cannot live in the past or bemoan the future. Life goes on, and the divorced person can be helped to identify and learn from past mistakes and to make immediate decisions about practical issues. Each person needs to learn the basic skills of life to move ahead in order to accomplish God's purpose, while incorporating work, housing, finances, and newly established life priorities.
- *Building new relationships.* It may be difficult to build new relationships following a divorce. Finding a new support group and friends can be a tremendous help in the recovery process. At the same time healthy recovery includes redefining and often initiating new relationships with the former spouse, friends, and relatives.

Discussing and dealing with a few practical issues and providing the opportunity for a person to set goals in regard to these issues will help motivate a person on the road to recovery.

Symptoms and Struggles

Rejection, one of the major emotional traumas that a person experiences in a divorce, is a deep personal hurt that stems from loss. Some describe their loss as a heavy sorrow. Others describe a deep sadness or a gnawing pain in the pit of the stomach that will not go away. However it is described, the grief of divorce is monumental. It is wearying and wearing on a person's emotional well-being, and without support can be a devastating emotional process. Some of the words used by divorcing people to convey their feelings include abandoned, accused, agony, defeated, fearful, rejected, failure, betrayed, angry, confused, embarrassed, pulled apart, deceived, worried, violated, tired, hopeless, sorry, offended, hurt, humiliated, incompetent, helpless, frightened, furious, jealous, lonely, lost, and out of control.

Many will question, "Why doesn't my partner feel as bad as I do? Is there something wrong with me?" There are two parts to this question. The person who breaks the relationship has often spent a long time, possibly even years, contemplating this step. The actual breakup represents the achievement of a goal and in some sense brings a feeling of relief. The reluctant participant may have been unaware that the marriage was moving in this direction. The suddenness and the shock of the revelation throws emotions into a turmoil. This, coupled with the unfairness of not having a chance to work things out, adds frustration to the depression and hurt. Many times a reluctant partner perceives the relationship as being okay and continues to love the initiating spouse even when the divorce is finalized.

For many people, divorce can be compared to getting caught in a hurricane with only an umbrella. The winds of change swirl with vengeance. Those winds can cause wild emotional swings—swings that hinder not only the two who are divorcing but also extended family members, children, parents, and close friends. After a divorce, nothing is ever the same again.

Many times these emotional swings seriously hinder people's ability to function properly. They may experience fear that immobilizes them or sadness so deep that they cry uncontrollably. At the same time, they doubt whether they will ever feel good again. They may at times experience anger that seems uncontrollable. Thoughts of murder and suicide are common. These emotions may sweep over a person like a tidal wave without warning.

This "wild and crazy time" may go on for months, which in some respects is to be expected considering the significance and depth of the bond being broken. Two people may have experienced both struggles and blessings during their years together. Their identities have been intertwined in almost every area: emotionally, sexually, psychologically, spiritually, and socially. Now that bond has been ripped apart. As one person put it, "The person that I gave my all to and the one who knew me the best just left and told me that I'm not good enough."

Many times it will seem as if one of the parties or the children are not experiencing the fullness of the pain. Frequently, though, these are the ones who are hurting the most. Their pain is so deep that they have gone into denial and withdrawal.

Counseling Suggestions

Counseling Can Be Lengthy

Over the years, I have found that those who seek counseling for divorce are primarily those who did not want the divorce. They are up in the air about many of the aspects of the divorce process as well as their impending singleness. The reality of the split, the loneliness, or the helplessness bring many to the counselor or minister.

Recovery can be a long and rocky road that most experts believe takes an average of two years. Many who have worked with those going through divorce think that it takes men slightly longer than women to fully recover. Many will enter into another relationship too soon after the divorce, hoping that a new relationship will take away their pain. Even though intellectually they may realize this can never happen, emotionally, they act as if it can. Relationships that are initiated shortly after the breakup of a marriage may cover up some of the pain of rejection and hurt that goes with it, but it will return to haunt the person in the long run. Encourage counselees to take the necessary time to process the feelings they are experiencing.

Recovery usually involves a period of feeling terribly sad, lonely, and hurt. Without warning, feelings of intense anger, resentment, frustration, and bitterness may surface. At this point, desires to kill, mutilate, or otherwise punish spring up in the minds of those who feel rejected. Fantasies of the ex-partner helplessly lying on the side of the road, having just been run over by a Mack truck, or of the ex-partner begging for forgiveness may flood the reluctant partner's imagination. Many individuals report being physically ill, while others report feelings of betrayal and bitterness. One woman put it this way: "No man had ever left or rejected me before."

Do not be surprised by the victims' desire for revenge and the fantasies of how they are going to exact that revenge. One of the recurring themes in these fantasies is that they regain the power they sense they lost when the spouse left. This feeling of loss of power can cause a person to get stuck in anger, bitterness, and revenge.

Although no two divorces are alike (the way a person reacts to a loss depends on many factors), I have found that the recovery process can be prolonged by certain types of divorce. Divorces that end abruptly, without any resolution or explanation, are likely to wreak prolonged emotional havoc on spouses who are left. They desire some explanation as to what happened or at least some closure, but get neither. Those who go through divorces that involve personal humiliation (infidelity) also take longer to heal or recover. Those people who try to reconcile the reasons for the divorce in their own minds and who are able to move into the letting-go stage are the ones who seemed to heal most rapidly.

The last stage in recovery is regaining a sense of identity along with dignity, hope, and peace. One man described it this way: "It was as if someone had swept all the dirt and garbage out of my home." For another, it occurred to him as he was driving that he hadn't thought of his ex-wife for a long time. From that moment on, he knew there was another day to live and other people to love.

Counseling Can Be Personal

It is impossible to describe every situation or particular that each person who comes in for counseling experiences. But certain dynamics occur on a fairly regular basis. If you are able to discuss some of these behaviors and describe different relationships, those you counsel might find common ground on which to gain an understanding of their marriage, their divorce, and some of the dynamics that affected their relationship.

Although men and women have different styles of ending a marriage and recovering from a divorce, both sexes find the road to recovery a long and rocky one. Both wounded partners may use lurid fantasies of revenge to help soothe the throbbing pain. Many will find it difficult to admit this, which may be the result of several things. First, professing Christians may find it very difficult to admit these feelings. Second, these feelings are so foreign that they cause a great deal of embarrassment. Third, by admitting these feelings a person may feel that he or she is no longer a "good person."

A Possible Scenario

During the course of a marriage, one partner recognizes that coping with the relationship and the marriage has become unbearable. Emotional closeness, communication, or sexual intimacy is frustrating and/or disappointing. The relationship no longer measures up to a premarriage ideal. Tension increases to the point that he or she makes a decision—the other partner is at fault for my pain and the failure of this marriage, and it will never be any better. The spouse who comes to this conclusion does not communicate to the other partner any of these negative feelings. Instead, an event occurs which he or she will later identify as causing the decision to someday break the marriage. Whatever that event is, it will occupy a high level of personal importance to the spouse desiring to terminate the marriage. The reason I say "personal importance" is because it is an event that the other partner may not even remember. If it is remembered, it was not considered to be of any consequence at the time.

As time passes, and when the marriage relationship enters a more difficult period, that event comes forth as contributing to the difficulty. As mentioned, this event may seem insignificant. For example, the initiating spouse . . .

- observed his or her partner in an awkward social setting.
- was hurt when his or her spouse did not listen during a time of personal hurt.
- had an opportunity to compare the spouse to a former romantic interest or family member.
- had a disagreement with the partner about spending money on an unneeded but desired object.

Feelings of abandonment or betrayal may arise. From those feelings comes anger that is either verbalized or suppressed. Then other negative emotions become a part of the initiator's lifestyle and behavior. This moves the marriage into an unfair and more complicated relationship that pits the spouses against each other in a win-lose proposition, which in reality becomes a lose-lose situation leading toward divorce.

Initiators, or angry partners, become "injustice collectors." Starting with personal injustice, they build up a portfolio of evidence. Although their spouses may realize that something is wrong, they never have enough specifics to identify the exact problem. Therefore the marriage continues status quo. The angry spouse, suffering silently and deeply, appears agreeable on the outside but on the inside is looking for the day the breakup will be announced. The unaware partner usually continues the normal pattern of life and unknowingly continues to hurt and disappoint the angry spouse even more. The shock comes when the angry spouse suddenly moves out and files for a divorce or separation.

Attempts at counseling are often useless at this point because the one who is breaking up the relationship either refuses counseling or provides a superficially cooperative attitude to show that outwardly everything was tried. By doing this the initiating spouse can be absolved of all guilt and look like the "good guy" in the eyes of others. Frequently, the angry spouse presents a very detailed list of remembrances (mostly subjective), bathed in a sea of disappointments, thus giving credence to what he or she is planning to do. The divorce may have been triggered by a final-straw event or by a growing interest in a third person. Sometimes this new interest forces a confrontation between the husband and wife when it is discovered or confessed.

Counseling Can Be Hostile

In many situations, the person initiating the divorce will go through a period of baiting the partner into arguments and fights for a double purpose. First, it may be intended to cause the passive partner to leave or request a separation or at least to begin to feel the same as the initiating spouse. This often relieves the initiator's guilt. Second, it may be an intentional effort on the part of the initiator to "pad" perceived violations in order to justify his or her own leaving when he or she has to explain the breakup to family and friends. It is not unusual for initiators to play the role of victim and to gain a great deal of emotional support from friends who wonder how they tolerated the situation so long. At this point, initiators may look like saints or martyrs to family and friends.

Attempting to counsel in this situation can be frustrating for everyone except the initiator. It can be especially frustrating to the counselor and the reluctant partner when they do not recognize the ground rules set by the initiator. When the ground rules are not recognized by the counselor, he or she can easily fall into a trap that is detrimental to the reluctant partner.

The goal of many Christian counselors is to bring the couple back together. However, in this type of situation, pressure from a counselor may cause more hurt and anger, which will further alienate the initiator.

There are situations in which reconciliation occurs, but unless the angry partner recognizes his or her anger and is willing to stop blaming and assume responsibility for part of the conflict, reconciliation more than likely will not occur.

Non-initiating spouses often come to the counselor or minister with the feeling of wrongdoing and want to be told what to do. Usually the list of infractions used by initiators to announce the breakup of the marriage causes non-initiating spouses to feel as if all the blame is really theirs.

Some people have come into my office willing to give away everything in the hope that this new loving and understanding attitude will win back the angry spouse. More often, the initiating spouse feels justified in receiving an inequitable share, rationalizing, "I deserve it after all I have put up with." It is important that a counselor not let the guilt-ridden party atone by giving away his or her rightful share of personal property or savings or agree to settlements without the advice of a lawyer.

Counseling Can Be Arbitrary

The one who comes for counseling is often the one who is having difficulty coping with the breakup of the marriage and is unable to handle the overwhelming emotions caused by the suddenness and unexpected announcement that divorce is inevitable. A therapeutic counselor or minister can provide objectivity and thus bring healing to the marriage or growth through the divorce. This usually depends on the cooperation of both partners. But even in situations where one partner is not cooperative, growth can take place.

Unfortunately, some of the worst things to do when a marriage is threatened are often the easiest. When faced with threat and hurt, it is often second nature to punish and hurt in response. Assure counselees that it is normal for them to feel anxious, depressed, fearful, hurt, and many other unpleasant emotions during divorce or marriage difficulty. Help them guard against behaviors that would be counterproductive to the goal of rebuilding the relationship or would make the divorce process even more difficult, including those that would confirm the initiating partner's decision to divorce. Several common mistakes made by those who are divorcing are based on emotional reactions to hurt and anger.

Mistake #1: Listening to Well-Meaning but Misguided Friends

People often are overly influenced by sympathetic friends who say, "I wouldn't take that. I would tell so and so to get out if it were me."

This may not be the best advice or what the non-initiating spouses want to do, but they could be easily influenced into temporary bravado because they do not want to lose their friends. Subsequently some irreparable damage may occur. Encourage counselees to keep their friends; they will need all the support they can get. But encourage them to try to make contacts with their spouses less emotional.

Mistake #2: Seeking Revenge

Many non-initiating spouses indulge their desire for revenge and will attempt to punish the estranged partner by telling aspects of their story to others when they should not. It is not wise to let it all hang out. By telling every sordid detail to friends and family, they will succeed only in closing the door a little tighter and making it even more difficult for a reconciliation or equitable solution. Often the details that are shared cause not only a loss of face for the other partner but also provide more ammunition to continue with divorce proceedings. Help the individual curb the desire for revenge and punishment.

Mistake #3: Giving In to Fantasies

Fantasies can be extremely destructive to the healing process. They will block any objectivity that is necessary for recovery. Imagination can convince an individual that his or her mate or ex has it better than he or she does; that the ex is out enjoying life to the fullest while he or she is sitting home suffering personal, spiritual, and financial loss. Imagining the spouse in a carefree lifestyle may increase the desire for revenge and cause the buildup of hatred. Trying to understand the ex-spouse's lifestyle only detracts from the recovery process.

It is a fact that divorce affects the standard of living of both spouses. Dwelling on who is suffering the most will benefit neither one. Even if the fantasies are true, dwelling on things that cannot be changed serves no healthy purpose, so lead the person to relinquish the desire to fantasize.

Mistake #4: Using the Children to Punish the Spouse

Try to keep the spouses from involving the children in revenge and power plays and from using them as a source of information or as a method of punishment. Children are torn apart when parents split. If they are civil to one parent, the other may accuse them of unfairness. They may feel as if their loyalties are being tested and that they are expected to choose sides.

Encourage parents to talk freely to their children but not to use accusatory speech. Parents must be aware of the children's hurts yet remain aware that they cannot be both mother and father. Many children will display regressive behavior. Help parents understand the great turmoil their children are going through and encourage them to let their children know they are aware of the conflict they are experiencing.

Two divorced parents can come together to set guidelines and learn parenting skills for the raising of their children. It may be difficult, but it can be done.

Counseling Can Be Practical

When people are going through divorce there is no such thing as "normal." Given the wide varieties in human nature, the differences in each divorce, and the fact that no two people are the same, there is no normal divorce and no normal solution. However, there are at least two areas in which all situations are alike.

The Need for Legal Advice

If your counselees do not have an attorney, encourage them to find one who will answer their questions. The lawyer must be one they are comfortable with, someone who will take the time to answer their questions and ease their fear. Do not give them legal advice; you are their minister or counselor, not their lawyer.

The Need to Prepare for Life Alone

For the woman, this may mean going out into the work force for the first time; or back into the work force after a long period of time; or changing to a career that will provide better financial support. This may mean going back to school. Statistically, a husband's monetary support lasts for about four years, so most women are going to have to find other means of financial support. Many programs are now available at community resource centers and local colleges to help those in transition. Help clients find support systems that will help them move forward in their lives.

Assist them in maintaining their relationship with God and His family, the church. Their first response may be to run. Acknowledge that such a response is normal, but at the same time encourage them to be cautious. Let them know the importance of staying close to something stable and familiar. Remaining in an atmosphere that can provide emotional and spiritual support can be a great asset in the process of recovery.

In all of this remind yourself and your clients that God wants the best for His children. He forgives those who confess and guides those who want His leading. Divorced persons and their counselors are not left alone to fend for themselves. The Holy Spirit is the constant guide and companion of committed divorced believers and their Christian counselors.

When divorce is inevitable, you can help counselees find freedom from condemnation and tortured emotions by helping them to experience God's grace and new life. Times of trial often bring people face-to-face with the real meaning of life and the insecurity of placing their trust any place but in God.

Dos and Don'ts for Counselors

Do encourage others in the church and on staff to monitor and minister to divorcing people and their families. Develop a network of support. Provide a restoration team that may include people who have successfully grown through divorce and whose divorce experience may be helpful.

Do encourage parents to let their children know they are aware of the conflict the children are experiencing. Help parents see how harmful it is to use children to acquire information about the spouse or to punish the spouse.

Do encourage divorced people to take the necessary time to process the feelings they are experiencing and to grow through the divorce.

Do be aware of the healing power of an appropriate touch, but remember that not everyone is comfortable with hugging and touching.

Do use appropriate and well-timed humor as an instrument of healing. When people can laugh again it means they have hope.

Do not condemn or listen judgmentally. Remain objective and listen carefully and with understanding.

Do not exhibit behaviors or emotions that will confirm the initiating partner's decision to divorce.

Do not give legal advice. You are a friend, minister, or counselor, not a lawyer.

Do not assume that any two divorce situations are the same. The process of healing is different for each person.

Do not allow discussions to run wild or focus on imagination or on fantasy. Keep discussions focused on reality and keep them practical.

Do not take sides.

Suggested Scripture

Psalm 27:10; 42:5
Lamentations 3:32
Mark 11:25
Romans 12:18
Ephesians 4:31–32; 5:1–2
Hebrews 4:15

Prayer Suggestions

I have counseled many who have entered into a new and deeper relationship with God through the spiritual strength that comes from a new commitment to Christ. Divorce never keeps a person who wishes to serve God from doing so. When praying for divorcing clients, look to the Spirit for wisdom. Help the person understand God's forgiveness and how to receive it. At the same time, gently lead him or her to forgive all those involved in the situation. Pray for the fruit of the Spirit to be manifested in the individual and pray for strength, guidance, and wisdom for all involved. Through prayer and Scripture, encourage the divorced or divorcing person to not neglect the most important resource available— his or her commitment to and relationship with God. Remind the person that God knows his or her suffering, that God will not forsake him or her, and that the God we know knows what we feel.

Recommended Resources

Burns, Bob, and Tom Whiteman. *The Fresh Start Divorce Recovery Workbook.* Nashville: Oliver-Nelson, 1992.
Divorce Recovery Videos. Say What Communications. Available through the Network of Single Adult Leaders, P.O. Box 1600, Grand Rapids, MI 49501.
Hart, Archibald. *Children and Divorce.* Dallas: Word, 1982.
Smoke, Jim. *Growing Through Divorce.* Eugene, Ore.: Harvest House, 1976.
Splinter, John. *Second Chapter.* Grand Rapids: Baker, 1987.

14

Dealing with the Ex-Spouse

Richard Matteson

When asked for advice concerning how to deal with ex-spouses, a group of single parents answered quickly, clearly, and emotionally, "Don't." But for many single parents this is not an option. Nor is it an option to go through a divorce without experiencing negative feelings toward the ex-spouse.

In marriage, two people are brought together and made into one. In divorce, that union is severed, and the wound always leaves a scar. Divorced people are all wounded—even though some do not show it on the outside. The severity of the wound depends to some extent on circumstances such as longevity of the marriage, extent and outcome of the divorce proceedings, the involvement of children, whether or not adultery was a factor, age of the partners, and financial situation after the divorce.

In using the word *ex-spouse*, most people immediately think of a person divorced from an official marriage. But in our day we need to expand our concept of this word to include common-law relationships, i.e., couples living together with no official marriage document. Such people will experience just as severe a reaction to separation from their mate as those with a certificate.

The counselor's role depends on the conditions surrounding the divorce. There are several categories into which all the encounters with the ex-spouse can be placed—sex, money, and children. When children are not involved, the separation of the two adults may limit much interaction, especially if one party moves out of the geographical area. But with children, divorce can be worse than death because issues that involve them—including visitations and discussions about their health and well-being—are ongoing.

Emotional feelings regarding an ex-spouse range from being like an open wound to being like a scar. In the separation period, the counselor begins to help counselees formulate methods of interaction with ex-spouses. (Note: Dealing with an ex-spouse means dealing with the couple's wounds and pain. When the counselee is able to bring healing to those wounds, there is a better chance that his or her interactions with the ex-spouse will be more positive.)

The process of emotional healing can be illustrated by the three stages of physical healing required for a cut to heal.

- *Stage one.* The first order of business is to stop the bleeding and to clean and close the wound. Cleaning and closure are always accompanied by pain and more bleeding. This is also true in divorce. Deep hostility, hatred, and the desire for revenge may permeate the hearts of a divorcing couple. The cleansing process goes far beyond the surface level and into the deepest part of the soul. There is great pain, and it is important to stop the emotional "bleeding" in order to deal with the past and heal. This cleansing is confession—agreeing on the truth—to God and others.

- *Stage two.* After a period of time, the wound scabs. This indicates that healing has started. Unfortunately, the wound is sometimes accidentally reopened, which causes bleeding again. Something like this also happens in dealings with former spouses. During interaction there may be an intentional or unintentional reopening of the hurt. It is important to the healing process that everyone be cautious and introspective in determining responsibility. There may be surface feelings of guilt (real and false) and even a tendency to feel sorry for the ex-spouse. It is important to keep the wound covered so that it does not become infected by foolish or negative thoughts and actions. Forgiveness is the salve that quickens the healing process. Without forgiveness, people will find themselves again and again in stage two, unable to pursue new goals, directions, and interests. Caught in the grip of their own bitterness and pride they will be unable to deal correctly with former mates.

- *Stage three.* Scarring is common, especially if wounds are reopened many times as this causes a weakening of the tissue. The size of the scar may be determined by how quickly the wound was attended to and how many times it was reopened.

Problems that may occur if counselees do not deal properly with the ex-spouse are:

- bitterness that can eat away at the strength of life and cause physical as well as psychological problems.
- an altered perspective toward the opposite sex.
- stunted growth in a stage of recovery. This will influence how clients respond to children and other adults and will affect emotional growth as well. First Timothy 1:5 says that love comes out of a "pure heart, clear conscience, and a faith unwavering." If dealing with the ex-spouse is a continual problem, having a pure heart and possibly even a clear conscience becomes very difficult, which further hinders the ability to have a pure love for a new partner.
- revenge that can ultimately destroy a person and seriously hurt the children. A heart gripped by revenge focuses on evil and continually sows bitter seeds of resentment and bitterness. Because God is interested in forgiveness, efforts to hold on to ill feelings will cause people to reject spiritual resources and influences: the Bible, God, prayer, worship, and godly friends. This rejection can damage a relationship with God.

Negatives and Positives

People who are dealing with ex-spouses may develop both negative and positive feelings and/or actions. Individuals, however, are quite different in personality, and it would be too bold to say that everyone experiences these or that these are always present or that these are all the symptoms there are.

Fluctuations between love and hate (the two strongest emotions) are there periodically for the ex-spouse. Love and hate are not far apart in regard to the amount of energy necessary to generate them. The person will be on a roller-coaster of emotional highs and lows. These fluctuations are present in the early months of separation and divorce, but both feelings should fade as time goes by.

Sometimes one or both parties keep strings attached to the failed relationship. For example, the ex may still have a key to the house, or still help with chores or repairs, or possibly the two go out to dinner "just to discuss the children." One party may still perceive the possibility of reconciliation, and this drives one spouse to maintain strings.

Unresolved matters concerning children or material possessions sometimes cloud the issues. What has been done with all the things that still belong to the ex but are present in the home? What has been done regarding the children? Having joint custody but being unable to agree on any direction for their future often builds hostility.

Bitterness toward an ex-spouse, which seems to extend to other people (especially those of the same gender), is another negative aspect of divorce. This is readily apparent in conversation, jokes, and focused discussions on that person's gender.

Finally, there is depression. Where there seems to be no interest, strength, or ability to move on with life, there is probably depression.

Among the positive signs that clients are having success at putting ex-spouses behind them are the following:

- They show a steady decrease in their amount of anger and revengeful talk concerning their previous mate.
- They pursue new areas of challenge and interest.

- New goals emerge. Help clients examine these to be sure they are not aimed at getting back at the ex-spouse. Motives are very tricky and should be carefully examined, especially if there has been a high degree of codependency in a former relationship.
- New friendships develop. Those who continue to be reclusive will quickly lose perspective on life and their fear of new relationships will grow, thus encouraging them to turn further inward.
- They make progress in their spiritual life. Church may become an intricate part of their new beginning. Spiritual seeds often sprout in the rocky soil of a divorce.
- They begin to date—for the right reasons. There can be a major problem in beginning to date too soon after divorce. A person needs to clear away the past before moving on to new relationships.

Counseling Suggestions

Encourage counselees to forgive and to accept forgiveness. Forgiveness is absolutely essential to the restoration of normalcy in life and emotion. Forgiveness is best encouraged in divorce recovery and is a must for every divorcing person. There must be a "rooting out" of bitterness and the "taking no thought" for revenge or else the wound will continue to fester and remain unhealed, which will make dealings with an ex hard and strained. Encourage counselees to choose to live in the present and in the future instead of in the past.

Encourage counselees to understand that their marriage and divorce followed a certain process. This process involved four levels of a relationship: acquaintance, casual friend, close friend, and intimate confidant. The relationship was progressively built and must be progressively dismantled. Therefore it is not something that can be dumped in one day, week, month, or year. Recognizing the levels of a relationship and initiating a reversal process may be the best way to begin building a new kind of relationship

Levels of Friendship

```
INTIMATE FRIENDSHIP
Commitment to development
of each other's character.
Correct each other.

CLOSE FRIENDSHIP
Mutual life goals.
Discuss/suggest mutual
involvement in projects.

CASUAL FRIENDSHIP
Common interests.
Discuss/ask specific questions
(opinions and goals).

ACQUAINTANCE
Periodic contact.
Discuss/ask general questions
(public information).
```

with the ex-spouse. The diagram above may be of assistance in viewing this progression and its retrogression.

Encourage counselees to see themselves as God sees them. They are valuable, important, distinct, and separate individuals. Each year that a couple is together, a little more of their identities are united through common experiences and common goals. To once again see themselves as separate persons takes time. But this is absolutely essential to their ability to deal properly with each other as an ex-spouse. If counselees cannot view themselves as whole persons, they will be unable to function as whole persons, and the ex-spouses will continue to influence their decisions.

Encourage counselees to cut unhealthy strings. Unhealthy strings become apparent through counseling or divorce recovery, and some are identified by friends. The divorce decree and its division of material properties initiates this process both physically and emotionally, but there are many emotional strings, some of which may not be initially evident. Some are actually good and include special dates that hold significance, such as an anniversary, a child's birthday, a memorable experience, a fragrance that reminds you of a special moment or a place you went together, or a certain color that brings to mind a certain gift. These strings need to be untangled and properly disposed of before the person can move forward with new directions and goals.

Encourage counselees to review the time they spent with their spouses while married. You can help them delineate the real, the hoped for, and the dreamed about, and encourage them to put everything in perspective. They should acknowledge rather than suppress the positive feelings they had in these memories. Help them understand that it is okay to have positive feelings about past experiences even if they include pain. Just because they are now divorced does not mean that everything that happened is to be "ex"ed out of memory.

Encourage counselees to see growth in their lives as an aid in dealing with ex-spouses. It will also help them as they view themselves as unique and special. Areas of growth are suggested by the chart below. Review the areas of their lives with them and encourage new directions. Advise them to set yearly goals and to move toward them through good planning and effective decision making. The following is a simple chart of the areas in which goals need to be set:

Six Areas of Individual Life

Encourage counselees to live up to the responsibilities stated in the divorce decree, whether they are financial, maternal, or paternal. Encourage counselees to see their spiritual responsibilities as parents.

Dos and Don'ts for Counselors

Do tell counselees that you care about them and will treat nothing they say lightly. An insignificant issue from your perspective may be insurmountable to them. This is also true if you are trying to counsel the opposite sex. You may have a tendency to mentally side with the other party because you are viewing it from a gender perspective.

Do refer counselees to another counselor if you believe they need more help than you can provide. If their need is simply to have someone listen to them, present them with the idea of finding a "caring friend" who will allow them to talk and express their emotions without offering prescriptions, analyzing their behavior, or reprimanding them.

Do encourage them to attend a divorce-recovery workshop, seminar, or counseling session at least once. In some cases it might even be helpful to do it several times after intervals of one year or more, especially if they have a tendency to get stuck in their growth process. Counselees' growth can place past situations in perspective, altering initial impressions about incidents and bringing knowledge of what was the truth. Forgiveness can then come.

Do help them understand that although the phases of divorce recovery are mentioned in a particular order—denial, anger, bitterness, depression, acceptance, and hope—they need not always stay in this particular sequence. Each can be revisited at any point in the process of recovery.

Do start a single parent fellowship or encourage them to attend one in your area. Much wisdom can be gained by interacting with a small group that faces the same dilemma. You can also try to link them to a more mature Christian through weekly meetings. They may become prayer partners.

Do help counselees look for successes in their dealings with their ex-spouses. These can then be heralded as steps forward.

Do encourage them to abstain sexually. They must not use their previous spouse as a means of "safe sex." Sex in these circumstances only deepens the hurt and is often offered for the wrong reasons (e.g., to get the marriage back together). It is unwise to use sex in any way to deal with the ex-spouse.

Don't pretend you can understand counselees' feelings if you have not experienced a divorce. Instead, simply acknowledge their feelings by saying, "Although I have not experienced divorce, I see that you are experiencing real pain in dealing with your ex-spouse." Even those coming out of a "good" divorce may be unable to understand those going through a bitter fight.

Don't assume that you understand all that has happened to bring a couple to the demise of their family unit. Divorce is never a simple issue. There are three sides to every divorce: his, hers, and the truth.

Don't assume everything will be okay after you offer them a prescription to follow. First, they have to be ready to accept the remedy. They must be at the right stage before they can take any positive action. Second, each individual is unique, so one prescription does not fit all. Third, the ex-spouse is the unknown in the equation, and your encouragement and suggestions to the struggling person may be frustrated by the ex's unchecked actions.

Don't encourage counselees to compete with ex-spouses in any way, including jobs, children, or revenge. The more the focus is on competing (winning), the less they can concentrate on their own growth.

Don't encourage counselees to isolate their children from the other parent. In certain cases, such as child abuse or where a parent is living with another person, special guidelines may be necessary during visitation times. Being unable to interact with the other parent is not in the best interest of the children. Don't deny visitation rights.

Don't allow them to use their children as messengers. However hard it is for parents to speak to ex-spouses, they should never cause children to feel as if they are in the middle. They don't want to be the conveyers of bad news to someone they still love.

Suggested Scripture

Psalm 5, 6, 7, 13, 17, 18, 22, 23, 25, 27, 28, 31, 37, 40, 46, 51

Prayer

Lord, I thank You, even though it's hard, for the situation I am now in. I know I haven't handled every dealing with my ex-spouse in the best way. But You know that I want my relationships to glorify You and become an example of Your unconditional love. Help me to see and take care of any remaining bitterness in my heart. Help me to forgive as You have forgiven me. Help me to focus on how You are using these dealings to make me stronger and more like You. Help my children to see Your love in me when we talk or act concerning my ex, their parent. Keep me sensitive to Your Spirit as I continue to relate to my former spouse. I pray that You would continue to deal in our lives to accomplish Your will for us. Amen.

Recommended Resources

Barnes, Robert G. *Single Parenting, A Wilderness Journey*. Wheaton: Tyndale, 1992.

Berke, Melvyn, and Joanne Grant. *Games Divorced People Play*. Englewood Cliffs, N.J.: Prentice-Hall, 1986.

Fagerstrom, Douglas, ed. *Singles Ministry Handbook*. Wheaton: Victor, 1988.

Flanagan, Bill. *Developing a Divorce Recovery Ministry*. Colorado Springs: NavPress, 1991.

Knorr, Dandi Daley. *Just One of Me*. Wheaton: Shaw, 1989.

Richmond, Gary. *Successful Single Parenting: Going It Alone*. Eugene, Ore.: Harvest House, 1989.

Smoke, Jim. *Growing Through Divorce*. Eugene, Ore.: Harvest House, 1976.

Stanley, Charles F. *The Gift of Forgiveness*. Nashville: Thomas Nelson, 1991.

Whiteman, Thomas. *The Fresh Start Single Parenting Workbook*. Nashville: Thomas Nelson, 1993.

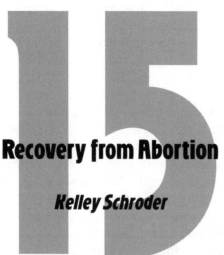

Recovery from Abortion

Kelley Schroder

bortion is the voluntary removal of a baby from the mother's womb. Although there are many different procedures for abortion, the results are always the same: an interruption of God's creation process. When a child is conceived, God's intent is for the child to develop safely in the protection of the mother's womb until it can survive outside.

Babies remind us of God's love for this world. Our family has a plaque on the wall in our house that says: "A baby is God's way of saying the world should go on." Abortion forcibly removes the baby, terminating both its life and the natural birthing process for the mother. Deep within her spirit a woman knows this and feels the loss of her baby. She knows that the baby is a part of God's creative plan for humanity, and to interrupt this plan creates a deep wound in the woman's spirit and emotions. Abortion simply is not natural.

Wounds caused by abortion are difficult to heal because the decision to abort is often made by the woman. A miscarriage is wounding also, but the woman does not have to deal with choices; it was not her choice to terminate the pregnancy. She has to deal with the loss of the baby but not the choice. A woman who has had an abortion has to deal with the loss of the child and the choice she made, regardless of the circumstances.

Those who have never experienced the trauma of an unplanned pregnancy need to fully understand what the mother and the father, if he sticks around, must go through. Keep in mind that a woman who becomes pregnant may not even suspect it for thirty to forty-five days, at which time her normal menstrual cycle ceases. Even at this point, she may very well ignore what her body is telling her because of fear, denial, or ignorance. So she waits, hoping and praying that she is not pregnant.

Another cycle is missed, and she begins to suspect she may be pregnant. She may tell the baby's father at this point. He may explode with anger and terminate the relationship or threaten to do so if she does not abort the baby. If she does not tell the father out of fear that he will break up with her, she begins to realize that their relationship is not healthy. Now she has to either deal with a breakup or the reality of a bad relationship. In most situations, he will pressure her to abort the baby, and there will be a breakup, either before the abortion or right after. Seldom does a father walk through the decision-making process with the mother. The men who do stick it out have a strength of character that is unusual and a love for the mother that will help tremendously with the healing process.

By now she may be sixty days pregnant. She may investigate getting an abortion and find out that the "safest" abortion is done in the first trimester, or within ninety days. She may consider going to her parents, but because of fear of rejection or criticism, this is difficult. She may tell a best friend, who probably knows less about the effects of abortion on women than does the pregnant woman.

She now has only thirty days in which to make a decision. Added to her boyfriend's abandonment, his pressure for her to abort, her poor relationship with her parents, and a friend's ignorance is the fact that her changing hormones are creating strange and unusual emotions. A woman often makes a decision in thirty days, many times alone, that will affect her for the rest of her life.

If the woman does not admit her emotional wounds following an abortion, they usually become infected, just like an untreated physical wound, and will negatively affect her emotionally, especially in future relationships. If she does not go to God with the choice she has made, she may live with a sense of guilt and shame that will paralyze her for the rest of her life, especially spiritually. Such a woman is a prime candidate for the healing grace of God, and needs to be pointed toward God.

Symptoms and Struggles

Two major symptoms in a woman who has experienced abortion are woundedness and shame. These will cause many struggles that should be signs identifying this issue.

The loss of the child she has conceived causes a wound that hurts for many years, despite efforts to deny it. She may have been "counseled" that she would not feel wounded because she was doing the best thing for herself and the baby. However, down deep, she hurts. There is a natural joy that a woman feels after giving birth to a child. Jesus refers to this in John 16:21. When a child is aborted instead, the woman feels no joy, only sorrow. She misses the baby, but she has been told that she is not supposed to. She tries to submerge the hurt, yet it rises to the surface, especially during certain times of the year—Mother's Day, the anniversary of the day on which she discovered she was pregnant, the anniversary of the day on which she had the abortion, the estimated birth date of the child, Christmas. She may weep uncontrollably or sink into a deep depression. I have seen these symptoms in women ten to fifteen years after an abortion.

The wound may drive the woman into *isolation.* She may become a loner out of fear of being hurt again. This is destructive because she needs people to help her acknowledge the wound. People can be used by God to lead the woman to healing.

The wound may drive the woman into a *second pregnancy.* She tries to replace the lost baby with another. The problem with this is that this baby will always be a replacement if the motive behind another pregnancy was to cover the past wound.

This woman also may *avoid emotional intimacy* with men. She may flirt with them, lead them on, but when they start to develop some emotional intimacy, she pulls back because the relationship probes the wound.

The wound may also drive the woman to *promiscuity*. She tries to heal the wound through sexual relationships with men. Every time she does, she may feel better for the moment, but every sexual relationship probes the wound also.

The woman who has this type of unhealed wound is often *depressed*. The depression may seem unexplainable and may create severe mood swings, but as long as she does something to temporarily soothe the wound, her depression may lift. However, if she does not, the depression may come back. Little things bring her to tears or anger; she overreacts. Her response to present circumstances is fed by the past wound of abortion.

Another major symptom is *shame,* which I see as unresolved guilt. A woman knows in her heart that the choice she made interrupted God's plan for that child. She not only feels a sense of loss but also a sense of wrongdoing.

This sense of shame may drive this woman to try to make restitution for the decision. She may become motivated by fear instead of love, which makes her susceptible to legalism. She may be the woman in your ministry who does everything right but still feels as though it is not good enough.

The shame may also give this woman a strong desire to be with children. She may work in the nursery, teach children's church, lead the children's choir, and still want to do more. She is trying to earn her forgiveness instead of confessing her sin and receiving forgiveness from God.

A woman who has experienced an abortion may have a hard time looking others in the eye. You can sense her shame. She is afraid to let others know about her abortion because she believes they will reject her. Her comment to people she tells about the abortion is, "Please don't hate me because of what I have done." She is truly a candidate for God's grace and forgiveness.

This woman needs to be led to God's healing. Psalm 30:2 (NKJV) says, "O LORD my God, I cried out to You, and You have healed me." In Psalm 147:3 we read that God "heals the brokenhearted and binds up their wounds."

Counseling Suggestions

The healing and forgiveness of a woman who has had an abortion must be led by God and covered with prayer and grace. She needs to first come to a point where she is willing to admit that she is wounded and needs God's healing. This usually happens as she begins to experience shame and hurt (as described earlier) on a regular basis or in a pattern, which many times surfaces in new relationships.

When counseling this woman, help her see the patterns of hurt and/or shame. She may realize that she is depressed but not understand where it is coming from. It is the task of the counselor to help her see the pattern of her depression. Telling her will not help. She needs to see it herself.

Ask questions about how she feels and if she has experienced these feelings before. Patterns of behavior reveal what is going on in regard to woundedness. If she has felt this way before, when? If she is depressed at Christmas ask her how she feels in May. What you are trying to do is get her to think. Do not ask specifically about Mother's Day, just the month of May. Remember, this woman may fear your rejection if you find out what has happened. If she thinks you are catching on too quickly, she may close up. During the early stages of counseling, let her lead. You may have a sense that she has had an abortion, but let her tell you.

Another area I dig into with a woman that I suspect has had an abortion is her relationships. How much has she dated? How is her relationship with her father? Some of these women had unsatisfying relationships with their fathers and are looking for any man to make them feel loved, accepted, and respected. Chances are good that she has dated many men in her search for one man to meet the needs her father did not. Chances are also good that she has become sexually involved in an attempt to gain intimacy in the only way she knows how. As a counselor, you must respond to her with grace.

Sharing the story of the woman caught in adultery in John 8:1–11 is usually helpful. Through it, a woman can know that God forgives her. A counselor who also forgives her will be able to lead her to God's grace. A counselor who responds with condemnation and judgment adds to her wounds.

As a woman tells about past relationships and how she became sexually active, the door is open for her to tell you about the pregnancy. As a woman talks about her sexual relationships, I ask her, "How did you prevent becoming pregnant?" This question many times opens the door for her to tell that she did become pregnant, thus uncovering the wound and opening it to God's healing.

Some women will be open and honest about their need for healing. Others, and I find them to be the majority, need to develop a trusting relationship with their counselor before admitting their wounds. It is a long process, but it is a must for healing and forgiveness to begin. They must admit that the abortion has hurt them or the wound will affect them as described earlier.

When a woman admits she is wounded from an abortion she may become very emotional. Allow that to happen and explain the reasons for her hurts (as discussed earlier in this chapter). She needs to know it is okay and natural to hurt. In fact, she needs to know that she will hurt. At this point, you are not focusing on the spiritual aspects of the abortion; you are focusing on how she has been wounded because the child conceived in her womb has been lost. She needs to experience God's healing grace, not hear someone tell her she is a sinner. Remember, she already may struggle with shame and guilt; you need not add to that.

I lead my counselees through a prayer of confession that leads to God. It is a simple process. They need to tell God that they hurt and that they want Him to heal them. I show them Scripture such as Isaiah 61:1–3:

> The Spirit of the Sovereign LORD is on me, because the LORD has anointed me to preach good news to the poor. He has sent me to bind up the brokenhearted, to proclaim freedom for the captives and release from darkness for the prisoners, to proclaim the year of the LORD's favor and the day of vengeance of our God, to comfort all who mourn, and provide for those who grieve in Zion— to bestow on them a crown of beauty instead of ashes, the oil of gladness instead of mourning, and a garment of praise instead of

a spirit of despair. They will be called oaks of righteousness, a planting of the LORD for the display of [H]is splendor.

Their prayer could be something like:

God, I am hurt. I miss my baby. I was created to carry that baby until it was born into this world. Not doing so has wounded me deeply. Lord, please heal me from the loss of this child. I trust You to keep Your promise of healing that You give in Scripture.

After admitting her hurt and loss, a mother needs to begin to seek God's forgiveness for terminating the pregnancy. Many women have already sought God's forgiveness for the sin of their abortion, but if they have not, they need to do so.

Sin, however, is deeper than just actions. It involves motives as well. Motives for sin need to be confessed also. There are many possible motives for the sin of abortion. One may be fear. Fear should not be a motive for making decisions; love and obedience should be. When a woman chooses to abort because she fears that her lover will reject her, she has to confess the sin of abortion and the fear behind it. Without confession, she carries the shame of the motive within her and she is not released for total healing.

When looking for the motives behind a woman's abortion, addressing the sexual immorality that led to pregnancy is helpful. Scripture is clear that sex outside of marriage is sin. Thus, the motive for the sexual immorality must be addressed. The motive may go back to the relationship between her and her father, which, to say the least, is usually not good. When the woman becomes involved in a relationship with a man who finally accepts her, she may become sexually immoral because of the fear of losing the much-sought-after acceptance. Sex is many times the only way in which she feels acceptance. For this woman, the motive of fear of rejection that led her into sin must be confessed.

For some women, the motive for becoming pregnant is to trap the man. Maybe he is married and telling her he will leave his wife soon, and she thinks that if she gets pregnant he will leave his wife and marry her. Or maybe he says he "isn't ready to get married yet," so she gets pregnant with the hope that he will marry her immediately. Usually the man dumps her instead.

The motives are as numerous as the women you will counsel. Ask your counselee why she made the choice she did, but do not be shocked or judgmental when she answers. Let her hear from her own mouth the motives that caused the wounds and shame she feels. Let God show her what her motives were and lead her to confess them as sin. Show her the promises in God's Word that He will forgive her. First John 1:9 says, "If we confess our sins, he is faithful and just and will forgive us our sins and purify us from all unrighteousness." In Psalm 103:12 we read that "as far as the east is from the west, so far has he removed our transgressions from us."

A prayer of confession may go something like this:

God, please forgive me for the sin of abortion. I know that Your plan for this child was to be born and I prevented the birth with my choice to terminate the pregnancy. Also forgive me for the motives of (list the motives here) that led me to the decisions I made. Please forgive me for the sin of sexual immorality and the motives of (list the motives here) that led me to sin.

At this point of healing, the woman has asked God to heal and has asked for forgiveness for the sin of both the abortion and the motives leading to sexual immorality and pregnancy. There is no set time frame for this to happen within the counseling process. Only God knows how long it will take the woman to heal and to fully accept God's forgiveness. The key is that she has asked for His healing and has confessed her sin and motives for sin.

A woman must also come to the point of forgiving others. Now that she is being healed and has been forgiven by God, she can begin the process of forgiving those who have wronged her, including the baby's father, her parents, the father's parents, and/or those who performed the abortion. She will know whom she needs to forgive.

To help her understand the process of forgiveness, help her realize that forgiveness is between her and God and is for her own good as well as that of the others involved. She needs to forgive as she has been forgiven. Luke 23:34 says, "Jesus said, 'Father, forgive them, for they do not know what they are doing.'" Along with this, we are admonished in Ephesians 4:32 to "be kind and compassionate to one another, forgiving each other, just as in Christ God forgave you."

There are volumes of books written on forgiveness. The key thing to remember is that forgiveness comes after the healing process has begun and usually after we have been forgiven by God, though they are very much connected to each other.

A woman needs to let go of the baby. This is difficult because she has never seen and held the baby. How does a woman let go of a baby that she does not really know?

There are several ways to do this. Some women know within their spirit whether the baby was a boy or girl. Validating this belief will help her let go of the child. It will also help the woman give an identity to the baby. She needs to be encouraged to name the child. Usually this is not difficult because she has already thought about it. If the woman knows the gender and has named the child, she has a child to release. Some women even know the color of the baby's hair and eyes. Some women have dreams from which they vividly remember the description of the child. This is not something to be feared but should be used of God to help the mother let go of the child.

Once the mother gets to know her child, she needs to understand that God loves children and the child is in heaven with Him. He loves children and brings them to Him. The New Testament confirms this in Matthew 19:13–14:

> Then little children were brought to Him so that He might put His hands on them and pray, but the disciples rebuked them. But Jesus said, "Let the little children come to Me, and do not forbid them; for of such is the kingdom of heaven" (NKJV).

It is obvious that Jesus loves children and welcomes them into His kingdom. The important thing for the mother to do is to prayerfully embrace the child and then let go of the child to be with God in heaven. A sample prayer is:

God, thank You for giving me this child of Yours. I am healing from the wounds created by my choices and You have forgiven me. For my own good I need to give (name the child here) to You. Thank You for taking care of (name the child here) and giving me a glimpse of this child. I look forward to seeing my child in heaven.

The mother may also want to perform some action of letting go. Some women have written a letter saying good-bye to their child. Others have conducted a funeral service for the child and have chosen a burial sight and a tombstone with the name engraved on it.

By this time the woman has gone to God for healing, has been forgiven, and has let the child go into the care of God. Among the many other issues this woman may need to deal with are those involving acceptance, sexual immorality, rejection, fear, guilt, anger, and so forth. Once a woman has healed from the wounds of the abortion, these areas can more easily be dealt with.

Dos and Don'ts for Counselors

Do approach these women with compassion and gentleness. Lead them to the healing grace of God. Remember that God desires mercy, not sacrifice, as seen in Hosea 6:6 and Matthew 9:13.

Do get the women into a support group with other women who are experiencing or have experienced the same grief. Give them books to read about what they are going through that include testimonies of other women. They need to know they are not alone in their journey. If there is not a support group available, have the women share their story with another trusted woman. This is critical for the release of shame. Every time they do this, they will feel less shame. Resources are given at the end of this chapter.

Don't act shocked. Some women have had more than one abortion. As they tell you about them, don't allow a look of shock or surprise to cross your face. Show them God's grace instead.

Don't make the abortion public knowledge. This will only add to the shame. One woman went to her pastor for help, and the next Sunday morning he had her stand while he told the whole congregation about her abortion. I do not think God was pleased, and I know what it did to the woman's spiritual life.

Don't judge. God alone can judge. He knows the hearts of these women. We have no way of knowing what motivated them or what their circumstances were when they made their decision.

Suggested Scripture

Psalm 32:5; 41:4; 103:2–3; 147:3
Matthew 15:19; 18:21
Luke 6:37, 45
Acts 13:38
Romans 13:13
1 Corinthians 6:13, 18; 10:8
Galatians 5:19
Ephesians 5:3
Colossians 3:5, 13
1 Thessalonians 4:3
Hebrews 8:12
1 John 1:9

Recommended Resources

Ervin, Paula. *Women Exploited: The Other Victims of Abortion.* Huntington, Ind.: Our Sunday Visitor, 1985.
Open ARM's (Abortion Related Ministries). National Headquarters: P.O. Box 19835, Indianapolis, IN 46219-0835. (317) 359-9950.
Women Exploited by Abortion (WEBA). National Office: 24823 Nogal Street, Moreno Valley, CA 92388. (714) 924-4164.

Part 4

Helping with Difficult Struggles

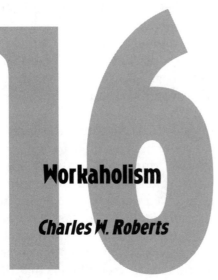

Workaholism

Charles W. Roberts

From time to time I hear people say to one another, "You'd better watch out or you're going to work yourself to death!"

Such is the impression we have of a workaholic—someone who is addicted to work; someone who is not concerned with results but with work itself.

Workaholics are different from those we would call "optimal performers" because optimal performers know how to relax, how to delegate, and how to surround themselves with competent people. Workaholics, on the other hand, are driven by the need to see their job as worthwhile. They view slowing down to relax as failure, so they push to reach new achievements without enjoying previous ones. Without treatment, workaholics will alienate nearly everyone, will be unable to experience happiness, and may indeed work themselves to death.

"I was getting between twenty and thirty minutes of sleep a night. That was all I needed. I had blood blisters on my feet from all of the time I spent running around on them. When someone would stop me and try to confront me about my schedule, about my pace, about the expectations I had for myself, I would only respond by asking them, 'Don't you want to succeed?'"

"My marriage failed as a result of my work addiction. Looking back I can see that my addiction to work was a replacement for my earlier addiction to alcohol. My happiness came only from externals, but they really did not make me happy because the minute I achieved a goal, I began to search for the next goal. I was on a treadmill that would not quit."

These examples describe the struggles faced by workaholics. Typically these people have in their background the lack of, or withholding of, full affirmation. Their parents were either unwilling or unable to show affection and affirmation. Sometimes the affirmation they received was conditional, resulting in a situation that could lead to workaholism. (For instance, many parents drive their children to get good grades by exhibiting disappointment over anything less than an A; or they offer monetary rewards for A's. The message this sends to children is that they are unworthy unless they perform up to a certain standard; anything less is unacceptable. This produces in children an inner drive to be continually at work, always trying to accomplish more.)

Gail Sheehy, in her book *Passages*, says this tendency toward workaholism comes at predictable stages. Sheehy suggests that as men approach forty they have an inner compulsion to be significant. Thus they throw themselves into work, which can easily result in workaholism. Women, too, especially single women who have not had children, feel the need to be creative and can easily fall into the trap of addiction to work.

Symptoms of workaholism are:

- *An inability to draw proper boundaries in relationships.* People become a means to an end, and any relationships that are not work related or that threaten a workaholic's devotion to work are no longer wanted and are often cast off.
- *A struggle with hypertension.* The body pays the price for stress. High blood pressure, chest pains, and many psychosomatic illnesses may appear. This is the way the mind communicates to the body that something is terribly wrong! (Do not assume, however, that someone with a type A personality is necessarily a workaholic, and do not expect him or her

to die early. *The New England Journal of Medicine* reported in January, 1988, that after twenty years of following control groups, there were more type A's alive than type B's.)

- *A total absence of joy.* Due to the unending drive to find fulfillment outside themselves, workaholics have no sense of inner peace. There may be superficial happiness, but there is no deep-rooted peace and joy. And why not? No one has ever told them they are valuable.

To break the pattern of workaholism, individuals will often have to change their place of work, so as to make a clean break and better effect a change in work habits. This extreme is not always necessary, however, and the chosen career path need not change.

As with any addiction, workaholics must often "bottom out"; that is, a crisis must occur to help them recognize that something is not right.

Suggestions for Counselors

To begin to address the issues surrounding workaholism, counselors must, of course, begin where the individual is. No two people are the same, so the following outline should be adapted to each individual.

Listen

This seems to go without saying, but sometimes counselors need to be reminded of the importance of listening to those who come for help. If you identify someone in whom you see workaholic symptoms, it is sometimes counterproductive to try to confront that person with his or her addiction. Intervention is possible but must be carefully orchestrated. I find it far better to anticipate the situation and to say something like, "Bill, it seems to me that you have been pushing yourself at work lately. Anything I can do to help?"

A brief offer to be of assistance may not result in any dramatic change, and it may not result in any immediate response. But frequently that kind of offer does let the person know that you care, which is something he or she will respond to later.

The key thing is to remember to listen when clients are finally ready to talk. Listen to their pain, their exhaustion, their shattered dreams, their sense of loss and lifelessness. Let them talk about whatever crisis brought them to you, and use the skills of active listening to help them see that you understand.

Probe

As mentioned earlier, the drive to succeed, which results in workaholism, often stems from a childhood trauma. This is not to suggest that all workaholic counselees have gone through a particular crisis; it is probably true, however, that they have at times had affirmation and/or affection withheld until a desired goal was achieved.

Part of the listening process involves probing the person's past in an attempt to understand what set him or her on this path of self-destruction. I probe at several points to gain a historical understanding of the problem. Typically, I work in reverse, beginning with today, and slowly working backward until I can pinpoint some kind of starting place.

Probing is not a neat and tidy process, so I take notes along the way. Some choose to write during the appointment. I prefer to write after an appointment because taking notes is sometimes a distraction to the process. Over time the notes can aid the counselor in establishing a history of how the counselee's addiction began. As soon as you get back to the beginning, you can move forward with caregiving.

Point Out

Counselees find it helpful to have someone point out to them where they went wrong or where they were led astray. As one individual told me, "Someone sold me a bill of goods!" This was his way of acknowledging that he understood what had transpired and that he was also ready to begin the process of changing.

Not until people reach this point is change possible. They may well be aware that something is amiss, but until they discern the source of their struggle they are not ready to move on.

At this stage, I point out to clients the "bill of goods" they were sold. I help them move from mere awareness to an understanding and acceptance of the process that led to their addiction to work. I affirm to them that I have never met anyone who chose to be addicted to work. Over time they either learned behavior that resulted in this addiction or something happened to cause them to move in this direction.

The intellectual awareness of what has gone wrong in their lives results in their readiness and willingness to change.

Teach

Once emptied of their story, and after they have invested themselves in you as a counselor and have accepted the truth of their addiction, they are ready to learn some new patterns of relating to others, to the world, and to work. They need to learn new ways of life in several areas:

- *Relating to others.* It is helpful to teach them, sometimes through roleplaying, new ways of interacting—with *everyone.* They need to learn new ways of interacting with peers, co-workers, siblings, parents, and others.
- *Relating to the world.* Once people decide to break the cycle of addiction to work, their entire framework for life is gone. Through reading Scripture together (particularly the creation stories where we see God resting and creating a day of rest) and examining alternative means to achieve goals, they begin to build a new way of relating to the world.
- *Relating to work.* Workaholics need help in establishing new expectations of work. Again, through readings and through discussions of what realistic expectations are or can be, clients can reframe their expectations of life and achieve a life that is more joyful!

Coach

The role of the counselor, like that of a coach, is to point out to the workaholic the things that need to be done without assuming responsibility for the person's life or actions. Coaches remind clients what needs to be done, help them envision those things actually taking place, and encourage them to go out to conquer the world!

The reality is that the best laid plans of mice and men often go astray. So do the dreams of recovering workaholics, so counselors must coach, encourage, affirm, rethink, and brainstorm with workaholics to conceive and implement a different plan.

Two particular areas of work must be addressed here: scheduling and priorities. The destructive patterns of workaholism have no place for the concept of rest. There is only one item on the schedule: work! So counselors and clients must spend time evaluating what it is that recovering workaholics want to accomplish and fleshing that out in terms of realistic goals (it may be helpful to use the S.M.A.R.T. plan, i.e., goals that are Specific, Measurable, Achievable, Realistic, and Timely). In Stephen Covey's book *The Seven Habits of Highly Effective People,* the chapter on "Begin with the End in Mind" offers some good exercises for establishing a personal mission statement that can be used not only to gain a better understanding of what one wishes to accomplish but also to create an action plan for pursuing those goals. Covey's next chapter even suggests a means of time management, which is a useful tool for scheduling the new priorities that the workaholic has developed.

Reprobe

It is not unusual for clients to regress a bit in the process of recovery. Workaholics are no exception. Counselors should expect counselees to get stuck at some point in the process. The process I suggest for working with workaholics is not neat and tidy. It is much like the grief process in that the person may jump around in it. The journey to recovery is often a one-step-forward-two-steps-back experience, which can be frustrating for counselors once they have seen improvement.

Be ready, therefore, to slip out of the teacher-coach mode at some point and begin reprobing. When a new crisis causes counselees to slip back into old patterns, listen and probe to find out the details of the situation. Ask, "What happened?" "What did it feel like when you were asked to do that?" "How do you feel about the way you responded to this?" "What would have been another way you could have dealt with this situation?"

Through listening and asking questions you can help them make the discovery themselves. They may very well recognize what they have done, what they could have done differently, and what they can do to self-correct the situation. If not, you must back up and teach again.

Affirm

Assuming that the workaholic has invested in the process and has discovered a new way of looking at work and rest, take time to affirm what he or she has accomplished. The workaholic has gone through the recovery process, has broken the cycle of addiction, and has begun to embrace a new way of relating to self and the world. This needs to be affirmed.

Of course, affirmation should have been part of the process all along. But at this point, when recovery has "taken" and the counselee no longer needs the counselor, it is appropriate to set aside at least one session for nothing but affirmation of the recovered workaholic.

One tremendously powerful way to affirm clients is to tell them their own story. Let them relive the process from destruction to wholeness by telling their story in narrative form. Show them the progress they have made, but be sure to affirm them for who they are—not for what they have accomplished. If workaholics are affirmed only for reaching a goal, they will probably continue in the cycle of destruction. Therefore, work to encourage them along the way, affirming them for who they are.

Dos and Don'ts for Counselors

Do listen to the person. I have said that before and I am repeating it because it is so important. You cannot help clients work their way through a crisis much less through a drawn-out struggle if you have not heard what that struggle is, how deeply rooted it is, and what the effects of the addiction are. If you get nothing else from this chapter, get this: *Listen!*

Do encourage them to give up things. Workaholics are among the most overcommitted people you will ever encounter. Their commitment to themselves, however, is low. In order to make a commitment to themselves, they have to give up something. The problem is, this happens very slowly. Encourage them to give up one thing (i.e., one hour of work or one book to be read) each week until they have slowly worked their way back to a realistic schedule. The choices must be their own.

Do remind them again and again of God's love for them and of the fact that God wants them to rest. Help them move first to the point of accepting God's love, then to the point of self-love. It is this self-love that will eventually allow them to grow in the grace of God and break the cycle of destruction.

Don't arrange the workaholic's schedule. This is a seductive trap and one that is all too easy to fall into. It may seem to be a natural and helpful service to perform for counselees who have trouble managing their time. Often they have been to time-management seminars and know all of the tricks of the trade but simply are addicted to work. A simple thing to do, it seems, is to manage their schedule for them during a weekly appointment so that there is some control over what they do. Unfortunately, this simply does not work and can backfire on the counselor by undermining the process when the schedule does not work out.

Don't agree to see workaholics during off hours, and be extremely cautious about accepting calls during off hours or on days off. If you bend or break rules that you tell them to follow, your actions will speak louder than your words. One young man (who was a workaholic) called me on my day off, wanting to see me that day; his fiancée had broken up with him the night before over his addiction. Had I agreed to see him that day, I would have been doing something which later I would tell him was inappropriate. Protect yourself; in doing so, you help others!

Suggested Scripture

Genesis 2:2–3
Exodus 20:2–4, 8–10
Psalm 46:10
Proverbs 3:5–6; 21:5
Ecclesiastes 12:12b
Mark 6:31b
John 10:10b
1 Thessalonians 4:11

Prayer

Merciful Lord, You who made this world and all that is in it, I thank You for this day. You alone are Lord, and You alone care for me more than any other. You know, Lord, the things with which I struggle this day. You know the mountains that I shall try to move, the massive tasks that I shall try to take on. You know, Lord, these are my weaknesses, and the things that come between me and You.

So Lord, protect me from this temptation. Remind me that You are truly Lord. Take from me the temptation to be my own god and to rule over my life. As David prayed so long ago, I pray that You will lead me to the places of still waters and green pastures. Restore my soul, Lord.

I admit that far too often I stray from Your will. Forgive me, Lord, and lead me in the way that You would have me to go that I may experience the abundant life You promise in Christ. Protect me from the tendency to self-destruct; fill me with Your Holy Spirit, that I may know, and follow, Your will. I pray this in the name of Jesus, Amen.

Recommended Resources

Exley, Richard. *The Rhythm of Life.* Tulsa: Honor Books, 1987.

Hart, Archibald D. *Adrenalin and Stress.* Dallas: Word, 1991.

Kushner, Harold. *When All You've Ever Wanted Isn't Enough.* New York: Summit Books, 1986.

MacDonald, Gordon. *Ordering Your Private World.* Nashville: Oliver-Nelson, 1984.

Nouwen, Henri J. M. *The Genesee Diary.* Garden City, N.Y.: Image Books, 1981.

Oates, Wayne E. *The Struggle to Be Free.* Louisville: Westminster, 1983.

———. *Workaholics, Make Laziness Work for You.* Nashville: Abingdon, 1978.

———. *Your Right to Rest.* Louisville: Westminster, 1984.

Peck, M. Scott. *The Road Less Traveled.* New York: Simon and Schuster, 1978.

Sanford, John A. *Ministry Burnout.* New York: Paulist, 1982.

Schaef, Anne Wilson. *The Addictive Organization.* San Francisco: HarperSanFrancisco, 1988.

Sheehy, Gail. *Passages.* New York: Bantam, 1976.

Winston, Stephanie. *The Organized Executive.* New York: Warner, 1983.

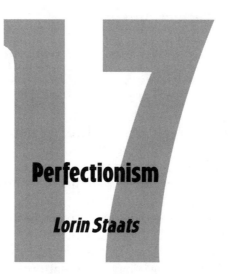

Perfectionism

Lorin Staats

Perfectionism is a broad-reaching compulsion—we are bred to seek it and trained to promote it. Standards of corporate and personal perfection are held high in our culture. From the board room to the body shop, images of Iacocca and Schwarzenegger say, "Go for the gold." The past generation's view of quality in property as diverse as cars and churches has changed radically.

As I work with single adults, I see perfectionism affecting programs, plans, and people in significant ways. It is an issue we must be equipped to address if we are going to effectively move people to healthy views of themselves and healthy relationships with others.

Perfectionism is a disposition that regards anything short of perfection as unacceptable.

The message that we must do everything perfectly comes from a variety of sources and produces a variety of problems.

Some people mistakenly believe that this message comes from the Bible because Scripture says, "Be perfect, therefore, as your heavenly Father is perfect" (Matt. 5:48). In this case, however, Christ was speaking about a position we gradually obtain as we come into relationship with Him. Perfection in Christ comes as we draw closer to Him through obedience and with the power of the Holy Spirit. God, however, accepts us in our imperfection. He does not say that He will accept us only if we do everything perfectly.

Results of Perfectionism

Fractured Relationships with God and Others

Christian institutions, both in practice and in proclamation, often provide a picture of a God who is distant, aloof, and dissatisfied. He apparently created the world, set it in motion, and now sits in judgment over it. His standard is perfection, and those who have not reached it can either live in fear or live afar. The impossible standard that perfectionists believe God has set for them becomes an insurmountable wall that separates them from Him. This same wall separates them from other people as well. Perfectionists believe they are not worthy of a relationship with another person because they cannot meet their own expectations, much less someone else's. They expect relationships to fail, so they engage in self-defeating behaviors. Relationship after relationship fails because the perfectionist finds fault in each person.

Fractured Self-Esteem

Perfectionists can never meet the impossibly high standards they have set for themselves or they have allowed others to set for them. Yet when they do not meet the standard, they are flooded by feelings of defeat. Each time they fail to meet the standard, their self-esteem receives another blow.

Stress

Stress develops because perfectionists can never be all they think they should be. Dominated by both societal and personal expectations, perfectionists suffer overwhelming stress. To let go of even one of these expectations might cause all the others to collapse as well. Therefore stress is a continual part of their lives.

Anxiety

Perfectionists become the victims of their own perfectionism when they feel shame for failing to meet the standards they have set for themselves. This shame results in anxiety which often triggers anxiety attacks. With an ongoing need to meet certain standards, and the likelihood of falling short, perfectionists often are subject to misplaced guilt as well.

Legalism

Legalism is excessive conformity to a set of standards. For perfectionists, legalism is a helpful tool for controlling themselves and others. Legalists say that a standard has been set, ostensibly by God, and that when the standard is not met, God is not honored. This drives the perfectionist to further striving, and the cycle begins again.

Anger

People who have been demeaned and made to feel unworthy due to real or perceived failure, respond with anger. The less progress they make, the more angry they become. They either bottle up their anger or blow up at the least provocation. When anger is bottled up, it is bound to resurface at a later time when the standard is not met.

Denial

Denial is a coping mechanism that helps perfectionists deal with their inability to reach perfection. Perfectionists who can no longer take the pressure of their failures look for ways to rationalize behavior that does not meet their standard. One way is to deny failure. They simply refuse to look at any ways in which they have not met the standard.

Depression

Depression is the final consequence of stress, anxiety, anger, and denial. An ongoing battle with perfectionism can lead to depression and despair because it produces a sense of hopelessness that makes people feel worthless.

Symptoms and Struggles

Dissatisfaction

Perfectionists struggle with broken relationships, dissatisfaction with their jobs, and so forth. They are continually looking for the right job or the right relationship. They are never satisfied with their own performance or that of others. They do not realize that their lack of relationships is probably due to their inability to find people who meet their standards. They also distrust people and are afraid of being deserted.

Compulsive Behavior

Perfectionists exhibit workaholism and other compulsive behaviors that reflect their drive to achieve perfection. Certain jobs lend themselves to perfectionism. Long hours, imbalanced priorities, severe competitiveness, and continual dissatisfaction with relationships characterize perfectionists on the job. Other compulsive behaviors such as organizing, straightening, and cleaning are also typical of perfectionists. Because they are always looking for ways to organize, they often want to organize possessions, people, and programs. Because they are always straightening or cleaning, their desktops may be the neatest or their houses may be cleanest.

Anxiety

Perfectionists often manifest extreme anxiety, which can lead to physical problems such as ulcers and colitis. The drive for perfection ultimately takes its toll physically.

Overloaded Schedules

There is always something that must be done, and perfectionists tend to overload their schedules. They find their worth in doing things and in doing them well. The more they can do well the better they feel about themselves. So perfectionists are often very busy people. They rush from one event to the next or from one meeting to the next, trying desperately to leave their mark or to get positive strokes for their work.

Demanding

Perfectionists are very demanding of others. They think their way is the correct way. Thus, they very seldom affirm others because no one else does the job as well as they do. If another person completes a job, perfectionists think the person could have done it better if he or she had tried harder.

They are also very demanding in relationships. Their expectations for others are as high as their expectations for themselves. Perfectionists are rigid in what they expect of their children. They are judgmental of everyone in their lives, and they judge everything from appearances to personal habits. They offer little affirmation in relationships because they believe everything can be done better and everyone can be better.

Inadequacy

Perfectionists feel a profound sense of inadequacy. They are unable to find personal satisfaction or lasting peace. They always have another job to do, another mountain to climb.

Poor Self-Image

Perfectionists have a sense of being defective, inadequate, and undeserving, which results in a poor self-image and a shame-based identity. To find personal worth, they base their values on externals—clothes, car, home, appearances. All these combine to create very unhappy persons.

Denial

As a way of protecting themselves, perfectionists learn to deny their feelings. They use different defenses to protect themselves from the hurt they carry within. They hide behind masks to keep messages of shame from permeating their fragile egos. Their disconnection from feelings makes life difficult for those around them.

Lack of Boundaries

Perfectionists have trouble setting boundaries in their relationships with others. Not only do their demanding natures make it difficult for them to act appropriately in relationships, but they also have expectations that sometimes overstep boundaries with others.

Counseling Suggestions

All counseling should be prefaced by prayer and be founded on scriptural principles. Counselors are dependent on divine guidance and empowerment to rightly and powerfully apply truth to meet needs in people's lives.

Help Counselees Clarify Their View of Self

Do they have healthy self-esteem or do they feel as if something is lacking? Do they see themselves continually striving to do more and to do better? Perfectionists do not allow mistakes.

Perfectionists use negative self-talk. Their self-talk is often a result of the rules they grew up with; for example, "I'm stupid," "People don't care what I think," "I don't have anything valuable to contribute," or, "I'll ruin it if I try."

Perfectionists:

- tend to be overly responsible.
- are unable to express their own needs.
- have a problem setting boundaries.
- feel guilty when they have fun.
- find it difficult to receive compliments.
- have a strong need for control.

When counselees exhibit these traits, perfectionism is probably their problem.

Help Counselees Understand
the Relational Causes of Their Perfectionism

What were the messages they received from their families about who they are? What were the family rules? For example, "Can't talk," "Can't win." How do they receive, process, and respond to continued dysfunctional behavior from within their family? For example, setting boundaries that are helpful and healthy, communicating openly and honestly, dealing with the often-negative responses they receive from their families.

Help Counselees Understand
the Situational Causes of Their Perfectionism

What brought on their perfectionist behavior? What self-talk did they experience as a result of this situation? What was the unhealthy response that came as a result of this self-talk? Have them replace the false self-talk with true statements about themselves. Have them act in respectful and accepting ways toward themselves.

Help Counselees Connect
with a Group or Individual for Accountability

Encourage counselees to find someone who will hold them accountable for reprogramming their unhealthy behavior. It is important that perfectionists have some positive supportive relationships that can perform two functions: build them up and challenge them to make necessary changes. They need to have models of healthy behavior as well as opportunities to relate to people in a healthy way.

Help Counselees Work
through Depression and Anger

Depression and anger may surface as a result of the discoveries surrounding perfectionism. Listen and be a sounding board for their anger.

Help Counselees Gain a Clear Understanding of God's Love and Forgiveness

Explore with counselees how God sees them. Study together Psalm 139 or Ephesians 1. Give them homework assignments that will help them reprogram how they view themselves. Have them begin each day by reciting the phrase, "I am a unique, unrepeatable miracle of God." Have them memorize Scripture that speaks of God's love for them. Have them read books and memorize Scripture on the subject of self-worth, and pray in a positive way that they might be brought through the process.

Counselees need to distinguish shame, false guilt, and biblical guilt from one another. Then teach them what forgiveness is all about. Counselors must be involved in the process of reeducating in this area.

Dos and Don'ts for Counselors

Do separate the person from the behavior. Value the person but challenge the behavior.

Do recognize the probable shame-based family structure that is part of the counselees' history and keep in mind the results it may have caused. Keep counselees focused on God's forgiveness that frees them from inappropriate shame.

Do help them understand the difference between guilt and shame.

Do surround all the counseling you do with prayer and biblical truth, both in preparation for and during the counseling session.

Do know your own limits and refer counselees to a professional counselor when you run out of expertise or time.

Don't expect quick progress. Perfectionism is a learned behavior that needs to be unlearned over time. Be patient with counselees and encourage them to be patient with themselves.

Don't give performance-based solutions. Give insight and direction but be careful not to give tasks on which their self-image may depend.

Suggested Scripture

Psalm 119:96; 139:13–16
Mark 14:8
2 Corinthians 12:9–10b
Ephesians 2:8–10
Philippians 2:13; 3:4b–11; 4:11–13

Prayer

Gracious heavenly Father, praise You that through Your Son You have shown Your free and unconditional love and acceptance. You understand the things that I struggle with and You accept me totally. Through Your Son You see me as complete, total, and whole. Keep me from expecting of myself and others more than You do. Remind me of the gifted person You have made me and help me to recognize when the expectations that I put on myself are not from You but from myself. Help me to find good models of people who have realized a good balance in their lives. Give me words of praise rather than of criticism for those around me. Keep me patient in the process. Amen.

Recommended Resources

Leman, Kevin, and Randy Carlson. *Unlocking the Secrets of Your Childhood Memories.* Nashville: Thomas Nelson, 1989.
Martin, Grant. *When Good Things Become Addictions.* Wheaton: Victor, 1990.
McDowell, Josh. *Building Your Self-Image.* Wheaton: Tyndale, 1986.

Seamands, David. *Healing for Damaged Emotions.* Wheaton: Victor, 1981.

Thurman, Chris. *The Truths We Must Believe.* Nashville: Thomas Nelson, 1991.

VanVonderen, Jeff. *Tired of Trying to Measure Up.* Minneapolis: Bethany, 1989.

18

Alcoholism and Chemical Dependency

Gary Winkleman

While caught up in the world of alcoholism and chemical dependency, I had one goal in life: to get enough money to support my habits, and it did not matter how I got the money. People were tools I used to get what I needed. I hated what I had become, but try as I might I could not stop the destructive cycle. Only the love of a younger brother, who, on his deathbed, told me about the unconditional love of Jesus, caused me to finally admit that I could not change on my own. I needed help—the help that could come only through Jesus Christ. It was then that my journey to wholeness and joy began.

I use the term *chemically dependent* to describe both the alcoholic and the chemically dependent, and the phrase *drug of choice* includes alcohol.

The chemically dependent person is caught up in a vicious cycle of depression, chemical use, guilt, depression, chemical use, guilt, . . . This cycle, if allowed to continue, will leave the person emotionally and physically bankrupt and perhaps in such a deep depression that suicide is possible.

People who are chemically dependent can actually reach a point where they believe they function better under the influence of the drug than without it. This belief, when acted on, can harm innocent people, as in when addicts drive a car while under the influence or lose control of their tempers and abuse someone.

231

Symptoms and Struggles

By the time those who are chemically dependent come for help, most of them have tried to quit on their own and failed. Their self-esteem is probably nonexistent. Most of them truly desire to quit and realize they need help. Chemically dependent persons who are attempting to kick their dependency face many struggles.

Living without Drugs

Chemically dependent clients must first learn to live without the drug. Usually the drug has become such a part of their lives that they do not know how to function without it. They are afraid of doing the tasks they did while under the influence. It has been so long since they functioned without the drug that they honestly do not know if they can. They are afraid to try for fear that they will fail again.

Fear of Losing Acceptance

Many people who become chemically dependent do so because they are lonely and want acceptance. They want to belong somewhere, and a sense of belonging exists among the chemically dependent when they use drugs together. It is likely that chemically dependent clients have a core group of friends with whom they use their drug of choice. When they are with these friends they feel as if they "belong." The fear of losing this sense of belonging is often a major stumbling block to those who want to quit but can never quite do so.

Denial

The chemically dependent know they have a problem, but they deny their addiction. They are much like a man I met in a counseling session at an alcohol-treatment center. He was willing to make the first step and admit that he had a drinking problem, but he denied that he was unable to quit. His exact words were, "I am an alcoholic. But I am different than the rest of you. I can quit when I want to." That was eleven years ago. He has not been able to quit to this day. His pride will not allow him to admit that he cannot quit on his own.

Integral to Social Life

The chemically dependent people do not realize the extent to which the drug has become an intregral part of their social life. The amount of time they spend acquiring and consuming it is enormous. When they try to quit, they end up with all kinds of time on their hands. Not knowing what to do with it often leads them back into drug use.

Guilt

Chemically dependent people usually are carrying a heavy load of guilt. They do not understand why they continue to do what they do not want to do. They have tried to quit, and each failure has added to their guilt.

Family Connections

Many who are chemically dependent come from homes where there has been some kind of abuse. Drug use is their way of not dealing with what has happened. Their parents may also be chemically dependent, so chemical dependency was the accepted way of life for them. They may have little or no understanding as to what life without drugs is like.

Counseling Suggestions

The following suggestions are parts of a process—a process that demands time and hard work.

Let counselees know that you are interested in them and that you also care. Listen to their stories. As is true in most counseling situations, they need to tell their story to release the guilt they feel.

Ask them why they want to change. Why do they want to quit? If the answer is something like, "My girlfriend wants me to" or, "It is wrecking my relationship with my boyfriend" or, "For my health," the odds are that they are probably not going to succeed in quitting. In order to quit, they must want to quit for themselves. They must realize that the lifestyle they are in is destructive and wrong and that there is forgiveness and help in Jesus Christ.

Ask them why they have been unable to give up this lifestyle. This will help you determine how sincere they are about leaving it. If they blame others or circumstances, chances are good that they are not ready to do what it takes to leave this lifestyle behind.

Find out if they really do want to change. Jesus asked the same question of the invalid at the pool of Bethesda in John 5:6: "Do you really want to get well?" Many chemically dependent people want to change. But there is a big difference between wanting to do something and actually doing it. The fear of facing life without the drug of their choice may keep them in their prison. The sad truth is that many today are so fearful of a new way of life that they would rather stay in their prisons of misery. Determine in the beginning if this is the case with your chemically dependent counselees. Then continue with the following questions to determine if they are ready to commit to what it will take to change.

Will they admit that they need help to change? If they say things like, "Yeah, I need help, but. . . ," you will have a good idea that they are not ready to change. They should say without hesitation, "I cannot change on my own. I need help."

Let them know that only one person can help them change and that person is Jesus Christ. Then make it clear that He not only *can* help them but that He *wants* to help them.

Ask them, "What do you think of when you hear the names God and Jesus Christ?" Their answer will help you determine their understanding of God and their level of faith. It can also reveal much about their childhood. The name of God strikes fear in some. All they think of when they hear the name is a father who is harsh and desires to punish them. It may bring to their minds thoughts of a father who could never be pleased. It may bring back feelings of anger. "If there really is a God who cares, why hasn't He helped me?" They also may not say much of anything because of their guilt and shame. They may never have known God as a loving and caring Father. They may have a terrible fear that they will fail God.

If their view of God is one of anger, fear, or shame, explain to them who Jesus is to you. Be careful not to preach. They need to hear your personal life story and journey of faith. Often they just need to see who Jesus is; that He does love them and care about them; that He is not sitting in heaven pointing fingers at sinners and looking for new ways to punish them.

When I counsel people who have little or no understanding of God, I use two pictures of Jesus. The first is in Mark 10:13–15. The people are bringing little children to Jesus and the disciples rebuke them for doing so. Jesus says, "Let the little children come to [M]e." And verse 16 says, "He took the children in [H]is arms, put [H]is hands on them and blessed them." Jesus loved children! He held them and He loved them! And that is exactly what He wants to do with us. He wants us to know that we are His special children and that He wants to hold us and love us. But those who are chemically dependent often have such a sense of guilt about their lifestyle and such horrible childhood memories that they cannot believe anyone would love them in such a way. They believe they are too terrible for anyone to love.

The second picture of Christ is found in Romans 5:6–8: "You see, at just the right time, when we were still powerless, Christ died for the ungodly. Very rarely will anyone die for a righteous man, though for a good man someone might possibly dare to die. But God demonstrates [H]is own love for us in this: While we were still sinners, Christ died for us." Let them know that Jesus loved them so much that He died for them before they ever believed in Him or desired to change. And if He loved them so much then, just think of how much more He loves them now when they desire to change. Then ask, "Do you want Jesus to be this kind of person in your life?" "Do you want Him to be your Lord and Savior?" "Do you want His forgiveness?" "Do you want His help in changing?" If the answer is yes, begin explaining the process of change to them.

The process of change starts with daily prayer. They may have no idea how to pray, or they may feel so guilty about life that they cannot pray. A good prayer to start with is one that simply agrees with God about where they are in their struggle, expresses their desire to live a new life, and asks Jesus for help. Encourage them to be as honest as possible in their prayers. If they are angry at life, they should say so. But always have them end their prayers with thanksgiving (Phil. 4:6). If they cannot think of anything to be thankful for, have them ask God to reveal something.

Help counselees write a list of goals for their journey to freedom from chemical dependency. Begin with simple, realistic, measurable goals. For example: (1) I will pray every day and honestly ask Jesus for help; (2) I will try to avoid the people with whom I use drugs; (3) I will not use drugs today; (4) I will keep a daily journal of my thoughts and actions; (5) I will call (name) when I am struggling.

Ask counselees how they feel about their family and friends. Many of them harbor intense anger at people in their past—especially their parents. Encourage them to write about their feelings. Then ask them how they can benefit from those feelings. Explain what anger does—how it sits and festers inside until they explode at people they really care about. If they really want to be free from the people who wronged them, there is only one way: by forgiving them.

Encourage counselees to either write a letter or go in person to anyone who has obviously wronged them. If they cannot do that yet, have them write a letter of forgiveness to the person, but not mail it. As they continue to progress in their counseling, periodically bring up the letter and ask them to read it. Then encourage them to send it or go to the person and ask for forgiveness.

Have counselees keep a daily journal of their actions and thoughts. They should begin the journal with their thoughts about themselves as they begin this journey. What are their goals for that day? Were there any answered prayers that day? Did something good happen? They should record their struggles. Have them use a highlighter to highlight all the positive steps they made that day. Review the previous day.

Explain the importance of finding new friends. They probably have no idea how much of their time and social activity were spent on drug use. They will need something new to fill that time. Encourage them to pursue new hobbies and ways to spend time. Exercise is great for relieving the stress of going without the drug. Encourage them to join a health club and work out or start walking each day.

Encourage counselees to attend a single adult small group. If they do not know of one, help them locate one.

Unless counselees are in a treatment center where they have no access to drugs, they may have a setback and begin to use the drug again. If this happens, they will be dealing with a tremendous amount of guilt. Some may never come back for counseling. But those who do come back and are able to admit that they blew it are on the road to freedom because they have been willing to own up to their failure.

Be very careful when this happens. The last thing they need is for you to add to their guilt by pointing a finger and telling them how foolish they were. Instead, remind them of 1 Samuel 16:7: "The LORD does not look at the things man looks at. Man looks at the outward appearance, but the LORD looks at the heart." Even when we do not do what is right, God sees our hearts and knows how truly sorry we are for our actions. Remind counselees that God looks at their hearts. And when He sees a heart that is broken, a heart that is repentant, He offers forgiveness.

Very few counselees who are not involved with a twelve-step program or a rehabilitation center are able to quit overnight. Many need to go through a healing process and deal with issues that run much deeper than the chemical dependency. That is why it is so important for counselors to continue to encourage clients and to emphasize God's grace for the brokenhearted.

Point out the positive steps they have taken. "You came back and were honest with me. That shows me that you are really trying." "Look, you were able to stay away from the drugs longer this time than ever before!" Then have them write in their journal exactly what happened. Where were they when they blew it? Who was with them when it happened? What happened earlier in the day that may have contributed to the fall? Were they angry at something? Ask them to describe the circumstances that led to the fall and have them tell you what they learned. Who or what do they need to avoid? Have them write in their journal what they have learned.

Next have them write down the steps they need to take to keep this from happening again. Have them go back through their journal and highlight the goals they have achieved. Also have them highlight the lessons they have just learned. Doing this will help them turn the negative experience into a positive one. Point out that they have learned a valuable lesson. They now know some things they can do to keep from falling again. Once again, help them see how far they have come in their journey to wholeness.

In counseling chemical abusers, you will learn that they are good at lying. The reason they are so good is because they have learned to lie to themselves. They have become good at blaming circumstances, other people, and even God for their actions. So how can you tell if they are honestly trying to deal with the issue?

Are they prompt in keeping their appointments or do they show up late or not at all? Do they often call and reschedule their appointments? These are usually signs that they are trying to avoid meeting with you or that their lives are so dysfunctional that they cannot carry out normal behavior. It may also indicate that they are again using drugs and want to avoid the guilt and conflict of meeting with you until they have had a short period of time off the drug.

When you ask questions about how they are doing, are their answers evasive? Do they try to change the topic to something other than themselves? Do they get angry when you bring up the topic of their actions? Do they attack you with questions of their own? These are signs that they are not dealing with the issue and not following through with the course of action you have suggested.

Do you catch them in lies? Are they keeping their daily journal?

Do they accept responsibility for their actions if they blow it? Or do they make excuses and blame other people or circumstances to justify their actions? If they do not accept responsibility for their actions this shows that they are still not ready to commit to the process.

Have they been willing to give up their old social circle? Do they make excuses for their friends' behavior and why they cannot give up that social circle? Unless they are willing to give up their old social circle, the odds are they will never get off the drug.

These are many of the signs that tell you when clients are not being honest about their efforts to be drug free. If clients do any of the above, you will need to firmly but lovingly give them your assessment of their actions. Let them know that you are willing to continue to see them only if they are going to be honest with you about their efforts. If the pattern of deception continues, you may want to terminate the counseling relationship.

Dos and Don'ts for Counselors

Do hold counselees accountable for their actions. Be loving but firm. They need to learn to accept responsibility for their actions.

Do point out their progress. List the positive steps they have taken, no matter how small they are. Pointing out the positive steps can be good for you as well as them, especially if you are losing patience. It can help you objectively determine what progress has been made.

Do pray with them and for them. Many people with a chemical dependency problem do not know how to pray and do not believe that prayer works. Praying with them and for them will help them become more comfortable with prayer. It is also a great opportunity to teach them about prayer.

Do use Scripture in counseling. Encourage counselees to read Scripture, especially passages that express God's understanding, love, and care. Great men in the Bible struggled with life. Use an example like Paul. The Psalms also are excellent. Psalm 13 is good for encouragement. Here David, the psalmist, feels as if God does not care. Four times in the first two verses he says, "How long, God? How long, God, must I deal with this problem?" But by the end of the psalm we see a man who, because he decides to trust in God's promises for his life, is able to say, "The Lord has been good to me."

Do be honest and say that you may have to terminate the counseling sessions if they are dishonest about their efforts.

Do pray for patience and understanding.

Do pray for the wisdom and words needed to help counselees.

Do let them know that they have a choice in life. They can trust in their own emotions, or they can believe in the promises of God.

Don't expect them to change overnight. Yes, it is possible, but not likely.

Don't "preach." Allow Jesus and Scripture to come alive.

Don't use guilt to get them to take the steps necessary for healing. They have to make the decision for themselves or they will not stay with the program.

Don't be afraid to refer a person to a counselor or agency with more experience in counseling the chemically dependent.

Don't be afraid to refer a person to another church that has a twelve-step program.

Suggested Scripture

Psalm 119:10–11
Proverbs 3:5–6
Mark 9:23
John 3:16–17
Acts 3:19
2 Corinthians 5:17
Philippians 4:1, 6

Prayer

Lord, I am tired of living this way. I have tried to change, but I can't. I have no strength left. Please help me to change. I know that the way I have lived has not pleased You. But Lord, You can see my heart. You can see the brokenness and sorrow that is there. I am truly sorry for wrong choices I have made. I want to know what it is to really care about life and people again. I want to know what it is to have joy and peace in my life. I want to be free. Jesus, I believe that You loved me enough to die for me. And now I just want You to be real in my life. I invite You to be the Lord of my life. I commit my life to You and accept Your forgiveness and Your gift of eternal life. Amen.

Recommended Resources

Alcoholics Anonymous. *The Big Book.* New York: Alcoholics Anonymous World Services, Inc., n.d.

Beattie, Melody. *Codependent No More.* San Francisco: HarperSanFrancisco, 1987.

Changing Lives Ministries, 8196 Grapewin, P.O. Box 2325, Corona, CA 91718, (714) 734-4300.

Collins, Gary. *Christian Counseling: A Comprehensive Guide.* Waco: Word, 1988.

Friends in Recovery. *The Twelve Steps—A Spiritual Journey,* rev. ed. San Diego: Recovery Publications, 1994.

Friends in Recovery. *The Twelve Steps for Adult Children.* San Diego: Recovery Publications, 1989.

Friends in Recovery. *The Twelve Steps for Christians,* rev. ed. San Diego: Recovery Publications, 1994.

Kritsberg, Wayne. *The Adult Children of Alcoholics Syndrome.* Deerfield Beach, Fla.: Health Communications, 1986.

Lasater, Lane. *Recovery from Compulsive Behavior.* Deerfield Beach, Fla.: Health Communications, 1988.

Liontamers, 2801 North Brea Blvd., Fullerton, CA 92635-2799, (714) 529-5544.

Overcomers Outreach, Inc., 2290 West Whittier Blvd., La Habra, CA 90631, (213) 697-3994.

Rapha, 12700 North Featherwood, Suite 250, Houston, TX 77034, (800) 383-4673.

Woititz, Janet. *Struggle for Intimacy.* Deerfield Beach, Fla.: Health Communications, 1985.

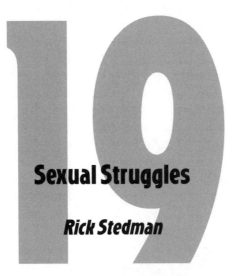

Sexual Struggles

Rick Stedman

Let's start with a little game, sort of like the TV game show *Jeopardy!* I'll list a few answers and you supply the questions. The category is "Singles and Sex."

- He wrote, "The more women with whom a man has intercourse, the greater will be the benefit he derives from the act."
- He wrote, "If in one night [a man] can have intercourse with more than ten women, it is best."

I'll give you a clue—the answer is the same for both questions. Have you figured it out? Some singles have guessed: "Who is Hugh Hefner?" "Who is Warren Beatty?" "Who is Madonna?" "Who is Howard Stern?" and "Who is Wilt Chamberlain?"

Sorry, all of those guesses are wrong. The right response was "Who was Lao-tzu, the ancient Chinese philosopher and author of the *Tao?*" Believe it or not, those two quotes are straight from the *Tao-te-ching,* the bible of Taoism, the official religion of modern China and Taiwan. Although the statements sound contemporary, they are more than twenty-three hundred years old. Sex was considered an important part of the healthy life; anyone who avoided sex was considered unhealthy. A similar attitude was held by the ancient Hebrews, who in the Mishna actually recommended the frequency of sex for a healthy marriage: "Twice a week for laborers, once a week for ass drivers, and every day for the unemployed" (maybe this helped them deal with recessions better than we do). Clearly the view was that an active sex life was the healthy way to live; abstinence was considered unhealthy and unnatural. That is why singles were almost forced to marry in ancient Israel—some rabbis taught that to be over twenty-five years of age and still single was a sin against God!

How modern this all sounds. In today's contemporary culture, an active sex life is seen as the norm, and celibacy is considered abnormal. This puts tremendous pressure on singles to either get married or be sexually active—many singles are even embarrassed to admit they are virgins. Movies, talk shows, magazines, and books all portray sex as normal and virginity as weird for singles. A friend of mine wrote to Oprah Winfrey to counter Oprah's implication that all singles were sexually active, and Oprah thought this woman to be so unique that she invited my friend to be a guest on her show! Oprah couldn't believe that virginity was anything to be proud of, or that there was a positive side to single celibacy.

This is true not only in the secular world but also in Christian circles. Single sexuality is viewed from an almost completely negative perspective. Singles are told all sorts of reasons why sex before marriage is *wrong*, how it is *harmful*, and how God has said *"No."* Although those negative reasons are all correct, single adults need more than negativism—they need to know the positive side of single sexuality, the positive things God wants them to work on and do during this stage of life.

We need to change the way we look at sexuality—we need a complete paradigm shift to a *positive* view of single sexuality.

If you are trying to counsel people struggling with homosexuality, sexual addictions, pornography, exhibitionism, voyeurism, pedophilia, sadism, or other serious difficulties, this chapter is not for you. Such complex issues cannot be handled in a brief or superficial manner. In fact, people struggling with those kinds of issues should be encouraged to seek treatment from professionals with expertise in those areas.

In this chapter, I simply want to present a new model that counselors can use to help singles deal with their sexuality from a positive perspective.[1]

Definition

To say that singles struggle with sexuality is probably the understatement of the year. A nationwide survey conducted in 1992 by the Centers for Disease Control in Atlanta polled 11,631 students in grades nine through twelve, and found that 40 percent of freshmen, 58 percent of sophomores, 57 percent of juniors, and a whopping 72 percent of seniors claim to have had sex. *Redbook* magazine reported in 1975 that 90 percent of women under age twenty-five admitted to being sexually active. This survey also asked the women to classify the strength of their religious commitment. Of those women who claimed to be strongly religious, 75 percent still admitted to sexual experience before marriage. More recent research shows that 90 percent of young women today have intercourse before marriage. A researcher in the Kinsey Institute stresses that sexual activity for women forty years ago meant sex with the men they would eventually marry, but today's woman has sex with a number of partners.[2]

The results of a questionnaire distributed in 1989 to national leaders of several denominations showed that only 40 percent of denominational leaders believed it was wrong for a man and woman to have sexual relations before marriage. This shows that there is a wide diversity among church leaders as to whether sexual activity before marriage is wrong or not, so it is no wonder that many Christian single adults feel frustrated and confused about sexual issues.

For years I based my counseling on the traditional, negative approach—in terms of what God has told us *not* to do. Most of the Christian books dealing with sexuality say, "Don't do it because God has said no." And, "In order to be healthy and happy, we need to follow His rules." Or, "Don't do it because it will harm you." And, "If you have sex before marriage, you will have sexual problems in marriage." Or, "Don't do it because of the danger of sexually transmitted diseases." Those are good reasons, and I do not wish to diminish their value. But in working with single adults, I discovered that they needed to hear more than just the negative side. They wanted to hear why God had given certain guidelines and why sexual activity outside of marriage would be harmful. They wanted to hear what they could concentrate on in a *positive* way.

Not only did I hear this need from the singles I counseled, but I also experienced it in my own life (I was single until I was thirty). In high school I thought, "I just have to hang on until I get out of high school, because I'll probably get married in college." Then in college I thought, "I'll just have to hang on until I get out of college, because I'll get married right after college." But when neither of those scenarios panned out, I realized that I might have to deal with this issue for years to come. I realized I might never marry. At that point the issue of single sexuality took on a much different meaning—what was God going to do in my life? How would all this be reconciled if I never married? What did God want me to do with all this sexual equipment that I was not allowed to use? These and other questions started me on the search for a positive side of single sexuality.

I quickly discovered that I was not alone in a desire to learn about the positive side. In fact, everyone needs to know that there is a positive side to each of God's instructions. God is not only all-wise and all-powerful; He is also loving. And like a loving parent, He instructs His children in ways designed to benefit us. He does not give rules without reasons. For instance, all the dietary laws given to the Israelites in the Old Testament were for their benefit; nutritionists today are seeing the value and reasonableness in those instructions. Another example is the Ten Commandments. They were not arbitrary rules; they are still sociologically valuable today as positive functional guidelines for relationships. As parents, we also have reasons behind our rules. I have a two-year-old daughter, Micah. If I say, "Micah, don't touch the stove," it is not because the stove is holy to me or because I am the only one privileged to touch the stove. I do not want her to touch the stove because she might get burned. I say, "Micah, you must eat your vegetables before you have dessert." I do not say that because it is an arbitrary order that I want obeyed but because I want her to learn to eat healthy foods.

In the same way, God gave instructions about sexuality, and those instructions are not arbitrary. He had positive reasons for them that singles can learn and appreciate.

Symptoms and Struggles

If singles are not shown a positive side of their sexuality, all sorts of troubles result. One of the more obvious results of a negative view of sexuality is that it can carry over into marriage. If singles approach sexuality negatively year after year and then get married, it is almost impossible intellectually, emotionally, and spiritually to instantly switch and begin to view sex positively. Many Christians who were always told, "Sex is wrong—don't do it," have a hard time after marriage believing and acting as if "sex is now good—do, do, do." Many Christian couples experience sexual dysfunction in marriage because prior to marriage they were never given any positive reasons for sexuality.

A second trouble area surfaces when Christian singles conscientiously try to live by the rules without having any rationale behind their efforts. They may become frustrated, confused, and even angry at God. They want to serve and obey God, but they also have natural bodily desires crying out for satisfaction. They ask, "Why did God create me this way and not allow me to be satisfied?" They feel that God has set this arbitrary limit in their life for which there is no rationale and which they find impossible to keep. Their unfortunate conclusion is that God is some sort of sadistic being who likes to watch people struggle. This obviously is detrimental to their personal relationship with God.

Third, the negative view can also be destructive in singles' relationships with other people. As they strive to live by guidelines that have no apparent reasons behind them, thoughts about sexuality can become obsessive. Or singles may function only mechanically in relationships, in effect isolating themselves from others. Or they can turn on themselves and feel extremely guilty, thinking, "I must have a terrible problem. I must have an extreme sexual drive. It must be all my fault." Or they may berate themselves because of their lack of faith—"This shows I'm not as good a Christian as I should be."

A fourth area of trouble is when singles are besieged with feelings of impurity and worthlessness. Divorced people in particular often feel as though they are "used goods" or "rejects" or even worse if they were mistreated or abused in their marriages. A great benefit of the positive view of sexuality is that it deals directly with this issue of impurity and charts a path for singles to recover a sense of self-worth. Our sense of self-worth as Christians is not something we can establish only on a spiritual or emotional plane. The way we view and use our physical bodies is a part of the process of discovering self-worth. If we don't feel we are valuable physically, we will have a difficult time believing that we are valuable as people.

Fifth, the negative view of single sexuality gives only conclusions; it does not help singles learn how to think through the issues ethically. As a result, some singles think that God's instructions to not commit sexual immorality means they are not to have intercourse until marriage; thus, they can do anything else they want—petting, caressing, disrobing, and so forth. They will not have intercourse but will be indiscriminate in other sexual areas, feeling justified that they are following God's rules. By failing to see the whole picture of God's desires for them sexually, they enter into destructive patterns.

A sixth problem is that many Christian singles decide this is an area of God's instructions that they can choose not to obey. One lovely, compassionate Christian woman who had everything going for her kept thinking she would marry in a few years. But when she got to be twenty-five and it was just not happening, she decided she did not want to miss out sexually any longer—even though she had been raised in a very conservative Christian home, had attended church every week, had a deep and sincere love for God, and had even been on the mission field for a time. She consciously made the decision to become sexually active. She first became involved with a man in her office, followed by a couple of married men who treated her very poorly. After a few years, she decided that the "swinging single" life was not at all what it was cracked up to be. She learned that the real result of being "sexually free" is a cheapening of the sense of personal value.

Many singles feel cheap as a result of their negative view of single sexuality, and many who have gone this route (even non-Christians) conclude that sexual freedom is actually damaging to the soul. Carolyn See, in her article in *Cosmopolitan* magazine entitled "The New Chastity," graphically described how sexual promiscuity affected her:

> What does all this mean in a discussion of the new chastity? What it means, I think, is that despite the Pill, legalized abortion, and economic freedom, our own bodies are trying to tell us something: They don't necessarily want to be tossed around like lost luggage on a round-the-world plane trip. That's why, maybe, after a long night of good times—six orgasms, say—with a Nick Nolte look-alike, when you get up and weigh yourself and find you've even lost two pounds from the exertion, and he left at five in the morning, but he did say he'd call, and you even work in the same office with him, so . . . But you go out for coffee in the kitchen, and something, someplace in your body feels like if it could cry, it would cry. It's not your genitalia feeling bad, it may not even be your "heart." It's in the vicinity of your lungs, your solar plexus, where some Eastern religions suggest your soul resides. In other words, recreational sex is not soul food.
>
> Yet, however difficult the choice, after close to two decades of sexual permissiveness (what a tiresome phrase; one gets "permission" to go to the cloakroom in grade school, not to go to bed with darling men!), more and more young women are opting for the new chastity. . . . "What's all this stuff about the new chastity?" asks a beautiful showgirl who was once married to a famous tap dancer. "I'm still working on the old kind! Save yourself for a man you love or at least one who makes your heart flutter. Otherwise it's meatloaf, under brand X catsup."[3]

See has described what many singles feel as the result of indiscriminate sex: overused and run-down like a worn-out suitcase, battered and torn from too many miles logged. They feel cheap and depreciated because sexual experiences do not reinforce a person's ultimate value.

A negative view of single sexuality may lead to a seventh issue: obsessive and problem behaviors. One such problem that many singles face is that of masturbation. During seminars on single sexuality, by far the most common question asked by singles when they are allowed to ask anonymously is, "Is masturbation okay?" Kinsey reported in a recent study that 97 percent of males and 83 percent of females masturbate. Of senior citizens over eighty years of age, 72 percent of males and 40 percent of females masturbate. These numbers represent the percentages of *all* adults who masturbate, so it would follow that the percentages of single adults would be significantly higher. In a study done among Christian adults, 92 percent admitted to having masturbated at some point in their lives, 88 percent had masturbated in the last year, 75 percent within the last month, and 52 percent within the last week.[4]

Although the practice is widespread, masturbation is such a forbidden topic in the church that it takes a major act of courage to bring it up, even in private counseling sessions. Very few books on Christian sexuality deal with the issue of masturbation—even though the perspective is very diverse as to what God's will is on the issue. Opinion ranges from, "It is always a sin and contrary to the will of God," to, "It is a necessary part of the single experience and a gift from God." Singles are confused and do not know who to listen to or trust on this topic. I think getting a positive perspective on sexuality will help with this dilemma as well.

Finally, singles who lack a positive rationale for celibacy can also get caught up in the more serious and dangerous world of pornography, prostitution, homosexuality, and molestation. If someone descends into this level of behavior, there is no easy way out. However, a positive view of single sexuality will help a person—even in these extreme situations—take the appropriate steps toward recovery.

Counseling Suggestions

Content

The most helpful tool for me in teaching single adults about a positive view of single sexuality has been the following true story:

There was once a woman named Pearl who owned an antique store. In the showroom, there was a special antique table that had been there a long time. Pearl needed more room and wanted to move some merchandise around, so she decided to sell the table. The price tag was marked $500. She crossed out the $500 with her marking pen and wrote, "Sale $400."

Later that day a man came in and saw the table with the price marked down. After introducing himself as Ted, he tried to bargain with her, saying, "I'll tell you what—I'll buy that table for $300."

Pearl responded, "$300! Oh, no. It's worth a lot more than that. This table is worth more than $1000. You would be getting a truly great deal for only $400."

"But it's got scratches on it!" Ted replied.

"It's an antique. Antiques have had a lot of use," she said.

"But I'll have to refinish it when I get home," he countered.

"It's made out of solid oak. They don't make tables like this anymore," she said, making a good point.

Back and forth they went—he kept trying to convince her to lower the price, and she kept giving reasons why it was worth more.

Finally Ted said, "You know, I'd buy this table if you would just change the price."

With a grin, Pearl said, "Talking to you has convinced me that I should change the price after all." She took her marking pen, crossed out the $400 price, and wrote above it, $600.

Ted was shocked. "Hold it, you can't do that," he screamed.

She responded, "What do you mean I can't do that? I own this table. I can sell it for any price I want."

"But you had it marked for $400," he cried.

"Yes, but talking to you has helped me see the real value of this table. Our discussion has reminded me how special this table is and that it is worth much more than $400. I realized that if I sold it for $400, I would be ripping myself off and getting less than I deserved. So thanks for reminding me how valuable this table is," she replied.

Ted thought for a moment, and then said, "Okay, you win. I can see you are quite a saleswoman. I'll tell you what. I'll buy this table for $400."

"Oh, no you won't," Pearl said firmly. "It's not for sale for $400. I will take nothing less than $600 for this table, and that is still a great bargain on a wonderfully special table."

Once again Ted became angry. He sulked and complained as he walked around the store. But eventually he bought that antique table for $600.[5]

In counseling sessions with singles, I follow this story with a simple question: "Now when Ted got the table home, how did he treat it? Like a $300 or a $600 table?"

Their answer is usually correct—he treated it like a $600 table because he paid that much, but if he had only paid $300, he would have treated it more poorly.

"But it's the same table. What determines the quality of treatment it receives?"

The point of the story is: In God's eyes, each individual is a person of incredible worth and value. But if we sell ourselves cheaply, we will not be treated in accordance with our full value. It was not the value the man placed on the table that mattered most. It was the worth that the saleswoman put on the table that determined how the man would treat it.

It is the same in relationships. The kind of treatment we receive is directly related to how cheaply we sell ourselves. So we ourselves select the type of treatment we will receive from others.

This has tremendous implications in the sexual arena for singles. If singles are to be treated as being valuable sexually, they will have to first believe they are valuable—valuable enough to hold out for someone who will treat them the way they deserve to be treated. Then, whether or not they ever marry, they will have a sense of personal and physical self-worth that no one can deny them.

The biblical basis for this positive concept is found in the Hebrew words for "virgin"—*almah* and *bethulah*. The respective root meanings are "to hide" and "to separate." God instructed the Hebrews to hide and separate the young women as a way of protecting and enhancing their worth—as a public declaration of their great value. Sexuality is related to personal value. And this is the revolutionary thought that has to be placed in people's minds to help them understand the purpose behind the practice of temporary celibacy, which is separating oneself from sexual activity to establish and enhance personal worth. This is the core of the positive approach to single sexuality.

This is very different from the way in which the church has historically viewed sexuality. The Catholics saw sexuality as being basically for procreation ("be fruitful, and multiply," Gen. 1:28 KJV). The Protestant theologians reacted against that and said that sexuality is not just for making babies; there is also a pleasure principle involved. The justification for this thinking was Sarah's response when she was told she would have a child: "Will I experience pleasure in my old age?" (see Gen. 18:12). Both of these views are correct, but insufficient. Sex is not just for having kids; otherwise those who cannot have children or are past the childbearing age would not be able to use their sexuality. The Protestant view has resulted in a hedonistic view of sexuality, which rates the performance of sexual acts according to the amount of pleasure experienced.

Instead, I suggest that God created sexuality as a way for us to learn to value ourselves and as a way of expressing that value to others. Value becomes the dominant and determining perspective concerning sexuality. The way in which I allow myself to be treated sexually, and the way in which I treat others sexually, either asserts and protects my value as a person or has the opposite effect and diminishes my value. Temporary celibacy is a positive way of asserting and enhancing personal value. Conversely, promiscuity cheapens and diminishes my sense of personal and physical worth.

This is not simply another way of saying, "Wait until you are married." The idea of temporary celibacy is like having a savings account. A single adult saves money in order to buy a house. She may have to give up driving a fancy car or having expensive clothes in order to save $100 a week for a down payment. At the end of five years, whether she bought a house or not, she would have a sizable amount of savings. She would feel a sense of security, stability, and worth by having that savings account. She has built a foundation for her future. Similarly, a person's sexual behavior should be that which most promotes and protects a sense of value—which for a single adult is temporary abstinence. Singles save themselves sexually to contribute to a sense of self-worth. Whether they marry or not, they end up with a sense of value.

When talking with engaged couples, I have found this positive approach to be the most helpful by far. Rather than try to convince couples that they must obey some arbitrary rule of God, I teach them God's reason for creating the idea of temporary abstinence. I stress the idea that their being patient and remaining pure until their wedding day will make a statement of mutual worthiness and will set the stage for a much more meaningful sexual relationship in marriage—with no guilt and shame to cast a shadow on the relationship. There is another positive reason for the couple to remain hidden (or separate) from each other before the wedding—even until the wedding night. They become more protective of their sexuality the closer the wedding date approaches. They may back off of heavy kissing and decide not to see each other very much during the last week before the wedding. This is another way of asserting worth and value through a "separating" process that is central to God's desires. It gives meaning to the tradition of the bride's not seeing the groom on the day of the wedding.

Engaged couples are often excited when they understand this concept and really want to save themselves for each other. It is seen not as denial, but as a deposit into the other person's self-worth account. They are saying, "I not only love you, I will prove it by not treating you cheaply and by separating myself from you until the wedding."

This positive approach helps to answer many questions that singles ask, such as, "Why did God leave my sex switch on?" "How far is too far?" and, "How do I handle the temptations that come?"

Approach

The positive approach—sexuality and how it relates to value—must be made clear to counselees.

At some point, it is mandatory for counselees to write and share their sexual autobiographies. Understanding the positive view of sexuality gives counselees the proper perspective with which to look at the past and determine what events diminished or enhanced their feelings of value.

Part of the counseling sessions should be dedicated to talking through the effects of the counselee's sexual history. Just verbalizing these feelings will be an enormously freeing and healing experience. Of course, the atmosphere must be one of great sensitivity and patience.

Then, the things that are going on currently in the sexual arena and how the person feels about them should be discussed.

The next step is to plan for and discuss what to do in the future. For instance, if someone is struggling with masturbation, I would not immediately give procedures for how to stop or how to cut down on the frequency. I would instead (1) lay the groundwork concerning the concept of value (the positive view); (2) explore their past sexual history; (3) decide how that is affecting their current sexuality; and (4) determine what that means to their future. It is important that they see for themselves how sexual experiences made them feel devalued and thus led to the current behavior. This approach enables singles to rise above feelings of shame and guilt.

Example

One single man, who was obsessed with the practice of masturbation, discovered through a discussion of his sexual autobiography that he had been molested as a young boy by an uncle. As he understood the positive aspects of his sexuality, he came to see for himself the connection between the past devaluing experience and the current obsession with masturbation. In a way, he was punishing himself because he felt so worthless. He was also using masturbation as a type of compensation because he felt that he would never be worthy enough for a sexual relationship. Through this discovery, he was able to gain control and release the feelings of guilt. We talked about how he could begin to assert his value as a person. He drew the conclusion that masturbation was not helping him do that but instead was causing him to withdraw more. He came up with some ideas of what to do, backed by positive reasons for doing so.

Dos and Don'ts for Counselors

Do write your own sexual autobiography if you have not yet done so. There is an enormous benefit in writing one's sexual autobiography, which is a confidential account of your sexual history, beginning with the first time you remember anything sexual happening in your life. It is so important for counselors who counsel singles with sexual struggles to have dealt with these issues themselves and to be aware of their own perspectives and how their sexual history affects those views. Do not let embarrassment or fear stop you. Ask yourself these questions: When did you first discover the difference between boys and girls? How was the issue of sex dealt with in your home when you were a child? Did you discuss your sexual thoughts and feelings with your parents? Did you have any sexual experiences on the playground at school? When and what were your first sexual experiences? How did you feel? Tell about your dating experiences, and so forth.

Do discern how your sexual experiences affected your sense of self-worth, how they contributed to your sense of importance, how they affect your view of sexuality.

Do discuss these issues with a trusted friend or counselor. This is extremely important. We cannot really counsel others on these issues unless we have dealt with them ourselves. An important part of this process is sharing them with another human being. As the Bible says, "Confess your sins to each other and pray for each other so that you may be healed" (James 5:16).

Do think through how to approach sexuality in a positive way. You may be able to think of a way that suits your personality more than the model I offer here. Behavioral change will come through a change of mind. What people really need is to change their whole mindset when thinking of their sexuality.

Do stress the power of God's forgiveness and love.

Do consider how to share appropriate vulnerability about your own sexual struggles. We all need to realize that everyone has probably been devalued sexually in some manner. Almost everyone has made withdrawals from their value account because of the barrage of peer pressure, media, and so forth. Each counselor will have to decide whether it is appropriate to share his or her own experiences in counseling sessions and how specific and detailed to get.

Do be especially careful with private counseling sessions concerning sexual struggles if you are a pastor. Some churches have rules that no pastor will counsel a member of the opposite sex privately with his or her office door closed. Some make sure each office door has a window so the people inside are in view to those who walk by. These are extreme solutions, in my opinion, but they at least reveal an awareness of potential problems in counseling. The other extreme is worse—to dismiss the problem and to not consider counseling a member of the opposite sex to be an issue. Many pastors who thought that counseling about sexuality would be no problem have fallen. So what is the best solution? The window-in-the-door solution is not very conducive to the confidentiality needed for counseling those with sexual struggles. For me, the do-not-counsel-members-of-the-opposite-sex solution is also faulty. In today's world, the prevalence of homosexuality and lesbianism makes many of the reasons for not counseling someone of the opposite sex just as problematic for counseling those of the same sex. Members of the opposite sex are not the only ones who can make sexual advances or falsely accuse someone of sexual misconduct. To avoid the problems, pastors would have to avoid all counseling. A better way of dealing with this thorny issue is somewhere between the two extremes. I handle it by telling my secretary that she has permission to interrupt me by coming through the door or calling me on the phone at any time. I also tell my counselees that my secretary could come in at any time. There is never an occasion that my office is off-limits to my secretary. She is a witness to the fact that I am never with anyone behind locked doors.

Don't counsel anyone concerning sexual issues if your own sexual issues are unresolved. If you struggle in the area of sexuality, it is best to refer these cases to someone else.

Don't talk too soon or too much. Allow counselees to set the agenda and decide how deep the conversation will go. Avoid the temptation to try to draw out sexual confessions or details about their sexual lives. If disclosure is to happen, it must be the choice of the counselee—not the coercion or manipulation of the counselor.

Don't try to deal with issues too complex or deep for your level of expertise.

Don't rely on guilt or shouldn'ts. If you find yourself using expressions like, "This is inappropriate because God said so," or, "You shouldn't do this because the Bible says it's wrong," or, "You shouldn't do this because this behavior will get you into trouble," your counseling model is relying too much on the negative approach to single sexuality.

Suggested Scripture

Genesis 1:27
2 Samuel 24:21–24
1 Corinthians 6:18–20
1 John 1:3–4
James 1:2–4, 13–15

Prayer

Dear God, thank You for loving me so much. I thank You that in Your eyes I'm a million-dollar table. You have created me as a valuable and worthwhile person. Help me to live in a way that will protect and enhance my sense of worth, rather than reducing and diminishing it. Help me to learn to forgive myself and to get to the point where I feel valuable again. Help me treat others in a way that will make them feel valuable and contribute to their sense of personal worth. Thank You for the forgiveness that You have offered so freely and for Your ability to wash me and make me as white as snow. Amen.

Recommended Resources

Beslow, Audrey. *Sex and the Single Christian.* Nashville: Abingdon, 1987.
Foster, Richard J. *Money, Sex, and Power.* New York: Harper and Row, 1985.

Goergen, Donald. *The Sexual Celibate.* New York: Seabury, 1974.

Hershey, Terry. *Clear-Headed Choices in a Sexually Confused World.* Loveland, Colo.: Group Publishing, 1988.

Jones, Thomas F. *Sex and Love when You're Single Again.* Nashville: Thomas Nelson, 1990.

Koons, Carolyn A., and Michael J. Anthony. *Single Adult Passages.* Grand Rapids: Baker, 1991.

Landgraf, John R. *Singling, A New Way to Live the Single Life.* Louisville: Westminster/John Knox Press, 1990.

Smedes, Lewis. *Sex for Christians.* Grand Rapids: Eerdmans, 1981.

Stafford, Tim. *Worth the Wait.* Wheaton: Tyndale, 1988.

Stedman, Rick. *Pure Joy! The Positive Side of Single Sexuality.* Chicago: Moody Press, 1993.

Tannahill, Reay. *Sex in History.* Lanham, Md.: University Press of America, 1982.

Thielicke, Helmut. *The Ethics of Sex.* New York: Harper and Row, 1964.

Zilbergeld, Bernie. *Male Sexuality.* New York: Bantam, 1981.

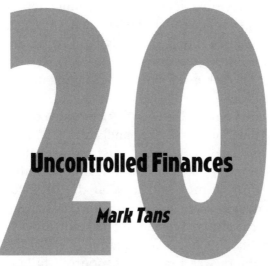

Uncontrolled Finances

Mark Tans

Kitchen stores are Don's favorite place to shop, even though he knows nothing about cooking. He is awestruck by the ingenuity of the gadgets and the possible things one can do with them. He loves to buy all sorts of gadgets that would outfit the best and most complete kitchen, home office, entertainment center, automobile, and hobby workshop. Don developed the love to organize and tinker as a child, and he was glad to get his first job so he would have money to buy the things he loved. Don's collection of gadgets grew as his pocketbook expanded, and he spent his paychecks within hours of receiving them.

Don grew up in a lower-middle income family. Family vacations were infrequent, but always paid for with cash. Don's parents rarely borrowed money for anything, except on occasion to buy a used car. The loans were short-term and quickly paid off. Money was always tight, but every basic need was provided. Don's parents handled money well because they grew up during the Depression and understood the value of money and the need to remain debt free. Money management was not openly discussed or taught, but Don's older siblings all learned to handle money well by following their parents' example. Don never caught on.

High school graduation shocked Don into facing the reality of providing for himself. His parents encouraged him to attend college, but they were unable to finance his education. Student loans were easy to get and seemed like a good option. Don lived inexpensively and when things got really tight he headed over to the financial aid office to borrow more money. He bought his first computer by using his savings and borrowing more student loan money for school.

Pride swelled within Don the day he received his first offer to receive a credit card. "I must be handling my money pretty well," thought Don, "or they wouldn't trust me with this." From that day on, Don always had a balance due on the credit card, except when he borrowed money to pay off the balance. Everything worked out okay except when the unexpected happened—like car repairs. The car always seemed to break down when money was the tightest. Soon Don was having to juggle monthly payments. The real problem was that Don's monthly bills exceeded his income, but he did not realize that yet.

The solution to car repairs came easily. Don decided to buy a newer car that would need fewer repairs. "Why not?" he asked himself. "I'm paying out about $100 a month in car repairs, and car payments would be only $129." What Don had not figured was the increase in insurance for a newer car and the new tires needed for the used car. Don also got tired of the cheap AM-only radio in the car and decided to buy a new stereo. Don was feeling down about himself and decided the stereo would be a nice pick-me-up purchase, so he plunked down his credit card and took home a new AM/FM-CD player for his car.

At age thirty, Don was over $37,000 in debt, still living in an apartment, and still making payments on a used, high-mileage car. His debt consisted of student loans totaling over $18,000 and a credit card balance over $4,000. Additionally, he owed $15,000 to a variety of companies for car payments, bill consolidation loans, and medical bills. All told, Don had over thirty-five creditors to pay each month, and doing so left him no money for food and gasoline. Don avoided paying bills because it made him feel depressed.

Definition and Results If Left Unattended

Don's case illustrates what can happen when people do not have financial priorities, a working budget, and the learned skills to manage and live within that budget. Out-of-control finances can occur very quickly with mismanagement, excess use of credit cards, unplanned major medical expenses, a devastating loss, or divorce. Single adults are especially susceptible to uncontrolled finances due to the lack of accountability to any other person. Many single again adults are separated or divorced because of poor money management. In his book *Debt-Free Living*, Larry Burkett reports that "approximately 50 percent of all first marriages fail, and finances are listed as the leading cause of divorce by a factor of four to one over any other cause, including infidelity."[1] "Nearly 80 percent of divorced couples between the ages of twenty and thirty state that financial problems were the primary cause of their divorce."[2]

Many of the single adults that come to you for help will be far down the road toward depression, loss of possessions, credit loss, and/or bankruptcy.

Finances that remain uncontrolled can lead to loss of secured loan items such as houses and cars. The possibility of bankruptcy increases as money problems multiply. Although bankruptcy may seem like a solution, the cost of it must be weighed carefully. Credit is rated on a scale of one to nine—one is the very best and nine is bankruptcy. After declaring bankruptcy a person likely will be unable to get credit for major purchases or home mortgages for up to ten years. A poor credit rating may also mean that a person will pay higher interest rates and down payments.

The losses go beyond finances. The increased stress affects a person's mental and emotional state, resulting in further financial problems. Decision-making abilities blur or become nonexistent. For married couples, uncontrolled finances can lead to separation and divorce. Forms of depression, emotional problems, or physical problems may increase as the person suffers from increased stress.

Symptoms and Struggles

Persons experiencing uncontrolled finances are difficult to detect, and by the time they finally seek help on their own the problem is often severe. Men are most likely to avoid detection because of pride in wanting to tough it out and be self-sufficient.

Persons suffering from uncontrolled finances can sometimes be detected through indirect symptoms. Churches that record giving can often detect a problem if a person's giving is low for his or her income level or if giving decreases. Deacons can note changes in giving and respond with loving concern, and, if needed, provide counseling referral or benevolent care.

Other symptoms are general depression, passive-aggressive behaviors, or a critical attitude. Obviously these symptoms may also be the result of any number of other physical, emotional, or mental conditions. But a counselor should not overlook finances as a possible source.

Financial struggles may result in decreased participation in social activities that cost money. Excuses will vary, but they rarely will reflect financial need. Some spending habits may also indicate a problem. People who constantly buy seemingly unnecessary things may be spending money to satisfy social pressures. This symptom is displayed in overspending for clothes, toys, expensive and frequent vacations, home furnishings, as well as in other areas important to social standing. Underspending may also be a symptom. Someone who always wears the same outdated clothes or drives a beater car even though he or she has a well-paying job probably has a problem.

Sources of Uncontrolled Finances

The sources of uncontrolled finances tend to be spiritual, temperamental, environmental, or circumstantial.

Spiritual

Greed and envy are the most common spiritual sources of uncontrolled finances. A common pattern among young-adult singles is to avoid marriage in order to buy and enjoy all the toys they want. They observe parents, friends, and co-workers buying and enjoying all the "good things" of life, and envy takes over. They easily justify new cars, jet skis, boats, condominiums, technogear, and whatever else is hot on the market and in their friends' possession. Envy soon leads to greed, the desire to have it all, and greed soon finds a way to get it. Out come the credit cards and in go the loan applications. Many loan agencies will let people borrow up to 40 percent of their monthly gross income, depending on housing costs, which are not included. Imagine what will happen to someone who borrows 40 percent, has housing costs of 30 percent, and taxes of 30 percent. One hundred percent of the person's paycheck is taken before anything is spent on tithe, food, clothes, gasoline, insurance, and so forth.

Setting selfish priorities is another spiritual cause of financial mismanagement. Without clear biblical priorities, people spend their money on personal needs, wants, and desires. Larry Burkett points out that "faithful management will yield a fifth portion. The creation of a *surplus* should be a major goal for the Christian. It is the surplus that allows us to respond to the needs of others."[3]

The lack of teaching and training about biblical concepts of money results in a misunderstanding as to the proper use of money.

Temperamental

The temperamental sources for uncontrolled finances develop from a person's personality, which includes a person's psychological, emotional, and mental natures. Temperament tests like the Myers-Briggs Personality Type Indicator or the Taylor-Johnson Personality Profile are very helpful for understanding how a person approaches decision making. Some personality types are more likely to make decisions based on subjective feelings than on objective information. The more subjective the decision maker the more necessary the external controls on finances. Feeling-oriented buyers will spend money to help them through times of depression. You can imagine what happens to feeling-oriented people who experience the trauma of separation, divorce, or death. Purchases come easily, frequently, and are large.

Brandon loved Terri and wanted the relationship to grow toward marriage. Terri was not that interested in the relationship but liked reaching into Brandon's deep pockets. He spent lavishly on her to win her heart. She took advantage of him until she grew weary of his desire to become more serious. When the relationship began to break up, Brandon grew depressed and frantic. In an attempt to save the relationship, he purchased a $25,000 boat that he knew Terri coveted. The ploy did not work, however, and the relationship soon ended. Brandon was left with high bills from Terri's use of his credit card, big payments on a $25,000 boat that he did not want or even like, and no girlfriend. His anger over the loss of the relationship was intensified due to his anger at himself for making an emotional decision to buy the boat.

Extreme temperaments reflect themselves in addictive behavior. Those addicted to spending have many credit cards from many places—department stores, service stations, and major credit companies. Their limits are as high as they can obtain and the balances near or at the top. The addictive behaviors of overspenders are very similar to the behaviors of those trapped in other addictions. Extensive therapy and external controls are needed to overcome these insatiable appetites. Many communities have Debtors Anonymous groups that follow a twelve-step recovery program. In the cases of addictive spending, I recommend that counselees seek the combined help of a therapist, a debt counselor, and a support group.

Environmental

Many individuals develop a habit of uncontrolled finances from a lack of training. Parents who do not teach or model proper ways to handle money frequently raise children who have no clue as to how to be financially responsible. And parents who do not discuss finances or include children in their discussions may also raise children who do not know how to manage money.

Even when people are not *taught* the proper use of money by their parents, they nevertheless *learn* many of their spending habits from their families. The level and extent of gift buying is one example. Some families give moderate gifts to immediate family members; others send gifts to every relative in the world. Some give gifts only on Christmas and birthdays. Others give for anniversaries, graduations, weddings, and new babies.

Two other factors related to environment are impulse buying and lack of accountability.

In some cases impulse buying is related to a person's temperament, but often it is learned. To combat impulse buying, whether it is caused by temperament or environment, counselees must learn the principle of purchasing only after a waiting period. In my opinion, the larger the purchase, the longer the waiting period should be. Twenty-four hours is the shortest period of time I wait before purchasing an item with discretionary money. This allows time to think about the purchase in relation to goals. Another helpful approach is to list all potential purchases, prioritize them, and then, when money is available, buy the one at the top of the list.

Impulse buying is very dangerous if left uncontrolled, but it also is fun, so don't legislate against it. Instead, encourage counselees to set aside some discretionary money (a rainy-day fund) for an occasional shopping day when they can spend the fund on whatever they want to. Doing this gives them control over the amount they spend and avoids the guilt they would feel afterward if they spent money they really needed for essentials.

Single adults who have no accountability system are also very susceptible to uncontrolled finances. One single adult told me that he rarely made a deposit to his retirement account until a close friend took the time to ask him if he was making deposits. Lack of accountability affects married adults as well. The lack of communication between spouses leads to numerous financial difficulties and marital stress. Far too often, divorce is the result of a lack of mutual financial accountability. The root of this problem lies in a misunderstanding of financial controls and budgets. Many people believe that budgets are restrictive and keep them from getting what they want. The opposite is really true. Budgets and financial controls reflect what people really want from short- and long-term goals. This enables them to use their money to do what they really want and not what they are pressured to do by well-meaning friends or a temporary lack of self-control.

Some single adults use a self-controlled system for accountability. If the single adult can maintain a management system and stick with the plan, he or she may not need or want outside accountability. This will not work, however, if the financial system is already out of control. In serious situations, creditors will not accept a payment plan unless a neutral third party is involved to assure accountability. To learn new habits and skills, most counselees will need an accountability partner for at least six to twelve months.

Circumstantial

Some single adults get caught in uncontrollable circumstances that develop into uncontrolled finances, for example, loss of income due to unemployment, separation or divorce, unexpected medical bills, and failed business ventures. Some may argue that these are the result of poor planning and therefore are controllable. I treat them as uncontrollables because no one can plan for everything. Sometimes resources cannot be stored up for future possibilities without neglecting current necessities. At other times the circumstances are truly beyond a person's realm of influence.

When challenged with a decreased income due to unemployment or other causes, most people have difficulty curbing their lifestyle. Denial keeps them from seeing the danger of using credit cards to "get themselves through" until their income returns to its original level. Self-denial is difficult during these highly stressful times. Intervention from an outside accountability partner can be helpful.

Counseling Suggestions

Open and Ongoing Communication

Open communication is essential among counselees, creditors, and counselor. It is imperative that counselees share with their counselor all concerns and changes regarding their finances. A counselor becomes ineffective if counselees hide debts, reallocate monies, fail to pay bills, or are late making payments. Any changes in the monthly financial plan must be discussed and, if needed, creditors notified in writing. In most instances, the counselor and counselees need to meet once a month and maintain telephone contact on an as-needed basis.

Encourage counselees to contact you whenever they face unexpected expenses, otherwise they may make a decision without looking at all the options.

On two occasions I went to a local muffler repair shop to have exhaust work done on my car. In one instance I needed a pipe replaced and the other time I needed the muffler replaced. Both times the salesman strongly encouraged me to replace the whole system because having everything done at once would save me some labor costs. He showed me the pipes and said they would last six to nine months. Money was tight, so I chose to do the partial replacements. I could have spent the additional money then and saved ten or twenty dollars down the road, but I would have placed myself in a very tight financial position. On both occasions the parts lasted over a year before I had to replace them. By waiting I protected my financial position and benefited from those old parts for a long time (in terms of muffler life expectancy).

Counselees under financial stress need to discuss these unexpected needs in order to make wise decisions.

Communication with creditors is also crucial. Counselors and counselees must keep creditors informed if they want to avoid legal action. Most creditors will not pursue legal action if counselees have a working plan and are sticking with it. The more communication with creditors, the more likely they will cooperate until the obligation is met.

Initially, the counselor may need to send a letter to the creditors to notify them that the counselee is working on a plan. In most circumstances, however, creditors will not contact or discuss the account with the counselor. The obligation for payments and communication remains the responsibility of the counselee.

Remind counselees that creditors have heard every excuse imaginable and don't care to hear any more. The only proof of sincerity is a regular monthly payment.

Flexibility of Budget

Budgets (and counselors) must remain flexible on a month-to-month basis. Learn to expect the unexpected and plan ahead as much as possible. Some months will require a shift of funds to meet an urgent need. When setting up the budget, do not commit every available dollar to creditors. Allow enough flexibility to meet ongoing needs, within reason. On a tight budget the counselee may not be able to save ahead for auto repairs or major clothing purchases for seasonal changes. Discuss the counselee's current needs and desires each month before making adjustments and allocations of available funds.

Knowledge of Rights and Responsibilities

One thing that few people realize is that the creditors who call the most generally have the least legal right to a person's money because the debt is unsecured. High pressure, therefore, is the name of their game. Even though they are regulated by federal laws concerning collection methods, they are not pleasant to deal with. In *Debt-Free Living*, Larry Burkett gives some excellent summary appendixes concerning the rights and responsibilities of debtors and creditors. Knowing these rights and obligations will help you and your counselees deal positively with the emotional pressure of frequent telephone calls and mail notices.

Be sure to remind counselees, however, that just because creditors are not calling does not mean they are not interested in receiving their money. It means that they have a better way of collecting: repossession.

Consistency in Payments or Immediate Notification

Counselor and counselees should work out a plan for meeting monthly needs and for repaying debts. Once a plan is established, contact creditors to inform them of your counselee's total debt, of his or her commitment to pay the debt in full in a timely manner, and of the amount the creditor will receive each month. The counselee's obligation is to maintain consistency in the monthly payments. If this becomes impossible, he or she is to notify the creditor in writing of the changes. For example, if income drops during a slow season, the counselee must notify the creditor that payments are changing for a temporary period, give the reason why, and supply the date when normal payments will resume.

Ownership of the Problems and Willingness to Change

The most significant factor in the success of any budget program is ownership of the problems leading to uncontrolled finances. In almost every circumstance we can avoid uncontrolled finances and even disasters. A person living on a floodplain without flood insurance is asking for future financial disaster. Someone failing to plan ahead for medical expenses is flirting with trouble. A person cannot, however, plan for every possibility, such as uncovered major medical expenses due to unusual illnesses. In rare circumstances it may be necessary to consider bankruptcy.

The key to the success of any plan is the willingness of the counselee to change old spending habits. Simple repayment of debts will not solve most problems of uncontrolled finances. If bad habits got you into debt, good habits will get you out and keep you out. Change does not come easily and accountability is a key to facilitating positive change. A minimum of six months is needed to establish new patterns of handling finances.

Guidelines for Budget Categories (see Form A at end of chapter)

Category 1—Payroll

Reverse an unbalanced budget by cutting expenses, raising income, or a combination of both. If practically possible, counselees should consider increasing income with a second job. This is not always a realistic choice because of other factors such as child care, required overtime in a first job, and the added stress of too many hours at work. They should consider the feasibility of sharing with their employer the struggles they are facing as well as their plan. They may unexpectedly find another source of encouragement and support.

Check your counselees' pay to determine if they are taking any voluntary deductions that can be eliminated or reduced. Also, be careful to not overestimate variable income when preparing the budget and payment schedule. It is easier to pay more to a creditor when excess income is received than to renegotiate a payment schedule several times.

Category 2—Other Income

List all other regular sources of income including alimony, child support, interest earned, and so forth. For example, my monthly mileage reimbursement will usually pay for all my gasoline and repairs to my car. If promised child support or alimony is not being received, assess the likelihood of obtaining that money without incurring additional legal debt.

Category 3—Tithe

Tithe is an important part of showing gratefulness to God. Depending on your counselees' situations, they may not be able to tithe 10 percent or more of their income. I suggest that they give something and increase the amount as debts are paid, income increases, or expenses decrease. Ten percent may become one of their future goals that God will honor through their commitment.

Category 4—Taxes

Examine your counselees' tax deductions to determine if they are underpaying or overpaying. Some are in the habit of overpaying as a form of savings. When they are on a tight budget, however, encourage them to pay only what is needed and use the rest to make their monthly budget work.

Those paying self-employment taxes should consider sending a monthly check instead of trying to save until the end of the quarter. The Internal Revenue Service will gladly accept their money at any time, and they protect themselves from spending the money and shorting themselves later.

Have them encourage their employer to develop a flexible spending account, utilizing Section 125 of the Internal Revenue Code, which allows people to pay medical, dental, and child care expenses with pretax dollars. The counselees elect to have money withheld from gross wages for these anticipated expense items. This allows them to reduce their gross income and therefore taxes (including FICA, federal, state, and local). The plan reimburses them after the expense is incurred. The tax savings can be 25 percent or more of the total amount they spend on out-of-pocket medical, dental, and child care expenses each year.

Category 5—Housing

Housing is a major expense but possibly a place to cut expenses. Moving to a less expensive home is an option, but not always possible because of the up-front expenses of selling and moving. For a guideline on housing expenses, Larry Burkett suggests, "the percentage of an average family's budget that should be spent on a house payment is no more than 25 percent of the net spendable income (after tithes and taxes). Add to the mortgage payments the cost of utilities, insurance, maintenance, and the incidentals, and the percentage climbs to around 35 or 36 percent."[4] Notice the percentages are *after tithes and taxes.*

Address counselees' home repairs as needed until a savings can be established to meet emergency and routine maintenance needs. They should consider buying used or refurbished appliances and items like vacuum cleaners. They should borrow or share whatever they can rather than purchase.

Category 6—Personal Care

The two major items in this category are groceries and clothing. Groceries are a place where counselees may be able to cut expenses. One family of four can live on $50 a week while another spends $200 a week. A beginning guideline is $125 per month for one person and $75 per month for each additional person ($350/month for a family of four). Special diets and geographic location may affect these numbers somewhat, and the more foods they make themselves, the lower their food budget will be.

The other major category is clothing. Your counselees should consider shopping garage sales for clothing, especially for little children. Making specific lists of what they need will help them avoid impulse buying. Purchase with cash only and buy a little each month. Clothing purchases can be drastically reduced for a short time, but they should avoid spending too little on clothing or they will create problems down the road when everything begins to wear out. Extended family may be willing to help out in this area while they are struggling through debt repayment.

Category 7—Transportation

In most cases, the least expensive auto to own is the one they have, even if it needs constant repairs. If they have two cars, they should consider selling one and using the cash to pay off debt. They should examine their insurance policy to determine if they can reduce coverage without jeopardizing potential losses. Also, counselees should compare prices of insurance companies and buy the least expensive insurance.

Transportation is a major expense that can use unexpected dollars at any time. A few years ago I went on a mileage-reimbursement plan for work-related travel. The Internal Revenue Service estimates and approves a per-mile rate each year for standard mileage reimbursements. The rate takes into account all the costs of owning and driving a vehicle. The reality of it costing twenty-eight cents per mile or more struck home as I counted each mile for work. I soon began consolidating trips for work and personal use to cut down on my operating expenses. It is easy to think that the only transportation cost is gasoline. The efforts to consolidate trips and save mileage will result in many dollars being saved.

Category 8—Insurance

Adult singles need to examine their situations to determine what kind and how much life insurance to carry. A single person without children needs very little life insurance—only enough to cover the obligations of the estate and funeral expenses. Many employers include a basic plan and your counselee may not need to purchase any additional policies. Single parents must consider the needs of the children and determine how much life insurance will be needed to provide for them until they are out of school.[5]

Disability insurance may also be included through an employer, but examine the coverage to determine when it is applicable since disability coverage varies greatly as to when it begins and how long it lasts. The younger the person is, the higher the risk of disability. Social Security will provide limited coverage under highly restricted situations, but should not be counted on. The counselee should find an agent who can be trusted and who is sympathetic to their situation if they want to purchase disability insurance, and then they should purchase only what they can afford. Even if it is not full coverage, it is better than none at all.

Major medical insurance is a must today. If your counselee is without medical insurance he or she is at high risk of major financial problems. Some people, however, do not believe in insurance for religious reasons. While I agree that we need to live by faith, someone will end up paying the bills in the end. One woman became single again when her husband developed cancer and died within a few months. They had no medical or life insurance because he had been self-employed and chose not to purchase coverage. When he died, the family was left with $20,000 in medical bills and no money. In this case, the church raised the money to pay their bills. Was their faith in God or in the church? My brother-in-law is a doctor and he tells me that they annually donate or write off about 30 percent per year. When this happens, everyone pays more to cover those without insurance.

Category 9—Medical

Failure to plan for unexpected medical expenses is one of the most common causes of financial problems. Having insurance coverage helps, but few policies pay for everything. And medical costs can eat up a sizeable portion of a person's income.

To manage the cost of insurance premiums, counselees should investigate the use of deductibles and co-pays. Those with a good health record and a healthy lifestyle (e.g., nonsmokers who exercise, control their eating habits, and have no hereditary diseases in their family history) have a lower likelihood of incurring health costs, so they may want to assume more risk by raising their deductibles, thereby reducing their premiums. Anyone who chooses this route should keep an amount of cash equal to the deductible in a liquid cash reserve. This reserve should also include money for uncovered medical and dental costs. A reasonable rule of thumb to follow when determining how much this should be is to set aside an amount equal to one month of take-home pay.

Eye care and eyewear are sometimes part of insurance coverage, but policies vary widely. In addition to insurance, employers sometimes join co-ops or other discount programs with opticians who offer special plans.

Remind counselees to keep all receipts for out-of-pocket medical expenses and to maintain detailed mileage records of travel to and from doctors' offices and hospitals. Depending on the person's income level, out-of-pocket expenses and mileage (9¢ per mile) may be used as an itemized deduction for tax purposes.

Category 10—Gifts

Going into debt on credit cards is a holiday tradition for Americans. Our family has learned to begin Christmas saving and shopping in January by planning a gift budget for each person on our list. In the past, we purchased gifts for almost thirty people each year; now we purchase for fewer than ten. When my extended family and friends understood that we went into debt to buy their gifts, they agreed that the gifts were not that important. Spending time with people is more important than gifts. Making things for them meant more than expensive gifts they rarely use. The holiday dread and the winter blues went away when there were no credit-card bills in January. We do the same thing for birthdays and special occasions. Prepare an annual gift budget and plan ahead to reduce stress and protect from overspending.

Category 11—Recreation

Instruct your counselees to allow something for recreation every month, even under the tightest of budgets. When under stress, the last thing they need is no relaxation. Help counselees find inexpensive forms of recreation, but also allow something for an inexpensive dinner or an occasional movie. The same applies to vacations. Single parents need babysitters to maintain some equilibrium. Consider creative babysitting such as adopt-a-single-parent-family or develop a middle-school service ministry of babysitting for them.

Category 12—Miscellaneous

Too many miscellaneous expenses can destroy a budget, too few are unrealistic. Any item they spend over $10 a month on should be listed in their budget. They should know where their money is going and plan for it. A few dollars here and there add up quickly in a tight budget. When things were tight for us, we eliminated the daily newspaper except for Sunday when the coupons were included. The savings of $7 was not much, except when combined with other miscellaneous cuts that totaled $50 per month. Everyone can cut expenses out of their budget and still survive. Someone once said that anyone can live on half of what they do now. I believe this is true after hearing that two-thirds of the world lives on less than $500 per person per year. We can live on less if we are willing to give up lifestyle.

Category 13—Debt

The key to long-term controlled finances is the control of debt and spending. Avoiding debt is a lifestyle issue in almost all circumstances because most, if not all debt, is the result of inadequate planning. People can never plan for everything, but the more planning ahead they do the more likely it is that they will survive the unexpected. They should make it a goal to become debt-free (except for housing) within three to five years. For some with large accumulated debt this will not be possible, but develop the shortest plan possible for their situation. Making a goal to be financially free will give them a new sense of liberty.

Category 14—Savings

Savings should include emergency funds, long-term investments, and money set aside for variable expenses. Those three areas represent a priority list for available monies and a goal list for developing future budgets. If your clients are using one savings account, they should be sure to record what budget areas the money is for to protect from inappropriately spending the monies for unbudgeted items.

Category 15—School/Child Care

Child care is a big expense for single parent families. After paying taxes and child care they may wonder why they are working. A church in my community began a latch-key program. The program was so well managed that the local public school discontinued their program and encouraged parents to use the one at the church. Many of the children do not go to church, so it also serves as a vital outreach program with little cost to the congregation.

Extra-curricular activities for the kids are important to their overall well-being. Have your counselees and their children choose the programs they want and that they can afford. Parents should share their financial limitations with their children and make them a part of the process regarding extra-curricular activities. The children may be willing to earn some of the money to offset the cost.

Category 16—Unallocated Surplus/Deficit

Your counselees may think that the word *surplus* is a joke when dealing with uncontrolled finances. However, if they set up a budget properly, even the tightest budget will allow for some surplus on occasions such as an extra pay period in a month. They should use any nonbudgeted funds wisely by developing a list of needs and wants ahead of time. When funds become available, they can look at their list and use it for the highest-priority items rather than for impulse items. They should not overlook the possibility of paying off a debt with those funds. They will be delighted at how good the freedom feels.

Only the government thinks it can live with *deficit* spending. Your counselees will need to make further adjustments in the budget to make it not only balance but work from month to month. Anything balances on paper, but making it work every day is the true challenge of reality.

Steps to Solving Financial Problems

Gather Information about the Counselee's Financial Condition

1. *List all debts on Form B (see chart at end of chapter) and summarize totals on Form A, "Current" column.* The counselee needs to bring a list of all debts and ongoing obligations, giving the creditor's name and address, total amount owed, monthly payment, due date, and date of last payment. The list should include mortgage or rent payments, utilities, credit cards, bank loans, family loans, and other miscellaneous past-due bills. Look for hidden debts that may be overlooked or forgotten. A counselee may have 25 to 40 creditors, and overlooking a couple is easy to do.

2. *List current income and expenses for each category on Form A.* The counselee should complete the column titled "Current" by estimating what is currently spent in each of these categories. A guess or desired level is adequate at this point. Do not worry about making this budget balance. The point is to think through

what is being spent and to establish what current priorities are for expenditures. A complete picture of finances will enable the counselee to determine new priorities and goals.

3. *List variable income and expenses.* The most difficult items for many people are budgeting for variable income and expenses. Variable income is received from sources such as wages based on commission, variable hours at a part-time job, periodic bonuses, or overtime. Variable expenses are items like insurance premiums, property taxes, some quarterly loan payments, auto repairs, and noncovered medical expenses. The goal for budgeting is to turn as many variables into fixed accounts as possible.

Variable income from commission-based wages or other regular income must be averaged and the budget based on the average or below. Your counselees should not shortchange a budget by expecting more income than they can be certain of over a period of time. Obviously the best time to begin a budget is during a high-income period when a surplus can be established to carry them through the low-income periods. Other variable income should not be used to figure a budget for monthly living expenses. I live in a community where one large manufacturer paid overtime and annual bonuses to all production employees for over a decade. Most long-term employees based their expenses on the planned overtime. In recent years, however, the downturn in the economy resulted in lost sales, lost overtime, and no annual bonuses for those who were still working. Nearly everyone suffered as a result. Periodic variable income should be used for debt reduction, surplus giving to God, savings, investments, or special purchases that fit into a person's goals and priorities.

Variable expenses should be listed and divided into pay periods as fixed expenses. Money should be set aside to pay the expense when it is incurred. Variable-expense items include such things as insurance premiums, tuition, self-employment taxes and year-end taxes, auto or home repairs, savings for auto replacement, and so forth. A few insurance companies will place people on a monthly payment schedule for a small fee. Property taxes and home-owners insurance should be built into monthly mortgage payments. Most companies will accept advance monthly payments without complaint. Any remaining variable expenses should be divided into a monthly payment/savings schedule.

Once your clients have their income and expenses down to monthly amounts, they will be able to effectively move to a workable budgeting plan. Most nonbudgeters have no concept of what they really spend or how much it really costs to live from month to month. This experience will be a challenge to the first-timer.

Discuss Priorities with the Counselee

Knowing where the money is spent provides counselees with the opportunity to consider what their spending priorities have been to this point. The lack of specific priorities leads mostly to self-priority spending based on wants and desires. Determining their goals and priorities will give them a framework in which to make decisions about what to purchase, how much to spend, and when to obtain an item.

To counsel someone with uncontrolled finances usually means arranging strict priorities to meet basic needs and to pay off debt. Usually there is not enough to meet all the obligations to the degree required by the creditors. Choices will need to be made and I would suggest that they consider the following priorities in making choices.

The first priority is to honor God. It is often necessary to confess the choices that led to uncontrolled finances and debt. God is willing to forgive if we repent and change our lifestyle. Giving a tithe back to God is important as a symbol of our gratitude, but the amount is not as important. I encourage the most indebted people to give something to God each pay period, even if it is less than 1 percent of their gross income. The spiritual value is beyond measure. Honoring God is also found in developing a written budget and using it to the fullest financial advantage. God will be pleased if they repent of their old ways and change their habits and lifestyle. Finally, they honor God when they pay their debts in full. God does not want us to sin by nonpayment. I do not believe that high contributions to God honor Him when compounding interest takes years of surplus money away from a person's future ability to give freely. Honor God by cheerfully giving while changing lifestyles and paying off debts.

Honoring God is their first financial priority and basic living expenses are their second. Everyone needs to eat, sleep, get to work, and provide for other basic needs of life. The difficulty many face is in determining what is a basic need and what is a want or desire. When faced with uncontrolled finances, I believe it is helpful to cut spending in every category to the point where they could not survive with anything less. That is the basic need level.

A third priority is to honor God-ordained government by paying taxes. As one tax accountant told me, "Avoid paying all the taxes you can, but do not evade paying the taxes you must." Nonpayment of obligated taxes is not something worth the hassle with God or the government. Your counselees should take the time to examine taxes and allowable deductions with a tax specialist familiar with their type of income and expenses and tax options.

Payment to their creditors and debt reduction is the fourth priority for spending. The goal is for them to pay all their creditors a monthly payment or more. If the remaining money after the other priorities will not meet the total required by the creditors, then they must prioritize their payment schedule and negotiate with creditors. Secured debts get first priority for repayment. They include such things as homes, cars, boats, furniture, or anything specifically listed on the loan papers as collateral for the loan. Unsecured debts are the opposite and include credit cards, medical bills, and some other loans. One approach to determining a payment schedule is to divide the total of the possible payments by the total of the unsecured debt payments requested. This will give them a percentage of what they are capable of paying each month. Pay each creditor the same percentage of available funds. It is best for them to explain to each unsecured creditor what the total debt is, how much they can afford to pay, and what the creditor's equal percentage would be. Then they should send the first check with the notice along with their cut up credit card, if appropriate. When the small bills are paid off, adjust the payment schedule to give more money to the remaining creditors.

Set Up a Realistic Weekly/Monthly Budget

Construction of a monthly budget is the key to successfully living by priorities and reaching goals. Since most bills are based on monthly payments, begin with a monthly budget. Work with the "Current" column of expenditures (Form A) and reduce wherever possible to lower the monthly expenses to balance income and pay off as much debt as possible. Trial and error will be necessary to find a workable trial budget in the "Adjusted" column. Once a trial budget is in place, they should use it and make adjustments each month until they are consistent.

Once your counselees have a monthly budget, divide the budget into pay periods. When developing a working plan, a rule of thumb is that monthly budgeting is good, bi-weekly is better, and weekly is best. I am paid once a month, so I arranged with all my creditors to pay within five to ten days after my payday. It means, however, that I must strictly budget my week-to-week cash expenditures to make it to the next paycheck. Bi-weekly budgets cause less problem in stretching out the money, but clients must save portions of each check to meet monthly needs. Weekly budgets are best because of the number of weekly living expenses such as groceries, gas, babysitters, entertainment, and so forth. A portion of every check must be saved to meet large monthly bills, and smaller bills can be divided up with different ones paid each week. Under bi-weekly or weekly pay periods they can arrange bonus income by setting up their monthly budget on two or four pay periods per month. This way the bi-weekly incomes will twice a year receive an extra check. For those on a weekly income basis, they will receive an extra check every three months. These extra checks may be used for variable expenses such as insurance, Christmas gifts, or savings. It is a good idea to use part of the extra check as a reward for meeting short-term goals. The incentive of a night out will strongly encourage someone on a strict no-frills budget.

Set Up a System to Handle Money

Develop a system for handling the money. A cash system using envelopes or jars is the best way to spend less money. Under a cash system, people are less likely to charge or write checks for unnecessary or unbudgeted items. This will avoid further debt and make them think twice before spending cash. We use a modified cash system in our home along with a checking account. Each month a check is received and the deposit is made, less the amounts for the cash envelopes. The deposit equals the amount paid by check for monthly bills. An additional deposit is made to the savings account for emergency funds and variable expenses. The only checks written are for bills mailed to the various utilities or creditors. The cash is divided into appropriate envelopes and used as needed. When the money is gone, we cannot spend any more in that area without transferring something from another cash account. This process always makes me stop and consciously decide whether to spend this money or not.

Checking accounts are acceptable, but hold some hidden faults. The fees for maintaining a checking account are costly if the minimum balance is not maintained. I learned the hard way that overdrafts are expensive. I wrote a $42 check one time that created an overdraft because of a missed entry early that month. The overdraft occurred the day before I made a small deposit, so I paid the fee and assumed the problem was corrected. A week later I received another overdraft notice from the bank and then the merchant for the same check, and I knew we had a significant problem. The final result was that I paid $48 in overdraft fees to the bank and the merchant to whom I wrote the check. My $42 purchase cost me $90. Forty-eight extra dollars on an already tight budget is disastrous. Checking accounts and bank cash cards also hide the effects of spending money because people do not realize they may be spending money that is budgeted for other items.

Credit cards must be avoided for anyone dealing with uncontrolled finances that are the result of overspending. Others with high debt should also avoid them because of the temptation to purchase things when they are unable to pay the balance in full each month, thus creating a new debt.

Arrange an Accountability System with Counselee

- To control consistency
- To maintain open communication

- To encourage progress
- To troubleshoot new concerns
- To review monthly adjustments to the budget
- To discuss potential purchases and avoid hasty decisions to spend money outside the budget

Contact Creditors Concerning Payment Plans

- Send a letter to each creditor where payments are overdue, stating that the amount being paid will change, or the amount will be less than requested.
- The counselee should keep open communication with all creditors.
- The counselee should not make any promises or change the payment structure over the telephone. Any agreement should be made in writing. Any changes should be discussed with the counselor. Creditors should receive notification of changes in writing.
- For further information on dealing with creditors see a summary of the Fair Debt Collection Act (1977) in Larry Burkett's book *Debt-Free Living*, Appendix C, page 21.

Allow for Flexibility

- If your counselee is behind on regular payments, you should plan to work with him or her for at least six months.
- Everyone is different, so adjust your approach to fit your client's situation.

Watch for Symptoms of Backsliding

- Not saving for variable expenses
- Using designated money for other categories
- Reduced communication

Dos and Don'ts for Counselors

Do actively listen and understand the root causes as well as how the counselee approaches money.

Do learn to feel their feeling. Most counselees are already suffering from low self-esteem and feeling hopeless. A solid plan will give the counselees a new assurance that they will make it.

Do accept the counselees and their conditions as unique human beings with solvable problems. Financial problems are common but rarely discussed.

Do maintain strict confidentiality. Keep all your discussions between you and the counselee unless you have a signed waiver. Most creditors will not talk to you unless you have a power of attorney.

Do let the counselees maintain control of the money and the final decision making. Encourage them to discuss any expenditures outside the established budget plan.

Do refer when you become overwhelmed. A counselee with $70,000 of credit card debt is probably out of your league.

Do make a feedback plan and follow up consistently.

Do build periodic rewards into the plan and give room for the counselee to occasionally save for something special like a weekend away with the singles group.

Do ask lots of questions. Many counselees will forget about small debts and even some regular bills because of the pressures they are experiencing.

Don't handle their money unless bonded, and in some states licensed. Many states have laws controlling how credit counselors may handle money.

Don't solve their problems for them by mediating with creditors or forcing decisions upon the counselees.

Don't give up on counselees too quickly. They will succeed if they are determined to succeed.

Suggested Scripture

Proverbs 21:5; 22:7, 26–27

Prayer

"Two things I ask of [Y]ou, O LORD; do not refuse me before I die: Keep falsehood and lies far from me; . . . give me only my daily bread. Otherwise, I may have too much and disown [Y]ou and say, 'Who is the LORD?' Or I may become poor and steal, and so dishonor the name of my God" (Prov. 30:7–9).

Recommended Resources

Blue, Ron. *Master Your Money,* rev. ed. Nashville: Thomas Nelson, 1991.
———. *Money Matters for Parents and Their Kids.* Nashville: Oliver-Nelson, 1988.
Burkett, Larry. *Debt-Free Living: How to Get Out of Debt and Stay Out.* Chicago: Moody Press, 1989.
Consumer Credit Counseling, (800) 388-2227.

FORM A
BUDGET WORK SHEET

MONTHLY GROSS INCOME	CURRENT	ADJUSTED	FUTURE GOAL
Salary/Wages			
1. Payroll Total	$	$	$
Interest/Dividends			
2. Other Income Total	$	$	$
GROSS INCOME TOTAL	$	$	$
	=========	=========	=========
MONTHLY EXPENSES			
Church Tithe			
3. Tithe Total	$	$	$
Federal Tax			
F.I.C.A.			
State Tax			
Local Tax			
4. Tax Deductions Total	$	$	$
Mortgage/Rent			
Property Taxes			
Insurance			
Maintenance			
Electricity			
Gas/Oil			
Telephone			
Water/Sewer			
Rubbish Removal			
5. Housing Total	$	$	$
Groceries			
Laundry/Cleaning			
Hair Care			
Clothes			
6. Personal Care Total	$	$	$
Auto Loan Payment(s)			
Gasoline			
Insurance			
Maint./Repairs/License			
Public Trans./Parking			
7. Transportation Total	$	$	$
Medical Insurance			
Life Insurance			

Disability Insurance _____ _____ _____

8. Insurance Total $_____ $_____ $_____

Deductibles/Co-Pays _____ _____ _____
Uncovered Medic./Dental
Prescriptions
Eye Care/Eyewear

9. Medical Total $_____ $_____ $_____

General Gifts
Christmas Gifts

10. Gift Total $_____ $_____ $_____

Entertainment
Vacation
Babysitters
Cable TV
Sports Teams/Equip.

11. Recreation Total $_____ $_____ $_____

Allowances, Children
Lunches
Subscriptions/Newspaper
Cigarettes/Tobacco
Pet Supplies

12. Miscellaneous Total $_____ $_____ $_____

Child Support/Alimony
Credit Cards (See Form B)
Loans (See Form B)

13. Debt Total $_____ $_____ $_____

Emergency Savings
Retirement Account
Investments

14. Savings Total $_____ $_____ $_____

Tuition
Extra-Curricular
Sports
Books/Materials
School Lunches
Day Care

15. School/Child Care Total $_____ $_____ $_____

TOTAL MONTHLY EXPENSES _____ _____ _____
========== ========== ==========

Total Income _____ _____ _____
Less Total Expenses _____ _____ _____
16. UNALLOCATED $_____ $_____ $_____
    SURPLUS/(DEFICIT) ========== ========== ==========

FORM B
LIST OF CREDITORS AND DEBTS

Creditor, Account #, Address	Collateral	Loan Balance	Normal Payment	Past Due	Due Date	Comments	Adjusted Payment

PAGE TOTALS $ _____ $ _____

GRAND TOTAL (last page only) $============ $============

Part 5

Helping Prevent Potential Problems

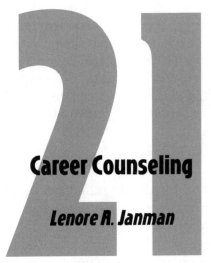

Career Counseling

Lenore A. Janman

By the time most people retire, they will have spent more than eighty thousand hours at work—more than at any other thing except sleep. Work is important to all of us. Work is a part of God's plan and nature. In Genesis 1:28 and 2:15, we discover that God created us to manage and care for the earth. Romans 12:6–8 talks about the different gifts that are evident in the body of believers and how, just as we are blessed with spiritual gifts, we are given different skills and abilities by God to be used in our occupations.

It is important for Christians to clearly understand the differences between vocation and occupation.

An occupation is not necessarily a vocation. There is an important distinction between the two. The primary vocation of Christians is to serve God, follow His commands, and love their neighbors. An occupation is a specific trade or profession. It can be an important means of fulfilling a vocation, but it is not a vocation in the strict sense of the word. An occupation is only one way of fulfilling a vocation. There are many ways of serving God and demonstrating His love. So even during periods of unemployment, a Christian's vocation can remain intact. He or she is still a child of God working to do God's will. Unemployment limits only one area that is available for expressing vocation.

Going through a job crisis is a traumatic event for people. Sometimes the crisis is unemployment due to "downsizing" or termination. Sometimes the crisis is a poor work environment that does not allow people to use all their skills and training and therefore provides no sense of personal fulfillment. Regardless of the reason, a job crisis is devastating and can be particularly isolating for the single adult.

When counseling people in a career crisis, you will need to be prepared to address the following matters:

- What it is like to be unemployed in a world where identity is closely tied to occupation.
- How it feels to work hard to afford college and then, unable to find a job in your chosen profession, end up working for minimum wage in an unchallenging job.
- How to help people figure out where God is when their job has been terminated or when they've been laid off or forced to resign.
- How to cope in a work environment that is hostile or where they are subjected to daily harassment.
- What to do when a job provides no sense of personal satisfaction.

These are just a few of the difficult issues that counselors need to be able to respond to in order to help those going through a crisis in employment.

Symptoms and Struggles

Most experts agree that losing a job triggers the same emotional reactions as does the death of a loved one. Elisabeth Kübler-Ross, in a landmark study on death and dying, identified these five stages of loss:

- Denial and isolation
- Anger

- Bargaining
- Depression
- Acceptance

These stages vary in duration and intensity from individual to individual, and it is even possible for someone to get stuck at one particular stage. A knowledgeable career counselor will help clients work through these stages and turn a negative experience into a positive one.

When people first receive word that they are going to be without a job, whether the news comes as a complete surprise or they are expecting it, their first reaction is usually denial: "This can't be happening to me!" "What did I do to deserve this?" The individual needs support from family and friends at this time, but the paradox for many people is that they may also feel some shame (even though they have no reason to), and they may want to isolate themselves from those who are in the best position to lend emotional support. Single adults living away from family members may feel particularly isolated, especially if their friends are co-workers who fear losing their own jobs.

The next and sometimes simultaneous reaction to the news of job loss is anger. This anger can be focused on the boss or the company, on themselves, and/or on God. Christians are vulnerable during this particular stage because anger may prompt them to say or do things that can damage their Christian testimony at work. If they allow this to happen, their anger can damage their relationship with God and others.

The third stage is bargaining. An individual may want to bargain with God. "If You provide me with another job I'll . . ." "If You cause my boss to change his mind I'll . . ." It is important for Christians to know and believe that God is in control of all circumstances, even this particular situation.

Especially damaging to those experiencing job loss is depression. People overwhelmed by depression may be unable to begin the process of searching for a new job. One adult who experienced this told me, "I couldn't even get out of bed in the morning. At first it was nice to sleep until 8:00 A.M. since I was used to getting up at 6:00 A.M. when I worked, but then I found I couldn't even get up at 10:00 A.M. When I did get up I wouldn't shower or get dressed because I had nowhere to go, nothing to do."

The final stage in this process is acceptance. It is waking up in the morning and saying, "Yes, I am unemployed, but this is only a temporary situation in my life. I will find another job that will meet my needs and through this experience I will grow and mature in my relationship with God and others." This occurs when people realize and believe that even though they have no job, they can still have self-esteem; they are made in God's image and they are children of God and He has a plan and a purpose for their lives.

Once people reach this stage of acceptance they can focus their energy on looking for a new job.

Unemployed single adults face many struggles as they cope with unemployment and search for new employment. Some authors talk about "stages of unemployment." For the first couple of months the attitude is, "I'm just between jobs." After six months, the attitude of the unemployed usually turns to hopelessness and a sinking feeling that they may never work again. The underlying struggle of the unemployed is to maintain healthy self-esteem.

No one likes rejection, yet the process of looking for a new job is filled with rejection. At a time when job seekers are struggling to maintain self-esteem they are forced to participate in an activity that tears it down.

A struggle of the single unemployed adult is dealing with isolation. For single adults, it is often co-workers who provide a support network that married adults find in their spouses and children. When singles leave the workplace, they are going to have another eight hours a day alone.

Inherent in the struggles of the unemployed are difficult financial problems. The individual is suddenly without a paycheck and health insurance. In most cases, individuals may be eligible for some type of unemployment compensation, but this probably will be considerably less than the money they earned while working and can require a change in lifestyle. A federal law enacted in 1985, COBRA, does require most employers to allow employees to continue insurance benefits, at their own expense, for eighteen months after leaving a company, but insurance payments can quickly drain a savings account.

Maintaining good health while going through this traumatic event is a struggle. Of all the events that create stress, loss of a job ranks close to the top. Long-term unemployment has a powerful impact on unemployed single adults. Without some kind of intervention or change, job seekers may begin to believe their situation is hopeless and give up. This can be avoided. There are constructive things that a career counselor can do to assist the unemployed adult through this crisis.

Counseling Suggestions

Single adults facing unemployment or a job crisis can benefit from a support group of others in a similar situation. Through local churches, unemployment offices, or local newspapers, clients can find appropriate groups.

In addition, the following strategies will help single adults conduct a successful job search. Counselors should advise their clients to:

- Develop a plan or strategy for how to go about finding another job. Write out the plan. Modify it as they go along.
- Think about their strengths and weaknesses. List them. This will help them in putting together their resume and in responding to interview questions.
- Contact local unemployment or job service offices, not only to see if they might be eligible for unemployment benefits, but as a source of job leads.
- Find a person or organization specializing in resume writing and production to help them develop a professional resume. Local telephone directories list this type of service.
- Make a list of all sources they can use to find job leads. According to the U.S. Department of Labor seven out of ten job hunters find jobs through networking, so do not overlook friends or colleagues.

- Find a counselor who can administer skills tests to determine what job they are best suited for.
- Talk to others who are working in the type of job they are looking for. Find out how they got started and what specific skills are needed for the job.
- Prepare for upcoming interviews by getting a list of typical interview questions (found in many books on the subject of interviewing) and think through their answers.
- Anticipate any difficult questions that their background and employment history may trigger. Talk to a personnel manager or employment counselor as to how they should respond.
- Collect as much information as possible about a particular business or company before going for an interview. Do homework.
- Send out resumes with well-written cover letters when applying for jobs. Follow up with phone calls.
- Learn to be assertive and consistent, and follow through on details.
- Not neglect family and friends—they can be a great source of support and encouragement.
- Manage time wisely during unemployment. Finding a job *is* a job—spend the appropriate amount of time on their job search and related activities.
- Read the Bible and pray. Ask God for guidance in each activity they pursue. Remember, God is in control, and He has a plan for their life.
- Budget financial resources carefully. The rule of thumb on job searches is that for every ten thousand dollars made in a previous job, it will take a month to find a new job at the same salary level. During times of recession this can take even longer.
- Consider further training or retraining in another field.
- Volunteer! Get involved with some community, church, or social group. Volunteering is a good way to meet new people and develop new relationships.

- Conduct a self-evaluation of their attitude. Look for signs of hidden anger, resentment, or cynicism due to previous experiences or the present situation.
- Keep circumstances in perspective. Success for a Christian is finding and doing God's will.

Dos and Don'ts for Counselors

Do show compassion to those going through a job crisis. Remember that most people lose a job through no fault of their own.

Do be available to listen; sometimes discouraged single adults just need someone to hear their frustrations and fears.

Do become aware of the range of emotions that can be experienced by a person going through a job crisis.

Do be sensitive to both the spoken and the unspoken needs of the unemployed.

Do assist clients in connecting with others in your church or with agencies that can help meet financial or physical needs.

Do assist clients in networking. Introduce them to people in your church who may be able to help in their job search.

Do help clients face reality in a loving way.

Do offer encouragement. Check up occasionally just to see how things are going. A phone call or note of encouragement can make a difference.

Do assist clients in connecting with a support group in your area.

Do pray with clients and help them search for God's will for their lives.

Do give clients a "nudge" when needed. Remind them that this period will not last forever.

Do help clients remain positive by nurturing their faith.

Do allow clients to express their emotions—to be angry or discouraged—but do not allow them to stay that way.

Do encourage clients to take care of themselves. Discourage unhealthy habits like overeating, smoking, or alcohol consumption.

Do encourage clients to consider part-time or temporary work.

Do encourage clients to center their lives on biblical principles that will create a model for effective living.

Do encourage clients to acknowledge mistakes and work to correct them.

Don't condemn or criticize clients.

Don't assume clients did something wrong, are lazy, or are unmotivated.

Don't allow clients to remain in any one stage of loss—except acceptance—for a long period of time.

Don't overlook liabilities that may be preventing clients from finding the right job.

Don't encourage clients to go after a job for which they do not possess the necessary training, skills, or temperament.

Don't allow clients to undervalue themselves or sell themselves short.

Don't allow clients to waste emotional energy looking back and asking, "What if . . . ?"

Suggested Scripture

For the unemployed
Job 23:10; 42:2
Psalm 37:23–24
Proverbs 3:5–6, 25–26
Jeremiah 29:11
Luke 11:10
Philippians 4:6–8, 11–13
James 1:2–5
1 Peter 4:19
To give direction
Psalm 37:5
Matthew 7:8
Romans 12:11–12

James 1:5
For those dissatisfied with their jobs
Ecclesiastes 2:22–26
Acts 20:35
Colossians 3:23
2 Thessalonians 4:11–12
2 Timothy 2:15
1 John 3:17–18
To help keep work in perspective
Proverbs 10:4–5; 22:6
John 6:27
2 Thessalonians 3:7–10

Prayer

Dear Lord, thank You for being sufficient to meet the needs in my life. I know that You have a plan for my life. Make me patient while You reveal it to me. Thank You, Lord, for being aware of each detail of my life, for being in control of my life circumstances. Thank You, Lord, for working in my life. Keep reminding me that You are in control. Lord, give me perspective on my circumstances. Open my eyes to see my strengths and weaknesses as You see them. Give me wisdom to know which jobs to apply for. Direct my actions and behaviors. And Lord, give me courage to do Your will. Remind me that my significance and value comes from You, not from my occupation or location. Give me strength to yield to You. In Jesus' name, Amen.

Recommended Resources

Beatty, Richard H. *The Resume Kit.* New York: John Wiley & Sons, 1991.
———. *The Five Minute Interview.* New York: John Wiley & Sons, 1986.

Bolles, Richard Nelson. *What Color Is Your Parachute?* Berkeley, Calif.: Ten Speed Press, 1993.

Covey, Stephen R. *The Seven Habits of Highly Effective People.* New York: Simon and Schuster, 1989.

Erlandson, Douglas. *The Job Shuffle.* Chicago: Moody Press, 1992.

Hosier, Helen K. *Suddenly Unemployed.* San Bernardino, Calif.: Here's Life, 1992.

Moreau, Daniel. *Taking Charge of Your Career.* Washington, D.C.: Kiplinger Books, 1990.

Morton, Tom. *The Survivor's Guide to Unemployment.* Colorado Springs: NavPress, 1992.

22

Premarital Counseling

John Splinter

By the time most couples arrive in a pastor's office for marriage counseling, they believe they have most of the skills necessary to make a marriage last a lifetime. Consequently, the opportunity for premarital counselors to truly shape the relationship is limited. A few hours of premarital counseling can do little to augment or erase twenty or more years of previous learning.

It is important, however, to set two objectives which you can accomplish in premarital counseling: first, provide a few tools—through counseling sessions, required reading, or other avenues—for the marrying couple to use; second, help the couple recognize some of the themes that will play out in their marriage.

To my knowledge, there are no longitudinal studies regarding the long-term quality or durability of marriages with premarital counseling versus those without. I am aware, however, of several couples who decided to postpone marriage after a few premarital sessions, and I would like to believe that the hours of work done with couples prior to their marriages make a qualitative difference in their marital relationships. Several couples have told me that this was true in their marriages, particularly during the first two or three years when they were making their greatest personal adjustments.

Symptoms and Struggles

Ample clinical research has demonstrated that the effects of parenting (from one's mother and father) will, for good or ill, be felt within one's marriage. Actually, people tend to carry into their marriages those issues with their parents that are most unresolved. Further, they tend to marry individuals who present an opportunity to resolve those unresolved parent-child issues. Whether the issue is with the father or mother is incidental.

Unresolved issues play themselves out in almost every aspect of marital relationships, from child rearing to money management, from housekeeping to sex. All of these issues weave into the tapestry of the couple's overall communication, both verbal and nonverbal.

Hence, when a relationship begins to falter, inadequate or impaired communication is almost always a factor. Other symptoms of relationships at risk include power inequity issues in which one partner is too strong and the other too weak; one partner overperforms and the other underperforms; marital priorities that are out of whack; the inability to "leave" one's parents and "cleave" to one's spouse; personal selfishness, self-aggrandizement, or other immature behaviors; triangulation of any form; chemical dependency; addiction; emotional, physical, or sexual abuse. The list could probably fill pages, but the symptoms listed here are the ones people routinely find in troubled marriages.

It is important for the premarital counselor to address both pathology and health. That is to say, it is important to address both the probable long-term effects of growing up with an alcoholic father (for example), and also the long-term effects of living in the image of Christ. To solely focus on either pathology or health will be to provide either no hope at all or an illusion of how easy marriage will be.

Counseling Suggestions

The following model is suitable for a fairly in-depth premarital counseling session. Each item should be answered by both members of the couple.

History of Parental Relationships

- How did you get along with your mom and with your dad? (Unresolved issues with either will be brought into the marriage.)
- Within the past two generations, has there been any alcoholism or other substance abuse? Divorce? Incest? Other major trauma? (Whatever happened "upstream" will in some way affect the fish "downstream.")
- If you could change anything in your mother or your father, what would it be? (This type of question often reveals areas of unresolved conflict with a parent.)

History of Dating

- How frequently, and with what level of intensity, did you date prior to your current relationship? How many dating partners did you have? How emotionally committed or intense was your relationship with the other person? How sexually active were you? (The more actively and intensely a person dates, the higher the probability that he or she is using dating, and/or attachment in general, to address other issues.)
- How long have you known each other? Has this been a fast-track relationship based on sexual or emotional need, or has there been time for reality to sink in? (Any relationship that is shorter than eight or ten months is probably not long enough and should be slowed down for a few months. Any relationship longer than three or four years probably has problems too—perhaps fear of intimacy or commitment.)
- What is your level of same-sex peer support? (Men who surround themselves with women friends, or women who surround themselves with male friends, are usually dealing with some major issues of low self-esteem and are almost always bad risks for long-term commitment. Healthy people usually have many same-sex peer relationships.)

- Is your relationship founded primarily on faith in Christ or on common interests and dreams? Do you treat the other person with respect, forgiveness, kindness, humility, gentleness, and so forth? Have you sexually consummated your relationship? (Relationships with a solid spiritual core are immeasurably more trustworthy than those based on common interests and dreams because interests and dreams often change as individuals grow and mature.)

- Have you been married previously? If so, have the issues that precipitated the previous divorce been addressed and healed? Has forgiveness been sought and given? Has the dust settled? (Second marriages are almost always more challenging than first marriages. If there are children from a previous marriage, multiply the difficulty factor by ten. If the divorce occurred within the preceding three years, multiply the failure probability factor by ten.)

Hidden Agendas

- What is your greatest joy as you consider being married? (Answers to this question often point out many other issues—e.g., desiring to get away from home; having control over the spouse; making babies.)

- What is your greatest fear as you consider marriage? (This question often brings out deep fears, e.g., fear of being unable to sustain a marriage; fear of losing control of one's life by becoming attached to another.)

- What one thing would you change about your future spouse if you could? (This question often leads to personal hidden agendas for changing the other person.)

- How might the traits that drew you to your partner become stumbling blocks to intimacy in the future? For example, his sure-and-steady nature may one day be perceived as stodgy and dull; her exciting, vivacious nature may one day be perceived as immature and eccentric. (The very characteristics that at first draw people to one another often become the things the pair eventually wants to change in each other. Today's "desire" often becomes tomorrow's "agenda.")

Specific Marital Issues

- Who will handle the checkbook? How much will you use a charge card? How much would you spend without consulting your partner?
- How will you handle discipline when you have children? Who will be the primary disciplinarian? How severe will it be? What type of behavior requires discipline? What is discipline? How does it differ from punishment?
- Who will do which household chores? When?
- Who is responsible for initiating lovemaking? How frequently might you make love? In what rooms? Under what circumstances?
- How do you communicate when angry? About what types of things should you communicate? What if your partner does not want to talk about it?
- What are your ground rules for arguments? Can one party have a time-out if needed? How long should a time-out last? Is there a "statute of limitations" on issues? What does Scripture say about fighting? (Read Ephesians 4:26–27.)
- How will you handle in-laws? What issues do you expect will come up regarding them? Who will deal with whose parents?
- What are your values? What things are absolutely forbidden within your marriage? What things are disliked, but might be tolerated once? What positive goals do you have for your marriage? What place does forgiveness have?
- Will you attend church? If so, which church? How often? Will you bring up your children in a church?
- Make a list of twenty things that your partner could do to say, "I love you." Give the list to your partner as a wedding present. Once married, pick one of the things to do each week. At the end of the first twenty weeks, make a new list.

Faith, or Religious History

- Describe your religious faith.
- Will your future religious orientation be the same or differ- ent from your partner's? For example, are you a Baptist and your partner a Catholic? Are you Islamic and your partner Christian? (The greater the mismatch in faith perspectives, the greater the probability of serious difficulty later on, espe- cially when dealing with child-rearing and financial issues.)
- Are you mildly religious or deeply committed to Christ? (Genuine faith in God, in and of itself, is usually a stabiliz- ing and healing factor in marriages. Does this couple have such a faith? Every marriage encounters stress and pain. Faith in God provides added strength to face these issues as well as added wisdom to help avoid many of the pitfalls in the first place. Minirth and Meier in their book *Family Founda- tions* indicate that although the divorce rate hovers near 50 percent, for those who pray together, worship together, and read Scripture together, it drops to 5 percent.)

System of Marital Priorities

Swiss psychologist Jean Piaget has done extensive research into the development of self-identity in males versus females. For a review of his work, see *The Moral Development of the Child.* The following system of priorities is closely tied to Piaget's research, but is combined with Ephesians 5:21–31. It has been field tested within a master's thesis. The more closely the system is adhered to, the stronger the marriage will be.

First Priority. Personal faith in and walk with God through Jesus Christ must always be the number-one driving force in marriage.

Second Priority. The spousal relationship must take precedence over any and all other relationships, including relationships with parents and children. No other relationship must be allowed to threaten or impair the spousal relationship.

Third Priority. No relationship other than with the spouse must be permitted to take precedence above the couple's children.

(Women are more prone than men to put children above spouse within marriage. When this occurs, it damages relationships with the spouse as well as with the children.)

Fourth Priority. The purpose of an occupation is to provide for the family. Family is the priority, not the occupation. If occupation supplants any of the above (God, spouse, kids), the marriage is at risk. (Men, more often than women, tend to put job above children, spouse, and/or God.)

Fifth Priority. All other interests and relationships, including hobbies, church activities, sports, close friendships, ongoing education, and so forth.

Community

Marriages, like life, are lived within community. The more isolated a marriage is, the more at risk it will be. Husbands need camaraderie with other males, wives need camaraderie with other women, and couples need camaraderie with other couples. Couples who isolate themselves from multiple caring relationships are often at risk. Relationships with other Christians are usually the best for beginning and maintaining a solid support system.

Scriptural Tools

Ephesians 5:21–31: Both partners are to be in submission to each other; wives are to submit to their husbands (attitude of respect); and husbands are to love and serve their wives. Sacrificial servanthood by the male is the model of Christian male leadership. Other approaches become counterproductive and dysfunctional. There is no place within Christian marriage for one partner to dominate or rule over the other.

First Corinthians 13:4–8: Love is never defined in Scripture as a feeling. Rather, it is defined and measured in terms of actions. It is a method of doing relationships. For example, "Love is patient. Love is kind." Loving feelings will eventually fade (see M. Scott Peck, *The Road Less Traveled*), and when they do, the relationship will have to depend on loving actions to sustain it. See also

Galatians 5:22–23 and 2 Peter 1:4–9 for other relationship characteristics that build healthy marriages.

Scripture mentions scores of relational traits. Some are positive and others are negative (see the appendix). Marriages that are built on the "wholeness" list will be much stronger than those incorporating pieces from the "brokenness" list.

Tools for Equipping Marriage Candidates

There are many good tools available for use in premarital counseling. They include:

- Myers-Briggs Type-Indicator—a psychometric tool for providing insight into personality function and probable relational style
- Taylor-Johnson Temperament Analysis—another good tool for marital preparation
- *Prepare/Enrich* seminars, if available
- Mentoring—"Adopting" a mature couple who has been married for at least fifteen years, a couple with whom the young couple can share openly and whose insights they will respect; this allows the young couple to "see into" a marriage
- An ongoing connection with a clergy person
- An ongoing connection with a group of Christian couples who meet regularly and talk honestly

There are also many good books to recommend to couples considering marriage. (See the recommended resources at the end of this chapter.)

Other Tips

Marriage is a decision to commit to a lifetime of ever-deeper maturing and ever-closer bonding. There are no guarantees in marriage. If or when a couple quits maturing and seeking deeper bonding, they are in trouble. It takes a daily renewed decision to commit to one's spouse and to maturity regardless of the pain.

Great childhood, adolescent, or previous adult relational pain usually means greater probability of marital struggle. The closer one can walk with God, the less traumatic will be the struggle, but it is probably going to be painful either way.

If there is substantial concern regarding childhood, adolescent, or previous adult emotional trauma, it is wise to establish a relationship with a Christian therapist prior to marriage so that when the storm hits, there is a lifeline.

Religion is a poor substitute for spirituality. Marriages based on religion rather than on God are at risk. Seek God, His will, His love, and His touch.

If there is ever a question of seeking after God versus following religion, seek God first.

Dos and Don'ts for Counselors

Do conduct a "history" with both bride and groom. This will help you get to know them, their childhood home situations, their past emotional scars, and their dreams and goals.

Do help the couple see how their individual issues, their issues with their own parents, and their issues with previous spouses affect their relationship with each other.

Do require that the couple read some good books. This should be an absolute—have them each buy and read at least two books that deal with marriage preparation.

Do provide the scriptural basis for happy and healthy husband-wife relationships. Help them see that marriage works best when based on God's instructions.

Do help the couple understand that their marriage will go through several "layers" or "stages," that this is to be expected, and that it is normal.

Do attempt to have other Christian couples mentor the unmarried couple and introduce them to a church if they do not have one.

Do challenge the couple to get help immediately whenever there is any reason to need it. They should not wait until the marriage is dead before trying to heal it.

Do slow things down if the couple is in too great a rush for all the wrong reasons. Doing so might prevent a later divorce.

Do provide the couple with tools for future use.

Do pray with the couple and encourage them to pray with each other regularly.

Don't take yourself too seriously. You won't have a major impact on every couple.

Don't believe that a couple's future success is contingent on your ability to prepare them for marriage.

Don't try to do more for them than they are willing to do for themselves.

Don't try to supplant the Holy Spirit's work in shaping the couple's lives.

Don't attempt to counsel at a depth for which you are not trained.

Don't generalize too much from your own marriage.

Don't attempt to hold together a couple that is obviously in relational or emotional trouble. Let them break up before rather than after marriage.

Don't assume that problems will be solved by marriage. Problems more often get worse after marriage.

Don't consent to marry couples who are living lives that will compromise your personal faith and/or integrity.

Suggested Scripture

1 Corinthians 13:4–8
Galatians 5:22–23
Ephesians 4:26–27
Ephesians 5:21–31
2 Peter 1:4–9

Prayer

Lord, we're planning on getting married. We believe we love each other and we believe we're mature enough to make a marriage last. We want to do the best we can in this marriage, Father. We ask You to bless us, and to bond our hearts and spirits together. We invite You to be the center of our marriage, and of our individual lives. We commit ourselves individually and as a couple to You.

Father, we each enter marriage with our own histories of hurt and failure. We ask that You will help heal the deep places in our spirits, our relationships, and our self-esteem. We ask that You would lead us to people who can help us in this endeavor. And again, we commit ourselves to walking as close to You as we know how to do, so that we may be healed.

Lord, we will be making vows to one another. Help us to live up to our vows. Give us the strength to commit ourselves to each other and to live out that commitment. Keep us from temptations that would weaken our marriage. Draw us to people and activities that will strengthen our union.

Father, we ask for wisdom. We invite You to give us enough hurts to keep us humane; enough tears to keep us tender; enough failure to keep our hands clenched tightly in each other's, and even more tightly in Yours. And Father, give us enough success, peace, and joy to confirm that we are indeed walking with You. Amen.

Recommended Resources for Counselees

Dobson, James. *Dare to Discipline.* Wheaton: Tyndale, 1973.
———. *Straight Talk to Men and Their Wives.* Waco: Word, 1984.
———. *What Wives Wish Their Husbands Knew About Women.* Wheaton: Tyndale, 1977.
Hendrix, Harville. *Getting the Love You Want.* New York: Holt, 1988.
Joy, Donald. *Bonding: Relationships in the Image of God.* Waco: Word, 1987.
———. *Lovers: Whatever Happened to Eden?* Waco: Word, 1987.
LaHaye, Tim, and Beverly. *The Act of Marriage.* Grand Rapids: Zondervan, 1976.

Peck, M. Scott. *The Road Less Traveled.* New York: Simon & Schuster, 1980.

Smalley, Gary, and Steve Scott. *For Better or for Best.* Grand Rapids: Zondervan, 1982.

————. *If Only He Knew.* Grand Rapids: Zondervan, 1982.

Wright, H. Norman. *Seasons of a Marriage.* Ventura, Calif.: Regal, 1983.

Recommended Resources for Counselors

Wright, H. Norman. *Premarital Counseling.* Chicago: Moody Press, 1992.

Remarriage Counseling

Nancy and Greg McPherson

The end of a marriage comes either through death or divorce. In the case of death, the surviving spouse and children must mourn. Spouses who mourn the end of a marriage resulting from death enhance their chances of success in subsequent marriages.

Those who divorce must heal also. To do so, they need to acknowledge the part they played in the death of their marriage. After divorce, there are generally many issues and problems to work through. Some of these are: (1) the counselee's family of origin and how it affected the marriage; (2) the lack of readiness for marriage and its commitments and responsibilities; (3) the causes of the divorce (drugs, alcohol, and financial difficulties are frequent causes); (4) accumulated bitterness and anger due to male-female differences that close down much-needed communication.

Healing from a previous marriage is the first thing that needs to be done before remarriage, but it's the last thing most people want to do. Some people may assume that just because they are older they know more about how to carry on a healthy relationship. But that is not necessarily true. Few people like to hear this about themselves, but if they want God to work, they must be open to His conviction and be willing to grow as well as to change. Make sure that divorced counselees have learned that they cannot change anything about their partner—only about themselves.

Those who do not heal from a first marriage may end up in another failed marriage, which will result in more hurt to themselves and to others, and more hopelessness regarding their ability to have a God-centered and God-honoring marriage.

The Bible says in Hosea 4:6, "My people are destroyed for lack of knowledge" (KJV). God wants people to use His Word to learn as much as they can about how to live and how to treat others—how to live in harmony in marriage and as a family. Living by the Word of God, "The Manual," is the only way.

Symptoms and Struggles

The number-one problem in Christian remarriages is a marginal commitment to the Lord. Living in disobedience to God's plan leads to all kinds of struggles. Due to their sinful nature, people are unwilling to see that living in *obedience* can lead to more order and peace.

The number-two problem that plagues second marriages is anger and bitterness toward an ex-spouse. Even though people genuinely believe they have let go of their anger, often it is only buried very deeply. Unresolved anger and bitterness will, eventually, be directed toward the new spouse. The Bible says, "out of the outpouring of your heart, the mouth speaks."

The number-three problem that married-again partners cite is not enough trust. Often the lack of trust has a direct relationship to anger and bitterness. Trust is deeply wounded when someone is hurt by physical and emotional abuse, abandonment, and infidelity. The wounded partner begins to think that all men or all women are alike. Thus, jealousy may become an ugly problem in a new marriage if one spouse even sees the other talking to the opposite sex. This alone may trigger memories of experiences that led to infidelity.

The fourth struggle for married-agains is idealism. Idealism reveals itself in unrealistic attitudes regarding marriage and unrealistic expectations concerning their ability to manage a blended family. There is much to be learned about what remarriage means and what blending a family involves, and not having a *teachable* spirit is the greatest downfall. Many couples have gone into remarriage thinking, "We have this all wired. We know what we did wrong before, and we're going to be a perfect family now." Unfortunately, this is seldom the case. The new family is not perfect because it is made up of two very different groups of people who think that their way of running a family is the right way. Also, seldom has every person in a remarriage or a blended family dealt with his or her own personal mourning and pain from a death or divorce. As a result, these family members take their anger out on the others in the family unit. Another common situation occurs when a person who has never been married marries someone who has been married before. This has its own set of difficulties because the never-married spouse often has unrealistic expectations of both the new spouse and the children. This leads to the fifth struggle, self-centeredness.

Self-centeredness is a problem because people who are accustomed to taking care of their own needs or are interested only in having their own needs met in a relationship will have difficulty in marriage. The Bible calls for the husband to be the ultimate servant to his wife. In Ephesians 5:25–31, Paul tells husbands to love their wives just as Christ loved the church and *gave himself up for her.* A true servant at all times gives, forgives, and forgets.

If there is a single thread of jealousy concerning attention given to the children, discuss the situation with your counselees and help them put it into perspective. Explain that the marriage is the relationship that will ultimately bring security to the children, so it must be cared for first.

Model and encourage compassion in your counseling of remarried people. Hurts may linger from the previous marriage. Something happens when people remarry that brings out feelings and memories that would not be triggered in singleness. By focusing on Galations 5:16–26 counselees can deal with self-centered thinking.

An absolute must in a remarriage and/or a blended family is flexibility. This is key to making remarriage work because changing circumstances, especially in a remarriage that involves children, are inevitable. Some issues will come up in blended-family circumstances that counselees will not like but may be unable to do anything about. One of these changes is child-custody arrangements. Another is change in child-support payments due to abandonment, unemployment, or irresponsibility. Others include discord between two ex-spouses and the difficulty of raising children in two very different households, with very different circumstances, rules, and often, values.

Dealing with the logistics of children's comings and goings can be a major difficulty in a second marriage. Couples who remarry today must be prepared for the changes in custody arrangements due to joint-custody laws, rulings on physical placement, and the fact that children now have the right in some areas of the country to choose which parent they want to live with. That being the case, your counselees need to realize that children will make the choice that offers them the most freedom, even though this is not in their best interest. When your clients are the ones who have established rules for the well-being of their children and the children choose the freedom route, a major problem develops. Children need structure, rules, and a family unit in order to grow up to be healthy adults.

Dealing with personality changes that take place as children go from one family to the other brings its own kind of stress. Counselees must be patient and understanding but also firm in their own standards. People who remarry need to get together, preferably before marriage, and set down rules and standards for how their home is going to operate, and go over this with the children so no one is surprised or left in the dark. This gives everyone an opportunity to speak up, and all of this makes a child secure. Children will watch for consistency between the parents and will be quick to take advantage of any inconsistency. The most important thing parents can do is to present a united front to the children and work out their disagreements concerning how to parent away from the children. (Consider Colossians 3:18–21.)

People who have never been married before will have trouble dealing with the antagonistic relationships that often exist between two divorced people. Even the best divorce relationships tend to take on a different flavor when one or both parties remarries. The new wife or husband must be flexible regarding the transporting or visitation of the children, or if there is joint custody, there could be issues of upbringing, schooling, medical treatment, discipline, and so forth. Instruct your counselees to stand behind one another and support and protect one another.

Struggles with financial difficulties and irresponsibilities are very big concerns in remarriage and blended families. Large debt, large support payments, late or nonexistent support payments, and whose money is going to whose account or to whose children are among the greatest causes of stress in a second marriage.

Child support or lack thereof is a never-ending story. If possible, the spouse who is to receive the money should establish a monthly budget that doesn't include it. That way, if it comes in, great, if not, the family can get along without it. This enables them to handle the problem in a more constructive way. If the support payment is not in their budget, they have the option of pursuing legal channels to get the payment or letting it go. If counselees go to lawyers "for the principle of things," they can figure that it will cost them money to get the money.

Large debts are common for single parents, and support payments are sometimes so overwhelming that parents feel as if they will never again get their heads above water. Some people may have to consider the possibility of not remarrying due to financial responsibilities. For example, clients who are unable to pay court-ordered child support should not consider remarriage until they have their finances under control.

Another potential problem remarried couples may have to face is that of ex-spouses who try to tap into the income of the new spouse if he or she earns a substantial amount of money. And if the new spouse's income is destined to increase in the future, there will be a constant source to tap into. Your counselees must consider how they will feel if this happens. Do not allow them to be uninformed or naive; these things happen to Christians as well as to non-Christians.

Another circumstance that often troubles counselees is when the ex-spouse is not using the support money in the best interest of the children. Counselees may need your help in dealing with that also.

Counseling Suggestions

Your first and foremost concern for counselees is that they have a right relationship with God. Make sure that they have a personal relationship with Jesus Christ and that they know what it means to have Christ as Lord of their lives. Clients need to understand that their first purpose in life is to bring glory to God. Quality of life improves with consistent study of the Bible, a daily prayer time, and obedience to God's Word. Couples need to find a church home where the Bible is taught as the inerrant Word of God, and where its teaching assists them in the Bible's practical application in their lives. Stress the need for total trust in God.

Healing from the former marriage is next in importance. This applies in cases of death as well as divorce. A personal relationship with Christ will aid in the area of forgiving their former spouses and forgiving themselves for their own sinfulness concerning the former marriage, because in knowing the One who forgives, we begin to understand what forgiveness is and how we, through the power of the Holy Spirit, can now forgive. People who lose a spouse to death feel left behind and abandoned and need to work through the mourning process and forgive the spouse for dying.

Letting go of the past is a process. It does not happen overnight. Everyone is different, but all should talk things through with a trusted friend, pastor, or counselor. Slow progress is better than no progress. Accepting the reality of the loss seems to be the hardest. Remind counselees that only God can change another person, but God can change things about themselves and assist them in healing.

Most of us want a quick fix, but it is not advisable to rush into a new relationship or marriage expecting this to cure the pain. Jim Smoke, in *Growing Through Divorce*, says, "Divorce is one of the most painful and emotionally draining experiences that a human can have. It is a hurt that goes deep, and is accompanied by the doubt that it will ever heal." Have your counselees answer these questions:

- Am I in a rebound relationship?
- Am I filling my "empty place" with another person?

- Am I looking for sexual fulfillment in this relationship?
- Is this relationship filling a financial need?
- Am I looking for a parent for my child?

These are tough questions, but let's face it, people in their sinful natures do use relationships for all of the above. If people are honest with God, and He honors honesty, they can learn to trust Him with their needs. He will provide for them while they heal. If they do not or will not trust Him, they are essentially saying that they cannot trust Him with their lives.

People who have experienced a loss need to know themselves and care about themselves. The hard questions I spoke about in the previous section involve real honesty, which is the only way for people to get to know themselves. The Bible says, "The heart is deceitful above all things, and desperately wicked: who can know it?" (Jer. 17:9 KJV). Clients need an accountability relationship with someone—someone to whom they can reveal their inner struggles and who will not only give feedback but also spur them on to work harder.

Men especially have difficulty getting to a deeper level of intimacy with themselves and with others. Getting counselees to share at a gut level in a trusting relationship with another man will involve some work on your part, but the long-term payoff will be great. Ask your clients if they are able to communicate about themselves on these points:

- Who am I?
- What do I believe?
- What are my likes and dislikes?
- What are my expectations?
- What are my goals in life?

It is virtually impossible for clients to care about another person or know them, as God calls them to, if they do not care about or know themselves. Many people will try to fill the needs of another person when they are drawing from their own empty well.

The next thing counselees need to do is study the subject of marriage. They should learn as much as they can by reading Bible passages that address marriage and how to treat others. They should look for solid Christians who have good marriages and ask them what works for them. They should read books on marriage found in any good Christian bookstore. Here again, they should ask themselves tough questions about how they did in their previous marriages. (Even in the case of the death of a spouse one can always look for ways to improve. Besides, even if the previous marriage was a good one, the relationship with the new mate will not be the same as it was with the previous one.)

Counselees should also learn all they can about choosing a mate. Knowing themselves is all important. They should not try to mold their personality to fit someone else's or vice versa. It is most important that counselees *be the right person*, not that they find the right person (which should be left up to the Lord).

Have counselees learn what God's Word says about loving unconditionally (see Eph. 5:1–2 and 5:21–33). Only through the power of the Holy Spirit can anyone carry out this kind of loving. Your counselees should be willing to communicate with their partners on an intimate level—spiritually, emotionally, and physically.

It is equally important for counselees to know what they are looking for in a mate. They know and the Lord knows that they have some specific needs and desires. The Bible says in 2 Corinthians 6:14–15, "Do not be yoked together with unbelievers. For what do righteousness and wickedness have in common? Or what fellowship can light have with darkness? What harmony is there between Christ and Belial? What does a believer have in common with an unbeliever?"

Major criteria for two people considering remarriage are that both have faith in Christ as Savior; want Christ to be the head of the home; have similar moral values, similar life goals and interests, good parenting skills, and be willing to parent another person's child.

Having a clear understanding of what commitment means is also important in marriage or remarriage, which in God's eyes is lifelong. Committed believers in Christ are called to love as Christ loved the church (Eph. 5:21–33). Marriage vows say: "Love, honor, cherish, and be faithful, as long as you both shall live," and if marriage vows do not cover this, the people hoping to remarry should evaluate their understanding of commitment. They should take time to learn together what God expects of husbands and of wives. Learn what God expects of parents (they may instantly become one). Commitment is tested in difficult times, so do not even cultivate thoughts of, "How can I get out of this marriage?"

Commitment in marriage means faithfulness, both in thought and in action. If counselees struggled with fidelity in the first marriage, this must be dealt with before they remarry. Sexual sin must be dealt with. Besides the counseling that you are giving, refer them to outside support groups and/or counseling that can be more specific in nature. If your counselees had unfaithful mates, they will have difficulty trusting again. Some very open communication on this issue must take place in the beginning and be ongoing.

Those considering remarriage should think clearly about the reality of parenting someone else's children because this is not a task for the faint of heart nor for a person who is hurt easily. Step-parenting is for the long haul, and it has few immediate rewards. Help counselees learn as much as they can about parenting and step-parenting. Many problems and questions will come up over this issue, and there are no quick solutions.

The key to blending a family is to plan in advance. The problem with many couples is that they become so involved with each other that they do not give enough thought to how their relationship will affect the children. One of the biggest problems I see is different parenting styles, including the different ways men and women parent. Counselees need to be open with each other about areas of disagreement and talk about their parenting skills or lack thereof. Studying a book on Christian parenting together should be considered.

Drawing up rules for their home, including how to discipline in certain situations that already exist, along with planning for other situations that might come up, *before* marrying is the ideal for clients considering remarriage. They should then agree to back each other up in front of the children—disagreeing and working out differences in private. A united front is an absolute must for the security of the children and the stability of the marriage. The children *will* try to divide you. It happens in *every* family.

Children of divorce or those who have experienced the death of a parent have issues of abandonment and have fears that they were somehow the reason that the parent left the family. The commitment that your counselees have for each other in marriage and that they display to the children will begin to give the children a sense of being able to trust again. Commitment is a very important area in a blended family; thus, your counselees should learn as much about it as possible.

Parents should consider the relationships of the children who are being put together. What are their ages and how far apart are they? They will not always get along, just like the siblings from the same household do not always get along. Teenagers from different homes who are put together can become sexually involved. This is a problem not often spoken about, but it does happen. Teens should be supervised and have same-sex roommates.

These blended family issues are many, but they must be considered, and should not be taken lightly, nor should blended families be created naively.

Dos and Don'ts for Counselors

The physical proximity of living with another person within marriage and the physical closeness of the sexual relationship will bring to light areas that need to be worked on. These things—fears; sexual, physical, and emotional abuses; addictions; anger; sinful thoughts; and so forth—are stuffed away and denied in singleness. They will surface again in marriage, causing partners to feel alone and alienated. This breaks the bond of oneness and true intimacy that God wants in marriage. God wants marriage to bring Him glory and to have that "oneness" He created. He wants partners to work hard at correcting their sin. He wants them to be honest and vulnerable before Him and heal.

Do ask many questions concerning previous marriages. In the case of a single who marries a previously married woman, ask about the single person's previous serious dating relationships.

Do give homework assignments for areas that need hard work and suggest more in-depth counseling where needed. Hold counselees accountable for doing the homework and for their commitments to get more help.

Do check for financial stability whenever possible. This is an area of great danger because people hide financial problems. Jim Smoke goes so far as to recommend running a credit check on both parties. If they cannot be totally honest, there is probably a problem.

Do consider fears of abandonment in people who are coming out of divorce.

Do consider the influence of ex-spouses on the new marriage/family, especially where children are involved.

Do ask if there has been sexual involvement before marriage. Hold them accountable in this area. Ask them to agree to stop before marriage because premarital sex will sabotage *true* communication and honesty, in addition to its being disobedient to God's Word.

Do encourage couples to become "best friends." This will help them get through the hard times. The ability to share on an intimate level, as only true friends can do, will allow them to enjoy laughing with each other, which will see them through much difficulty.

Do try to determine if one or the other has a critical spirit. This characteristic is a relationship killer and will break down the other person before he or she knows what happened. No bond can form in the true sense until this is solved. Encourage them to be each other's greatest fan.

Do have them say at least one positive thing about the other each day. Have them make a habit of saying "I love you" and of paying each other compliments every day.

Don't allow them to sidestep the healing process from previous marriages.

Don't allow couples to say they are all taken care of.

Don't let them go into this without making a plan for their family.

Suggested Scripture

Joshua 24:15
Psalm 37:4; 40
Isaiah 40
Jeremiah 29:11–13
Matthew 22:37–39
1 Corinthians 13
2 Corinthians 4:7–18; 5:7
Galatians 5:13–25
Ephesians 5:21–33
Philippians 4:8, 11, 13
Colossians 3

Prayer

Dear heavenly Father, I want to come before You and thank You that You sent Your Son Jesus to die for my sins and to make a way so that it is now possible for me to approach Your throne of grace. Lord, I can't do all this myself. I can't do much of anything in my own strength. I confess my need to change, and to grow through the power of Your Holy Spirit. Only through the power of the Holy Spirit can I confess the pain, hate, anger, disobedience, and other areas that I need to submit to You. I need to grow and change my heart, so please help me to be totally honest and transparent with You, Lord, so You can do a cleansing work in me. Amen.

Recommended Resources

Adams, Jay E. *Marriage, Divorce and Remarriage in the Bible.* Grand Rapids: Zondervan, 1986.
Crabb, Larry. *Inside Out.* Colorado Springs: NavPress, 1991.
———. *Men and Women: Enjoying the Differences.* Grand Rapids: Zondervan, 1991.

Dalby, Gordon. *Healing the Masculine Soul.* Waco: Word, 1988.

Dobson, James. *The New Dare to Discipline.* Wheaton: Tyndale, 1992.

——. *Parenting Isn't for Cowards.* Waco: Word, 1987.

Elliot, Elisabeth. *Passion and Purity.* Old Tappan, N.J.: Revell, 1984.

Frydenger, Tom, and Adriene Frydenger. *The Blended Family.* Grand Rapids: Chosen Books, 1985.

——. *Resolving Conflict in the Blended Family.* Old Tappan, N.J.: Revell, 1991.

Hart, Archibald. *Children and Divorce.* Waco: Word, 1985.

——. *Healing Adult Children of Divorce.* Ann Arbor, Mich.: Servant, 1991.

Houck, Don, and LaDean Houck. *Remarriage with Children.* San Bernardino, Calif.: Here's Life, 1991.

Hybels, Bill, and Lynn Hybels. *Fit to Be Tied.* Grand Rapids: Zondervan, 1993.

McDowell, Josh. *His Image . . . My Image.* San Bernardino, Calif.: Here's Life, 1984.

Minirth, Frank, and Paul Meier. *Happiness Is a Choice.* Grand Rapids: Baker, 1978.

Morley, Patrick M. *The Man in the Mirror.* Brentwood, Tenn.: Wolgemuth and Hyatt, 1989.

Rainey, Dennis. *Building Your Mate's Self-Esteem.* Updated and expanded ed. Nashville: Thomas Nelson, 1995.

Seamands, David. *Healing for Damaged Emotions.* Wheaton: Victor, 1981.

Smalley, Gary, and Steve Scott. *For Better or for Best.* Grand Rapids: Zondervan, 1982.

——. *If Only He Knew.* Grand Rapids: Zondervan, 1982.

Smalley, Gary, and John Trent. *The Hidden Value of a Man.* Colorado Springs: Focus on the Family, 1992.

Smedes, Lewis. *Forgive and Forget.* San Francisco: HarperSanFrancisco, 1991.

——. *Shame and Grace.* San Francisco: HarperSanFrancisco, 1993.

Smoke, Jim. *Growing Through Divorce.* New York: Bantam, 1986.

——. *Growing in Remarriage.* Grand Rapids: Revell, 1994.

Streeter, Carole Sanderson. *Finding Your Place after Divorce.* Wheaton: Shaw, 1992.

Warren, Neil Clark. *Finding the Love of Your Life.* Colorado Springs: Focus on the Family, 1992.

Crisis Counseling

Mike Popovich

Nobody schedules a crisis a week in advance—it is always unplanned, and it always overwhelms and consumes the people involved. They generally show up unannounced at your home or office. And if they do call ahead, they demand to see you immediately. They say to your secretary, "I know _____ is busy, but this is really important and it will only take a minute." They will stop you in the parking lot as you head home to dinner and say, "I'm in a crisis; I need to see you first thing in the morning."

Handling people in crisis is a much-needed ministry skill. Understanding how to deal with single adults in crisis can be intense, but do not shy away from it. Even if you have not experienced what they are going through, or have not dealt with the particular crisis, you can help them.

There are two types of crises. First, the out-of-the-blue type. It may be the sudden death of a loved one, a teenager in a critical accident, a job firing, a set of divorce papers being served without prior discussion, a daughter who announces she's pregnant, or learning about the cancer that has invaded a loved one's body. All of these situations occur unexpectedly.

The second type of crisis is the last-straw type. This too comes as a sudden shock, but as the story unfolds you discover that the person has been dealing with the issue for a long time. This is not a crisis of sudden discovery, but one where the method of coping (or denying) has broken down and the person can no longer keep the reality of the hurt or problem under control. It has demanded center stage.

Of the two types of crises, the first is easier to overcome. When knocked off balance by an event, people stumble for a while, but given the right help and some time, they recover. It is the second type of crisis, the one that builds to the point of breaking, that requires the most recovery time. Once people's coping mechanisms are overwhelmed by reality, they must learn new ways to handle their problems. It is up to you to determine if counselees can handle the crisis with the tools they already possess, or if they need to be taught new skills.

Symptoms of People in Crisis

When single adults in crisis walk through the door, they are in a panic. It may be hard for them to breathe, focus, sit still, or explain exactly why they are there. Overwhelming and erratic emotions become the norm, and counselees express discomfort regarding their display of emotions. Comments like, "I just can't seem to get control of myself," and "I feel like I'm drowning," indicate that they need help in order to stabilize their emotions.

People in crisis continue to demand immediate attention for a period of days or weeks. If a phone message from a person you met with yesterday reads, "Call me at 5:05 P.M.," you will know they have lost their perspective on time and want everything to be handled immediately. There is no clear differentiation between the past, present, or future for them.

Counseling Suggestions

Do Not Get Caught in the Crisis

If someone says to you, "My husband (wife) just served me with papers and kicked me out of the house," do not choose sides and join the fighting. To help people, you must remain as objective as possible. There is always at least four sides to every story; hers, his, yours, and the truth. You can never fix a problem by becoming involved in the crisis yourself. You are there to point the individuals back to their relationship with God. They will need comfort, hope, perspective, and assurance that they are not going crazy.

Your ability to listen can be a great help to single adults. Much of a crisis involves the overwhelming nature of the new information. When it hits, an overloaded mind cannot process all the thoughts at once. Having someone to listen as they describe the foaming sea of hurt, emotions, and facts can relieve them of the burden and bring some peace. As they talk, they may begin to draw some conclusions about what they need to do.

Avoid Giving Answers Too Quickly

When people come for help, counselees often feel obligated to help them find the answer to their problem. You may even be inclined to help them find *the one* right answer to their problem. Be cautious—the problem presented may not be the real reason for the crisis. If you try to formulate a solution too quickly, you will not solve the crisis and may add to it. If you do come up with an answer to their problem without making them a part of the process, they may reject it.

In the initial shock stage of crisis, most people are not ready for answers. They need to be a part of the process of arriving at the answer. Ask reflective and gently probing questions to help them identify the underlying theme of the crisis. A simple observation such as, "You're really overwhelmed right now," or, "That must leave you feeling very hurt inside," will help people describe to themselves what is already obvious to you. They need help attaining perspective. You can do this by using questions, having them write the events surrounding the crisis in a journal, or by drawing pictures. Drawing pictures may seem childish, but any exercise that helps people pull out their thoughts and feelings will help them focus on the real crisis.

Leading people through a crisis is not so much searching for an answer as it is helping them reestablish a proper view of their problem in relationship to God. Their gaze should be on God with only momentary downward glances at their problem. If you feel pressured to give the right answer to every crisis you will burn out in your efforts and become discouraged when people do not even try to implement your solution.

Counsel for a Cure, Not Just Relief

I have learned that there is a significant difference between counseling for relief and counseling for a cure. Counseling for relief is short-lived and must be repeated to remain effective. Relief occurs when we listen to folks and let them lay down their burdens for a while. They leave feeling a little better but not cured. In his book, *When You're Tired of Treating the Symptoms, and You're Ready for a Cure, Give Me a Call,* Dr. Henry Brandt refutes the myth of complexity surrounding the counseling process. Most counseling involves a long process as people reveal their history to try to determine how they reached the crisis.

The truth is, no one can ever really know what happened in the past. I once listened to five people in one family talk about the same problem, only to conclude that they must have been talking about five different instances because no account of it was like any other.

Counseling for a cure is about discovering where clients have failed to conduct their lives according to God's principles. Once the discovery is made, they are to repent and begin living as God directs them. The cure to any hurting heart is to discover the sin and confess it.

When a single mother and her teenage daughter enter the counseling office to have me referee their disagreements, I am in a no-win situation. So instead of determining who is right, I listen until I can determine the most prominent biblical principle they are violating. I listen a little longer to be sure that I am on the right path. I then stop them from embellishing their own versions of the story and confront them individually with their sin.

I ask each of them if she is angry with the other. Does each feel hurt and taken advantage of by the other? How long have they both felt this way? They will refer to the beginning of the conflict and recite again all the reasons their anger and bitterness are justified. I tell them: "The Bible says to 'be angry, and do not sin: do not let the sun go down on your wrath' (Eph. 4:25 NKJV). By the most generous of margins, this means that you only have twenty-four hours to address your anger with the one who has hurt you." They may not resolve that conflict, but they can get on with the process of dealing with it instead of letting their anger take root and grow into bitterness.

At this point, both mother and daughter are looking at me like I have wounded them. No matter the validity of their accusations, they must first, individually, deal with God, confessing their own sins of anger, bitterness, pettiness, jealousy, and whatever other sin God points out to them. Notice I did not judge their hearts. Only God can do that. I ask them if these were their feelings, and they are happy to claim them and rationalize why they deserve to feel that way. If people do not take responsibility for their own responses when they are hurt, they will forever be saying, "That person has made me angry."

God does not hold people responsible for the circumstances of their lives, but He does hold them responsible for their responses to life. If He did not, we would be at the mercy of anyone who wanted to hurt us. God will always give us a way to escape the sin that would ensnare us. He wants us to live with hearts that reflect the fruit of the Spirit—love, joy, peace, patience, kindness, goodness, faithfulness, gentleness, self-control (Gal. 5:22). This fruit can exist despite circumstances. There is no excuse for being impatient or unkind. Whenever we are, it is sin.

So what is the cure for the mother and daughter in my office? I instruct both of them not to talk to each other until God has done His work in their hearts. I give them a worksheet to help them expose their hurts and feelings. Only after they have forgiven each other will they be ready to properly address each other. The difference is that they will be ready to talk about the problem. If I try to negotiate a contract between them to modify their behavior toward each other, they will have the same venomous hearts and the relationship will not improve.

It is important to give relief to people who come to you in crisis. But when they have violated a biblical principle, it is not loving to rationalize their behavior and fail to confront them with it. After all, it is likely a pattern of sin has led them to this crisis.

Remember, I am not saying that what has happened is some kind of judgment on them. I am saying that their way of responding to hurts has allowed them to pile up until they can no longer carry the load. Is it the last straw that breaks the camel's back or the first one?

When Jesus was being falsely accused, tried, and condemned to die, was He in a major crisis? In the midst of hanging on the cross in excruciating pain, with a tender and loving heart, He forgave all those who put Him there. Can we be expected to do less?

A Crisis Is Not an Event

It is odd to think that when Jesus was on the cross, He was not in crisis. It was a horrible event, but Jesus never responded improperly. He struggled deeply with the prospect of the cross, but He never sinned. A crisis, in this sense, is not the circumstance we face, but how we react to it. If this is true, counselors should be less concerned with the details of the crisis and more concerned with how clients are reacting. Our perceptions of events determine how we act. If God can change our hearts, events will have no power over us.

I use the following illustration in every divorce recovery workshop we have.

Imagine that you are about to enter the freeway. You notice in your rearview mirror a car coming up quickly. The driver does not slow down but attempts to pass. As he does, he runs you off the road into the ditch. You bump your head, your axle is broken, and you are angry. You jump out of the car and see a teenage boy, probably in his parent's station wagon, speeding down the freeway. You are so angry that you want to chase him down on foot and wring his neck.

In the midst of your shock and anger you look again at the car. In the back seat there is someone else. It is the boy's father doing CPR on his wife. The boy is speeding down the freeway to the hospital. Now, how do you feel? Are you still angry? In some ways you are. Physiologically your adrenaline is pumping, your eyes are dilated, you still have a bump on your head, and your car is still in the ditch. But now you feel differently. You feel compassion for the boy and his father as they try to save this woman's life. Instead of chasing them down, you pray for them.

Even though the circumstances are the same, you experienced two different reactions based on what you believed was happening.

What if you had not looked up to see the reason for the reckless driving? You may have developed an attitude toward all male teenage drivers. Suppose one year later you meet this young man and he tells you the rest of the story. Now think of all the anger and malice you have shown to other drivers who had nothing to do with hurting you. You could have rationalized your behavior by telling them what had happened to you, but would it have made you right?

Many events happen to us each day. We choose how we will respond to each one of them. It is the accumulation of hurts in our heart that can explode and push us into crisis. The event cannot be blamed; God holds us responsible for how we respond.

If this is true, counselors must focus on how people are responding to the crisis and not on the crisis itself.

Following are three of the most commonly misunderstood and violated biblical principles I deal with in counseling.

The Crisis of Guilt

Guilt is a prime motivator in society today. Commercials make us feel guilty by showing us how we *should* look, what we *should* wear, what we *should* drive, what toothpaste we *should* use, and on and on. Employers use guilt to get us to work overtime for no more money. Even clergy use guilt to pressure people into moral behavior. Why is it that guilt is such an effective motivator? Why is it that so many people feel guilty today? I believe it is because they *are* guilty. How profound! I am amazed, though, at how many people are willing to live with their guilt.

When I ask Christians, "Who created guilt?" they often say, "Satan."

Apparently guilt makes people feel so bad that they conclude it must come from Satan. But guilt was created by God. Guilt is meant to be a warning when we sin. We need to acknowledge our guilt, recognize our sin, and not allow it to come between us and God.

But a word about sin. The concept of sin can be described by comparing it to an arrow. When the archer shoots at a target, any arrow that does not hit the bull's-eye is a miss. It doesn't matter if it missed by an inch or by a foot. A miss is a miss.

The same is true of sin. Every time our behavior misses God's perfect mark, it is sin. Godliness is not a matter of being pretty good. We must submit totally to God and let Him live through us. Guilt is God's way of pointing out sin in our lives, no matter how small. Guilt has become so much a part of our society that even Christians accept it as a way of life. But as the apostle Paul would say, "May it never be."

Christians are confronted by two kinds of guilt: *conviction* and *condemnation*. To understand the difference, we must consider them in a legal context. When persons are tried for a crime and found guilty, we say that they have been *convicted* of the offense. In the second phase of the trial, the judge will determine the sentence they must pay in light of their conviction. As Christians who have been forgiven, we are accountable only for the guilt that comes from conviction.

Let's evaluate the feeling of guilt as we would experience it. We all know what it is like to look in the rearview mirror and see flashing red lights. Do you feel that knot in your stomach? It is what we do next that determines whether guilt will be a fleeting experience or a constant nagging companion.

When humans experience guilt, they should turn to God and ask, "God, what is it I am feeling guilty for?" God is not interested in playing hide-and-seek with our sin. If we have sinned, whether it be by commission or omission, He will point it out to us immediately. This guilt is conviction, and conviction comes from God. "If we confess our sins, He is faithful and righteous to forgive us our sins and to cleanse us from all unrighteousness" (1 John 1:9 NASB). When that is done, we are back into a right relationship with God.

If at this point we still feel guilt, we turn again to God and ask what it is from. He replies that based on the confession of our sins and His forgiveness, the guilt we are experiencing is not from Him. This guilt is condemnation. As Christians, we are no longer condemned under the law because Jesus paid the penalty for our sin. "There is therefore now no condemnation for those who are in Christ Jesus" (Rom. 8:1 NASB). God no longer condemns us. Condemnation comes from another source. It can come from Satan, society (others), or ourselves. In all three cases, it is not valid guilt and must be rejected in light of God's declaration that in Him we are clean.

The problem is that we have had many experiences of living under guilt. A parent can scold and discipline a child for a wrong behavior, only to continue to be outwardly angry with the child when the stated discipline is completed. This teaches children that the real discipline is the prolonged anger against them. Children learn to live under the prolonged guilt. In our home we work very hard to give hugs directly following discipline. If God forgives and restores us to full fellowship with Him, should we not give the same kind of love to each other? Guilt can be used to keep an employee working long hours or a church member under a leader's control. Guilt is deep within our social fabric and often is a misunderstood part of the Christian's life.

Once people learn to deal immediately with conviction and reject condemnation, they no longer live under the dark cloud of guilt that keeps them wondering what it is that they have done wrong. Guilt is a spiritual sensor that God designed to keep people in close relationship with Him. People in crisis may be suffering because they have not accepted, or will not accept, God's pardon of their sin. They impose guilt on themselves or wrongly accept it from another source.

The release from condemnation can be an almost magical lifting of a tremendous weight. When we lead counselees to confess their sins and reject the condemnation they are experiencing, we have led them to a cure. It takes practice for them to keep from falling into old habits, but it is a freedom that once experienced will not be easily relinquished.

The Crisis of Forgiveness

People do not handle hurts very well. Christians who have been hurt will at some point try to forgive the one who has hurt them. I believe that forgiveness is misunderstood, misapplied, and the source of a lot of frustration for Christians. The most common cliche attached to forgiveness is "forgive and forget." If people who are deeply hurt try to measure their ability to forgive the offender by the degree to which they can forget the offense, they will experience a very defeated life.

Dr. Archabald Hart defines forgiveness as "surrendering the right to hurt back." I like to say "forgiveness is giving up my right to get even." The first thing you and your counselees need to see is that the definition assumes we have a right to get even. We must begin here in order to apply forgiveness properly. Do we have a right to get even when we are hurt? The answer is yes, we have the right, based on God's justice. But if we actually get even, we sin. Is this a little confusing? Stay with me as I describe how to apply this definition.

Have your counselees write down the hurts in their lives. I recommend they use a journal because it accomplishes two things. One, it puts them in touch with all of the feelings and facts that we may have been trying to forget, deny, stuff, or walk away from. Two, it establishes a record of the event so they do not have to keep it in their minds. They can relax a little knowing that they have a record to refer to when they need to argue that what happened to them was not right.

Once the hurt is fully exposed, we must consider justice. God is holy and all sin must be paid for. When people have been hurt, justice demands restitution. They have a right to get even.

In my office I have an eighteen-inch Dodgers souvenir baseball bat. I pull it out of the drawer and hold it as if I'm ready to hit a home run. While holding it I ask, "Do I have a right to get even with the one who has hurt me?" The dilemma is now clear to them. Counselees sitting across from me can visualize the use of the bat in evening up the score. Yet, Christians realize that there is something inherently wrong with those feelings. I then ask, "Is vengeance right or wrong?" Most will say it is wrong. The truth is, it is right. Romans 12:19 says, "Never take your own revenge, beloved, but leave room for the wrath of God, for it is written, 'Vengeance is mine, I will repay,' says the Lord" (NASB).

Desire for vengeance is the correct response to an injustice, but only God can carry it out properly. With the bat firmly in our grip, we are faced with a decision. Do we get our own revenge and defy the instruction of God? Or do we pass the bat of revenge over to God and trust Him to apply His justice?

I bring people to the point of holding all the hurt in their hands. Then I hand them the bat of revenge and ask them to decide what to do with it. They can hold on to it or give it to God. When they give their need to get even to God, it is not a decision based on feelings. It is a decision of the will. It is at the point of proving that we do have a right to get even, that we must give up that right. Getting even would not hurt the offender much, but the revenge would destroy us.

I then have counselees write out forgiveness statements.

I, _____ , give up my right to get even with _____ for _____ (event). Signed _____ , Date _____ .

Forgiveness is a process that begins with a technical and legal statement of giving up the right to get even. The moment that is done there is a change. Counselees who give to God their right to revenge are left only with the hurt. They will not necessarily feel better, but they will feel different. They will change from the bitterness of hurting to the pain of the original hurt which they have buried under the anger. The difference is that now they can walk through the hurt and leave it behind them with God's help.

When people claim the right to get even, God cannot help them because they have their hurts locked up in the same hands that hold the bat of revenge.

There is one other response to look for. Christians often try to display forgiveness by not picking up the bat. The problem is, the bat of revenge must be passed on to God. When it is ignored, stuffed, denied, or not released, the need to get revenge is not released and it continues to control their lives. Make sure the person in crisis has picked up the bat and has actively passed it to God.

The crisis of forgiveness occurs when Christians, intent on doing the right thing, do not know how to execute it. Someone will say, "You just need to forgive them." They try, but ten minutes later they again feel angry at the abuser and want to get even. They despair because they cannot even forgive the right way. They become guilt-ridden and even more depressed.

The Three Myths of Forgiveness

Myth #1: *You have to feel like forgiving.* Forgiveness is an act of the will, not an act of emotions. So no one has to feel like forgiving in order to do so. As people work through the hurt, they will never feel like forgiving because their feelings scream out for revenge. That is why forgiveness is so critical. People must forgive in order to release their feelings, work through them, and put them in the past.

Myth #2: *If you haven't forgotten you haven't forgiven.* If an offense is bad enough to require forgiveness, it will never be forgotten. Through forgiveness people will change the way they think about the offense, but they will never forget the event. In time, it will take a proper place on the shelf of their memory.

Myth #3: *If you've truly forgiven a person you have to fully trust him or her again.* The act of forgiveness does not immediately restore trust to the same level as before the offense. It must be earned. If I loaned my truck to you, and you brought it back totaled and asked my forgiveness, I could grant that to you. But if you then said, "Whew. That's great. Can I borrow your car tomorrow?" I would refuse. You might accuse me of not forgiving you as a Christian should, but that would be unfair. Many people, including Christians, misunderstand the nature of forgiveness in this regard. When I forgive you for wrecking my truck, it means I will not require you to buy me another vehicle. But your actions have violated the trust between us. I would be foolish to trust you with my car. Trust must be earned. The problem is that trust can be earned only when I give you some responsibility. You have a transportation need. God says I must take steps to restore our relationship but at a prudent level. So I loan you my skateboard. If you bring that back in one piece, I may loan you my scooter. Eventually you may earn my trust to use the car.

I have seen a sixty-five-year-old woman sign a forgiveness statement for parents who, though dead for years, still controlled her life. She came in because she was not treating her husband right and she didn't know why. She was taking out the hurt she experienced from her parents on him. She needed to forgive them.

A man who was adopted at birth and grew up in a loving Christian home needed to forgive his birth mother. He felt she should not have given him up even though she was young and unmarried. He came in because he was a compulsive spender, especially around his birthday. He had always been told he was special. One day he said, "If I am so special, why did my mother give me up for adoption?"

A young wife who would not let her husband near her physically, wrote out pages of forgiveness statements for all the abuse she endured from boyfriends, neighbor boys, and her parents.

Do you see the pattern? People in crisis will come in with a wide range of problems. At the root of many will be a crisis of guilt or of forgiveness. Over 90 percent of the time, my counseling focuses on one of these very basic yet profound biblical principles. You know how the world approaches many of these problems. Can you begin to see why counseling provides some relief but never a cure? A cure comes when we reconcile ourselves to the principles of God's Word. We need to study to show ourselves approved, workmen who handle the Word of God well. Our brothers and sisters in Christ are depending on it.

The Crisis of Trust

Every relationship is built on trust. In a crisis, trust is usually violated. We trusted a person to tell us the truth and love us forever. But then they leave us for someone else. We trusted our children to tell us what is going on in their lives. Instead they sneak out at night and experiment with drugs. When a spouse dies, we feel deserted and betrayed for being left to handle the business, the kids, and the funeral. An unfortunate event can shake us to the point that we do not want to trust anyone ever again.

When people in crisis have a history of abuse and trauma, they may have a difficult time forming bonds of trust. Children place unquestioning trust in parents, teachers, adult relatives, and any significant adult that is within their sphere. They view them in the same way they view God. When abuse occurs, children will not blame the abuser because that person is perceived as perfect, like God. Instead they blame themselves and the result is shame, contempt (often for themselves), and guilt.

This can destroy a child's ability to trust in the future. A child younger than the age of twelve does not have the cognitive ability to filter out the wrong motives of an abusive adult. The result is the impaired ability to form bonds of trust deep enough to satisfy the child's desire to love and be loved.

The fear of extending trust can be so deep that it seems irrational. The violation of trust that a child experiences goes straight to the heart. As an adult, it takes great courage to give trust to someone else, even God.

People with a crisis based on an inability to trust will often be very articulate about the hurt they have experienced. The only way trust can be restored is for them to prudently give it to someone. Often they must begin by giving it to God. This will seem an impossible task for the person in crisis. The decision to trust will have to be one of the intellect and not the will. Every bit of emotion and feeling will fight the decision to trust someone. It is important that you guide counselees in making a wise and prudent choice when selecting a relationship on which to rebuild their trust. If their choice is a poor one, the relationship will fail and the failure will allow counselees to say that they tried and no longer need to try, ever again.

On the Path Together

When people come to you for help, they are taking a significant step. You can represent God's presence in their life. In a crisis, people often lose all sense of God's leading and direction. In coming to you, they are open to God's help. In Galatians 6:1–5, we are told to bear one another's burdens. The picture here is of a person who has fallen under the weight of a heavy load. Bearing one another's burdens does not mean that we take the load from others. Instead we are to come alongside and help them up. As we begin to move down the path, holding them up on either side, we help them carry the burden they bear. As the burden is removed, not just relieved, the load becomes bearable and soon they are walking unassisted. They may even find themselves helping someone else along the path because of what they learned when they fell. Isn't that discipleship?

Dos and Don'ts for Counselors

Do empathize with the single adult in crisis.

Do help them attain a broader perspective on their problem.

Do pray with them and for them. God is our only source of healing. Pray for wisdom, comfort, timing, and direction.

Do let them formulate their questions. Help them learn all they can about the crisis they are experiencing.

Do tell them what they can expect in the weeks ahead as they move through the crisis.

Do make sure you involve them in the process.

Do loan them your faith while they are struggling. They will face some tough questions and doubts.

Do give them permission to express their hurts and doubts.

Don't take responsibility away from them. We may help them along the path, but do not allow them to become dependent on you.

Don't just give them a verse without dealing with their problem. Show them where it fits.

Don't answer a question that has not been asked. You must lead them to the point where they can ask the question before you answer it.

Do not avoid them or their problem. You may not be able to give them an hour, but comfort them and leave them with the hope they are desperately calling out for.

Don't tell them exactly what they need to do. Take them on a journey where they can discover it with you.

Don't tell them to move on, it's over. Help them through the process. They will move when it is time.

Don't tell them their anger will not come back.

Don't make them dependent on you.

Suggested Scripture

God knows me
Psalm 139
Jeremiah 29:11
John 10:7–15
Anxiety
Philippians 4:4–8
Psalm 46:10
Matthew 6:25–34
Guilt and cleansing
Psalm 32; 51
Isaiah 53:5–6
John 3:16–21
1 John 1:9
Grief
2 Corinthians 4:7–18
Isaiah 43:1–2
Isaiah 53:4
Help one another
Galatians 5:13; 6:1–5
1 Thessalonians 4:18
Hebrews 10:24
Forgiveness
Matthew 6:12; 18:21–35
Romans 12:19
Hebrews 12:15

Prayer

Dear Father, I often wonder why You have called me to this place of service. The responsibility often seems too great to bear. Thank You for Your love, acceptance, patience, caring, and gentle Spirit. We need Your wisdom, Father. Help us to keep our eyes on You while we take short glances at our problems. All healing is found in relationship with You.

I lift up those who come seeking relief from their problems. May they discover the cure of a heart in crisis by seeking You. Give us a desire to walk faithfully by Your side. Don't let us think too highly of ourselves or believe we are the ones helping these dear people. Let us show them Your grace and mercy as You have given us, so they might desire it also.

Father, I truly do not know why some people open their hearts and lives to You and experience healing, and others find the courage to trust You. God, give them the courage to let You in. Dear Father, make us one with You in mind and spirit as You and the Son are one. In the precious name of Jesus, Amen.

Recommended Resources

Allender, Dan B. *The Wounded Heart: Hope for Adult Victims of Childhood Sexual Abuse.* Colorado Springs: NavPress, 1990.

Brandt, Henry. *When You're Tired of Treating the Symptoms, and You're Ready for a Cure, Give Me a Call.* Brentwood, Tenn.: Wolgemuth and Hyatt, 1991.

Munger, Robert Boyd. *My Heart, Christ's Home.* Minneapolis: Billy Graham Evangelistic Association, 1980.

Nouwen, Henri J. M. *In the Name of Jesus.* New York: Crossroad, 1992.

———. *Wounded Healer.* Paper ed. New York: Doubleday, 1994.

Smalley, Gary, and John Trent. *The Gift of the Blessing.* Nashville: Thomas Nelson, 1993.

Smith, Harold Ivan. *Singles Ask.* Minneapolis: Augsburg, 1988.

Wright, H. Norman. *Crisis Counseling: What to Do and Say During the First Seventy-two Hours.* Ventura, Calif.: Regal, 1993.

Defining the Role of Spiritual Director

Doug Fagerstrom

In his book *How to Be a People Helper,* Gary Collins writes, "Helping people with their problems is everybody's business." And often it is just that. Whether we want to or not, we are constantly being called to come alongside single adults who need help. Sometimes we feel confident to provide just what the individual needs. Other times, we find that we are inadequate or ill-equipped.

Then we discover a startling reality. Someone else in the single adult ministry gave the needed help. It might have been the person's best friend or possibly a casual acquaintance. We're surprised, but why should we be? People are helped through the rough days of life more often by friends, business associates, and relatives than by professional counselors or single adult ministry leaders.

So what then is the role of the single adult leader?

First of all, there's one thing it isn't. The role of the single adult leader is *not* to be everything to everyone. That is impossible. However, as you successfully help people with their needs, it is natural for them to want you to meet more of their needs. It is also natural for you to respond with maximum effort to meet more and more needs until you hit a wall, burn out, wipe out, or drop out. So it is important to define your role with each person God brings into your life and ministry.

Five Relationships Everyone Needs

Throughout life, people need five different types of relationships, or five distinct "one anothers," in their lives. It is possible for one person to take on more than one role, but not advisable. Shifting from one role to another can become confusing to both parties.

ROLE	Childhood	Adolescence	Adulthood
1. Parent Figure	Parents	Friend's Parent	Authority Figure
2. Role Model	Sibling	Folk Hero	Colleague
3. Casual Friend	Playmate	Member of Clique	Neighbors
4. Intimate Friend	Best Friend (imaginary?)	Buddy/Date (often changes)	Soulmate (married or unmarried)
5. Spiritual Director	Teacher	Counselor	Pastor

I clearly remember the key influences, or the "one anothers," in my life. First of all, there were my dad and mom. They made sure that I was toeing the mark and that my life was in order. Second, there was my only sibling, my brother. Being seven years older than me, he was my ideal. I wanted to be like my brother; he was my role model. Then there was Davey, my best friend. Every week we sat together in Sunday school. Five days a week we were next to each other in grade school. Every other year we would be separated by our teachers for overpracticing fellowship. We just had good times together. My first intimate friend was Ron. Yes, I shared and did everything with Ron. We got into trouble together, talked about girls together, and together explored our thoughts about what we might do with the rest of our lives. We told each other stuff we never told anyone else. Finally, my spiritual director was Ken and later his son Bob. They were the directors of Youth for Christ. They encouraged and guided me through all of my spiritual quests and adventures.

One, two, or three of these roles are not enough. All five are imperative, especially for a person going through a crisis, a difficult struggle, or for an unhealthy person seeking wholeness. God created us with a need for this family-caring unit in our lives. Each *role* carries a very specific and worthwhile *function* necessary for growth and maturity.

ROLE	Purpose and Key Question
1. Parent Figure	Provides oversight of personal needs, such as diet, personal hygiene, maintaining a job, and other domestic needs. *KEY QUESTION:* Are you eating, sleeping, and keeping your basic commitments?
2. Role Model	Identifies where a person would like to be in one to five years. It represents the goals a person has. *KEY QUESTION:* Where do you see your life going in the future?
3. Casual Friend	Brings much joy and personal fulfillment. It is a nonthreatening, stress-reducing role that allows time-out from the difficult issues. *KEY QUESTION:* How about going out for pizza with me tonight?
4. Intimate Friend	Provides opportunities to share most secret and personal issues, thoughts, and concerns. This role of intimacy welcomes and receives any thought or idea without rejection and without critical counsel. *KEY QUESTION:* What is really bothering you? What are your dreams?
5. Spiritual Director	Meets the inner need of discovering the real person. It defines self-worth and value. This role helps the person identify his or her relationship with God, positionally for eternity and practically for today. *KEY QUESTION:* Are you closer to God today than yesterday? Why or why not?

The difficulty of filling more than one of the above five roles in a person's life becomes apparent when the person needs all of the above at one time. For example, a person in a crisis may try to make a casual friend into an *intimate friend, parent figure,* and/or *spiritual director.* The casual friend was not expecting it and does not have the time, energy, or other resources to take on the additional roles. Another example is when the person in crisis expects the spiritual director to become the *casual friend, intimate friend,* and/or *parent figure.* One person should *not* be expected to fill more than one or two roles. Leaders in the church must help people define the needed roles and find people to serve as the *various* one anothers in their lives.

Suggestions

This chapter is to help single adult leaders define the role and purpose of the spiritual director.

Most single adults can identify people who fill the first four roles. Most of them have a parent figure. For many it is indeed a biological parent. For others it may be a job supervisor. Many adult singles also have role models. Unfortunately, however, some of the people they name are more like religious heroes. For example, some might name Billy Graham, who, though admirable, is not reachable. Casual friends, if sought, are abundant for some single adults and obtainable for most. Intimate friends exist among single adults but are not as abundant because many tend to hold friends at a distance due to skepticism based on previous negative close encounters. A spiritual director, however, seems to be nonexistent for most single adults. This role also seems to be the least understood and least identified. Many individuals identify people as their spiritual directors who are not actually a part of their lives. For example, some people might consider their spiritual director to be a spiritual leader out of the past like Oswald Chambers, who is dead. Only limited help can be gained from a person's books or life story because interaction is nonexistent and there is no opportunity for individual counsel, direct observation, or personal touch. People like Billy Graham and Oswald Chambers are less than ideal as significant one anothers.

Purpose of a Spiritual Director for Single Adults

Chuck Colson writes, "There is today a widespread belief that one can be a Christian or develop one's own faith system apart from the church. The proposition is ludicrous. It is not a matter of choice or membership."[1]

Christians are members of one another. We are a body and a family. Both of these scriptural metaphors are germane to our faith and Christian life, where God is our Father and Jesus Christ is the head. As Christians, we are all connected and related to one another, both positionally and functionally (1 Cor. 12). There are no lone rangers in the Christian church. No man is an island. A "single Christian" is an oxymoron. A single adult Christian who is connected to one anothers is God's design for every single adult. Single adults need to learn the importance and means of this vital union of faith and life in the church of Jesus Christ.

Therefore, a spiritual director is imperative to spiritual life and growth. All believers need someone to point out their blind spots, weaknesses, and strengths; hold them accountable; and remind them to keep their eyes fixed on Jesus Christ (Heb. 12:1–14). People naturally fall into controlling and secret habits of the flesh and of the world's system (1 John 2:15–17). Single adults without an accountability system are vulnerable to slipping away (Heb. 2:1) and pursuing a life that is not guided by the Spirit (Gal. 5:16–26).

In chapter five of *Sacrifice and Delight,* Alan Jones points out that many people do not know enough about Christianity to reject it. That is my experience. Many single adults today do not have enough information or knowledge about the gospel to believe or not believe. *They need spiritual direction.* And it is not coming from our pulpits or classrooms with politically correct sermons. Jones goes on to say, "I need community and tradition. I need friends and colleagues. If I am to be a midwife of persons, I need all the help I can get to think, to feel, and to act. I have to be a confessor and a spiritual director."[2]

Criteria for a Spiritual Director

Erich Auerbach says, "Spiritual direction is the *task* of helping a person take seriously what is treated dismissively by the publicity-infatuated and crisis-sated mind, and then to receive this mixed, random material of life as the raw material for high holiness."[3] About a spiritual director he adds, they are, *"duty bound to take an interest in the specific detail of every day."* Spiritual direction concerns one anothers with the events of everyday life and brings those into a spiritual focus, acknowledging the Creator and Savior in everything.

As stated above, spiritual direction is a *task*. It is not some mystical union between believers and God. It is a duty to take an interest in the life of another person and to help one another grow and mature in a relationship with Christ (Col. 1:28–29). Single adults need to identify their spiritual director. The single adult leader needs to know how to be that person.

"To involve yourself in spiritual direction, it is necessary to select another individual to be your director," says Steven Harper, who goes on to say, "This [must be] a person who is mature in the faith, someone you trust and feel comfortable and at home with, and who can help you grow in Christlikeness. The main thing is that the director not be a novice in the faith."[4] Harper brings out a subtle element that most may not see. The one in need of direction is to seek out a spiritual director. It is not the task of a spiritual director to seek out willing "disciples" to tutor and lead through the imperatives of the Christian life. Single adults need to hear this point. Spiritual direction does not come through osmosis or by signing up for an eight-week course in biblical studies. Harper continues, "What occurs in the spiritual-direction process is largely *up to you*, for your own growing edges are the agenda for the relationship."[5]

Over a brief period of time, single adults seeking a spiritual director should develop a *personal spiritual agenda.* The spiritual agenda is simply a list of those areas of the spiritual life that need attention. For example, prayer may be on the agenda. For some people prayer may be a number-one need for maturity in the Christian life. For others, prayer may already be a vital part of their spiritual life but they seldom meditate on biblical truth, so they need to make that a priority.

Two steps are involved in developing a spiritual agenda: first, a devotional quest; second, asking yourself tough spiritual questions.

The devotional quest is a time set aside to seek God's will and general direction. It is a personal spiritual analysis that examines purpose and fulfillment in life and a personal relationship with God. (It is not a career assessment.)

The tough spiritual questions single adults need to ask themselves should be similar to the following:

- What are my areas of strength?
- What are my areas of weakness?
- Am I closer to God today than one year ago? Why or why not?
- Where am I going in my spiritual walk with Christ?
- Is the Holy Spirit working in my life?
- What major sin am I struggling with?

The answers to these questions and the reflections from a personal devotional time will begin to form a spiritual agenda.

After the agenda is formed, it should be simplified into several practical goals and objectives. The seeker should then begin praying for a person who is mature in these areas and who would be willing to make a commitment and begin working through the spiritual agenda. I believe that a clear agenda and faithful prayer will produce one person with whom the other person can begin a one-another relationship of spiritual direction.

It is not assumed at this point that you, the ministry leader, will be the spiritual director in a single adult's life. The single adult may identify a person in the church other than you. Your role is to assist and help begin and develop that relationship if possible.

Once the single adult has in mind a person who might fit the role of spiritual director, he or she should evaluate the person by using a personal preference list similar to this one:

- Do I feel safe and comfortable with this person?
- Do I recognize and respect his or her spiritual maturity?
- Will I respect his or her spiritual counsel and suggestions?
- Do others respect and admire this person as godly?
- Am I able to be myself around this person?
- Can I communicate with this person or do I have one-way conversations?

- Does this person exhibit the strengths to help guide me through my weaknesses?
- Is this person accountable with another for his or her spiritual walk?
- Are my motives strictly spiritual in inviting this person to be my spiritual director?

If the answers to the above questions are affirmative, the single adult seeking a spiritual director is ready to take the next step.

Matching the Single Adult with a Spiritual Director

Once the spiritual director has been identified, the single adult should meet with the single adult ministry leader for discussion and prayer to affirm God's leading in this choice. It is also wise for the ministry leader to share the name of the possible spiritual director with other leaders to determine if there is any known reason why the relationship should not be pursued. If everyone agrees to the relationship, the ministry leader should set up a meeting at which the spiritual director and single adult meet with the ministry leader.

Please note that the ministry leader plays an important role of accountability in the relationship even though there may be very little direct involvement. The ministry leader serves as a resource person and cheerleader. The leader can also serve as a neutral party if or when difficulties arise between the one anothers.

After the above interview, and after everyone has agreed that a relationship of spiritual direction is a viable option, the following relationship can be established between the spiritual director and single adult.

A Spiritual Contract between the Spiritual Director and Single Adult

"Be *devoted* to one another in brotherly love" (Rom. 12:10). Devotion is at the heart of a spiritual relationship between two one anothers. A loving bond of commitment will bring the two faithful followers of Christ through anything. That commitment means more than intimate sharing; it means a vulnerable keeping. Vulnerability means that what is shared by another can be used to hurt the one who has shared a part of his or her life. The single adult says to the spiritual director, "I entrust to you some of the most significant areas of my life; treat them with care."

Eugene Peterson wrote, "I wanted someone who would take my life of prayer and my pilgrimage with Christ as seriously (or more seriously) than I did, who was capable of shutting up long enough to hear the distinct uniqueness of my spirituality, and who had enough *disciplined restraint* not to impose an outside form on me."[6] That is what it is all about: *an honest set of loving rules and caring serious devotion* about developing the imperatives of the spiritual life without getting burned or burned out in the process.

Two areas of a contract are important. One is the rules agreed on by the one anothers and the other is the challenge to be held accountable for personal development.

There are two types of rules—team rules and personal rules. Team rules are the rules that one anothers both agree on. An example of a team rule may be the time and place of meeting. Both agree to this rule. Another rule may be that the cancellation of meetings will be done by phone at least twelve hours in advance. Another rule may be related to confidentiality, and so forth.

Personal rules are requested by one for the other. For example, one person may request not to have to pray audibly until ready. The other may feel free to pray audibly. One person in the relationship may request not to be forced to mention a certain topic. The other may be open to that area of discussion. "If members of a team are committed to each other, there is a price to pay. One price is that a team member help to establish and follow the team rules."[7] Without rules, people operate on assumptions, which are often inaccurate. Agreed-to rules help people move ahead feeling much safer and with more confidence and enthusiasm.

Following are five imperatives for spiritual growth and maturity:

Prayer	Communicating with God
Bible study	Learning about God and His will
Basic doctrine	Building faith's foundation
Spiritual formation	Discovering the inner work of the Holy Spirit
Reproduction	Becoming another's spiritual director

These are the road signs for a spiritual journey. They are all important for spiritual balance. The challenge is to set certain spiritual goals in the above areas of spiritual maturity. Begin with the easiest to accomplish. Timelines are not that important. Making progress toward godliness is important.

Terminating the Spiritual Director

This can be difficult, so I will quote Steven Harper who said it succinctly and well: "Whenever you sense that you are being squeezed into the mold of your director's preferences, it's probably time to end the relationship."[8] For this study, enough said.

One Conclusion and a Final Note of Hope

Jesus Christ can and does fill all five roles in our lives. For those who cannot find the five people needed, Jesus is there to meet these very important roles.

Father. Jesus said, "the Father and I are one. As you see Me, you see the Father." (See John 8:12–30; 10:30; 14:9–14.)

Role model. Jesus calls us to be like Him (Mark 1:17–18; Eph. 5:1–2; 1 Thess. 1:6).

Casual friend. Jesus calls us His friends (John 15:12–15).

Intimate friend. Jesus said, "Remain in [M]e, and I will remain in you. . . . apart from [M]e you can do nothing" (John 15:4–5). No relationship can be more intimate than that.

Spiritual director. Jesus said, "I give you another comforter, one who will guide and lead you into all truth, convicting of sin, righteousness and judgment." (See John 14:15–27; 16:1–16.) With the work of the Holy Spirit, and Jesus as our advocate before the Father in heaven (1 John 2:1), we have a sovereign and personal God who leads and guides us through every spiritual concern of our lives.

Am I just sermonizing? I think not. The good news (gospel) of the character of God is vital to single adults who find themselves very much alone. Loneliness often comes as a result of rejection. Sometimes this rejection comes when the one in need imposes too heavy a role on another to become the one another and assume many roles that no one person can fulfill. Again, Jesus can and does fill all the roles. Often He chooses members of His forever family to extend the warmth and love of those roles. The single adult leader needs to be sensitive, aware, and a resource for single adults to help identify their one anothers that are so needed.

Suggested Scripture

Proverbs 27:5–6, 17; 9:8
Malachi 4:6, 18
Matthew 28:19–20
Luke 9:23–24
2 Timothy 2:2
Hebrews 10:24–25
1 Peter 2:2

Recommended Resources

Foster, Richard. *Celebration of Discipline.* New York: Harper and Row, 1978.

Harper, Steven. *Embrace the Spirit.* Wheaton: Victor, 1987.

Henrichsen, Walter A. *Disciples Are Made, Not Born.* Wheaton: Victor, 1974.

Jones, Alan. *Exploring Spiritual Direction.* New York: HarperCollins, 1992.

Nouwen, Henri. *In the Name of Jesus.* New York: Crossroad, 1989.

———. *Life of the Beloved.* New York: Crossroad, 1992.

Stanford, Miles. *Principles of Spiritual Growth.* Lincoln: Back to the Bible, 1991.

Appendix

Spiritual, Personality, and Relational Traits

Note: All of the traits listed below, with the exception of "worldly sophistication," have been taken verbatim from Scripture. They are *highly* relational in nature.

Ways of making marriages stronger and happier

Ways of making marriages weaker and more painful

Wholeness Listing:

Affection (warmth)
Blamelessness
  (actions & character)
Comfort (offering it to others)
Compassion
Contentment
Dignity
Discretion
Encouragement
Equity
Fairness
Faithfulness
Forgiveness
Gentleness
Good deeds (actions)
Goodness (character)
Grace
Graciousness
Honor
Hospitality
Humility
Innocence
Integrity
Justice
Kindness
Knowledge of God
Lovingkindness

Brokenness Listing:

Abusiveness
Arrogance
Bitter words
Bitterness
Boastfulness
Bribery
Brutality
Callousness
Conceit
Corruption
Covetousness
Craftiness (sneakiness)
Crookedness
Cruelty
Deceit
Destructiveness
Divination
Duplicity (double-
  heartedness)
Envy
Evil (deeds, actions,
  thoughts, plans)
Falsehood
False witness
Favoritism
Foolishness
Greed

Meekness
Mercy
Obedience to God
Patience
Peace
Peacemaking
Peace-seeking
Pleasantness (words/actions)
Praiseworthiness
Prudence
Purity (heart, mind, actions)
Reconciliation
Respect
Reverence
Righteousness
Self-control
Sensibility
Slowness to anger
Steadfastness
Sweetness of speech
Temperance
Tenderheartedness
Thankfulness
Trust (of others)
Trustworthiness
Truth
Truthfulness
Understanding
Uprightness
Wisdom
Work (work ethic)

Haughtiness
Hypocrisy
Idolatry
Immorality
Impurity
Injustice
Insubordination
Lying
Malice
Maliciousness
Maligning
Meanness
Murmuring
Oppressiveness
Partiality (in judgment)
Pleasure-loving
Pretense
Pride
Pridefulness
Pugnaciousness
Quarrelsomeness
Quick-temperedness
Rebellion
Religiosity
Ridiculing
Scoffing
Selfishness
Self-righteousness
Sensuality
Slander
Sloth
Spite
Spitefulness
Strife-maintaining
Strife-making
Talebearing
Treachery
Ungratefulness
Vengeance
Vengefulness
Violence
Wickedness
Worldly sophistication
Wrathfulness

Notes

Preface

1. Pia Mellody and Andrea Wells Miller, *Breaking Free: A Recovery Workbook for Facing Codependence* (New York: Harper and Row, 1989), xvi.

Chapter 5: Low Self-Esteem and Self-Worth: Am I Valuable?

1. Harold Ivan Smith, *Life-Changing Answers to Depression* (Eugene, Ore.: Harvest House, 1985), 130, 132.

2. Jim Towns, "Self-Esteem," in *Singles Ministry Handbook* ed. Douglas Fagerstrom (Wheaton: Victor, 1988), 90.

3. Jason Towner, "I Am Alone," *Warm Reflections* (Nashville: Broadman, 1977), 15.

4. Janice Harayda, *The Joy of Being Single* (New York: Doubleday, 1986), 7–8.

5. Clyde Narramore, *The Psychology of Counseling* (Grand Rapids: Zondervan, 1979), 30.

Chapter 6: Bitterness and Pain: I Hurt So Much

1. Paul Welter, *How to Help a Friend* (Wheaton: Tyndale, 1983), 101–102.

Chapter 7: Depression and Anger: Down and Dangerous

1. Jerrold S. Maxmen, *Essential Psychopathology* (New York: W. W. Norton & Company, 1986), 174.

2. Ibid., 175.

3. Ibid., 173.

4. Roy F. Baumeister, "The Optimal Margin of Illusion," *Journal of Social and Clinical Psychology* 8, no. 2 (1989): 76–189.

5. Lauren B. Alloy and Lyn Y. Abramson, "Judgement of Contingency in Depressed and Nondepressed Students: Sadder But Wiser?" *Journal of Experimental Psychology; General* 108 (1979): 441–85.

6. W. E. Vine, *An Expository Dictionary of New Testament Words* (Nashville: Thomas Nelson, 1985), 466.

Chapter 10: Death and Dying: The Loss Is Too Great to Bear

1. William Cutler and Richard Peace, *Dealing with Grief and Loss* (Littleton, Col.: Serendipity House, 1990), 10.

2. John D. Canine, seminar at Ward Evangelical Presbyterian Church, April 1993.

3. Wayne Oates, *Pastoral Care and Counseling in Grief and Separation* (Minneapolis: Fortress Press, 1976).

4. Canine, seminar.

5. Haddon Robinson, *Grief* (Grand Rapids: Zondervan, 1976).

6. James Townes, *Growing Through Grief* (Anderson, Ind.: Warner Press, 1976).

7. Cutler and Peace, *Dealing with Grief*, 20.

8. Ibid., 20–21.

9. William Greenman, grief tapes, Ward Evangelical Presbyterian Church, summer 1986.

10. Cutler and Peace, *Dealing with Grief*, 40.

11. Ibid., 42.

12. Ibid., 50.

13. John D. Canine, *I Can, I Will* (Geneva, Ill.: Ball Publishing, 1990).

14. Cutler and Peace, *Dealing with Grief*, 51–52.

15. Canine, seminar.

16. Cutler and Peace, *Dealing with Grief*, 59–64.

Chapter 12: Abused and Feeling Used

1. The section on dos and don'ts was adapted from *Soul Survivors* by J. Patrick Gannon (New York: Prentice-Hall, 1990).

Chapter 19: Sexual Struggles

1. For a more complete discussion, see Rick Stedman, *Pure Joy! The Positive Side of Single Sexuality* (Chicago: Moody Press, 1993).

2. Stedman, *Pure Joy!*, 72–73.

3. Carolyn See, "The New Chastity," *Cosmopolitan* (November 1985), 382–83.

4. Harold Ivan Smith, "Dealing with the Question of Masturbation," speech to the National Association of Single Adult Leaders Consortium, San Francisco, 12 May 1992.

5. Stedman, *Pure Joy!*, 27–28.

Chapter 20: Uncontrolled Finances

1. Larry Burkett, *Debt-Free Living: How to Get Out of Debt and Stay Out* (Chicago: Moody Press, 1989), 8.

2. Ibid., 16.

3. Larry Burkett, *The Financial Planning Workbook* (Chicago: Moody Press, 1990), 7.

4. Burkett, *Debt-Free*, 144.

5. For a further discussion and helpful formulas, see Ron Blue, *Master Your Money* (Nashville: Thomas Nelson, 1991), or Burkett, *Debt-Free Living*.

Chapter 25: Defining the Role of Spiritual Director

1. Charles Colson, *The Body* (Dallas: Word, 1993), 69.

2. Alan Jones, *Sacrifice and Delight* (New York: HarperCollins, 1992), 156.

3. Erich Auerbach, *Mimesis* (Princeton, N.J.: Princeton University Press, 1953), 92.

4. Steven Harper, *Embrace the Spirit* (Wheaton: Victor, 1987), 44.

5. Ibid.

6. Eugene H. Peterson, *Working the Angles* (Grand Rapids: Eerdmans, 1987), 117.

7. Patrick Handley, *Team Rules, Insight Building Materials* (Kansas City, Mo.: Insight Institute, 1989), 1.

8. Harper, *Embrace the Spirit*, 46.

Contributors

Phyllis Alderman
First Baptist Church Indian Rocks, Largo, Florida

Jim Carlson
Calvary Church, Grand Rapids, Michigan

Kay Collier-Slone
The Episcopal Diocese of Lexington, Lexington, Kentucky

Robert Duffett
Northern Seminary, Chicago, Illinois

Jim Dyke
Grace Church, Edina, Minnesota

Doug Fagerstrom
Network of Single Adult Leaders, Grand Rapids, Michigan

Dennis Franck
Central Assembly Christian Church, Boise, Idaho

Lenore A. Janman
Grand Haven Public School System, Grand Haven, Michigan

Larry Kent
First Presbyterian Church, Flint, Michigan

Richard Krieger
Calvary Church, Grand Rapids, Michigan

Richard Matteson
Village Baptist Church, Portland, Oregon

Nancy and Greg McPherson
Elmbrook Church, Milwaukee, Wisconsin

Jacquelyn A. Meurs
Calvary Church, Grand Rapids, Michigan

Andy Morgan
Christ Church of Oakbrook, Chicago, Illinois

Contributors

Michael Platter
First Church of the Nazarene, Pasadena, California

Mike Popovich
First Baptist Church, Visalia, California

Charles W. Roberts
Peachtree Presbyterian Church, Atlanta, Georgia

Jerry Schreur
Calvary Church, Grand Rapids, Michigan

Kelley Schroder
Central Wesleyan Church, Holland, Michigan

Jim Smoke
Growing Free, Southern California

John Splinter
Central Presbyterian Church, St. Louis, Missouri

Lorin Staats
Elmbrook Church, Milwaukee, Wisconsin

Rick Stedman
Crossroads Christian Church, Corona, California

Mark Tans
Christian Reformed Church, Hudsonville, Michigan

Gary Winkleman
Westside Christian Church, Springfield, Illinois

Norm Yukers
Rehoboth Baptist Church, Atlanta, Georgia